Cultivating Empire

EARLY AMERICAN STUDIES

Series editors:
Kathleen M. Brown, Roquinaldo Ferreira,
Emma Hart, and Daniel K. Richter

Exploring neglected aspects of our colonial, revolutionary, and early national history and culture, Early American Studies reinterprets familiar themes and events in fresh ways. Interdisciplinary in character, and with a special emphasis on the period from about 1600 to 1850, the series is published in partnership with the McNeil Center for Early American Studies.

A complete list of books in the series is available from the publisher.

Cultivating Empire

Capitalism, Philanthropy, and the Negotiation of American Imperialism in Indian Country

Lori J. Daggar

PENN

UNIVERSITY OF PENNSYLVANIA PRESS

PHILADELPHIA

Published by
University of Pennsylvania Press
Philadelphia, Pennsylvania 19104-4112
www.upenn.edu/pennpress

Printed in the United States of America on acid-free paper
10 9 8 7 6 5 4 3 2 1

Cataloging-in-Publication Data for this book
is available from the Library of Congress

Hardcover ISBN 9781512823295
eBook ISBN 9781512823301

For my family

CONTENTS

Introduction

> You see, my red children, that our fathers carried on this scheme of getting your lands for our use, and we have now become rich and powerful; and we have a right to do with you just as we please; we claim to be your fathers. And we think we shall do you a great favor, my dear sons and daughters, to drive you out, to get you away out of the reach of our civilized people, who are cheating you, for we have no law to reach them, we cannot protect you although you be our children. So it is no use, you need not cry, you must go, even if the lions devour you, for we promised the land you have to somebody else long ago.
>
> —William Apess (Pequot), *Eulogy on King Philip*, 1836

In the midst of Andrew Jackson's presidency, the Pequot writer and Methodist minister William Apess offered, in twenty pages of speech, a history of North America and the emergence of the American empire to date. He delivered his *Eulogy on King Philip* twice to New Englanders who were then consuming the news of the Second Seminole War in Florida and the U.S. federal government's efforts to forcibly remove Creeks and Cherokees from their homes.[1] His history was not, however, one that most Euro-Americans would have celebrated or recognized. At the center of Apess's *Eulogy* was the tragic hero King Philip—a Wampanoag leader whom nineteenth-century Euro-Americans embraced only as a noble remnant of a supposedly vanished people. Apess's King Philip, however, was a thoughtful, complex leader wronged by the greed and violence of New England's Pilgrims and a coterie of ill-intentioned Christians. Both times he delivered the *Eulogy*, Apess turned white New Englanders' ideas on their heads—ideas regarding themselves, their ancestors, people of color, and their young republic: His history of the Wampanoag described a United States that inherited both the Pilgrims' cruelty and the lands that they stole. Apess's oration—delivered by himself, a Pequot—belied white New Englanders' belief that Native Americans had vanished from their midst.[2]

Apess's history of the United States stood in stark contrast to that of Euro-Americans, many of whom believed that the United States' engagements with Indigenous peoples—including the policies of Indian removal—were among the most benevolent of the world. And their rhetoric reflected their belief.[3] When Apess put the words "father" and "my dear sons and daughters" into the mouth of President Jackson, he mobilized the paternalistic ideas and language that had driven U.S. Indian policy since Henry Knox became the nation's first secretary of war under the Constitution in 1789. When Apess claimed that the president wished "to drive you out, to get you away out of the reach of our civilized people, who are cheating you," he laid bare white Americans' own camouflaged quest to obtain Indigenous lands; he exposed the duplicity of the president's claim to do good while manifesting the disaster that was Indian removal.

While Apess drew upon the discourse of benevolence and exposed its hollowness, his *Eulogy* reserved particular scorn for white Christians and their missionary counterparts. Apess was a follower of the Methodist Church, yet the *Eulogy* betrayed his disillusionment with Euro-Americans' Christianity.[4] Not only was he angered by the Methodist Church's split views on slavery, but he also harbored personal disappointment with regard to his treatment by white society. He remarked that "in vain have I looked for the Christian to take me by the hand and bid me welcome to his cabin, as my fathers did then, before we were born."[5] He chastised missionaries for their costly work and their complicity in Indigenous removals: "The poor missionaries want money to go and convert the poor heathen, as if God could not convert them where they were but must first drive them out. If God wants the red men converted, we should think that he could do it as well in one place as in another."[6] Excluding no religious sect from condemnation, Apess issued a firm conclusion that "missionaries have injured us more than they have done us good."[7] While Apess seized Jackson's voice to reveal the horror of white Americans' linked campaigns to civilize and remove Native peoples, he simultaneously underscored missionaries' complicity in those efforts. In doing so, the Pequot man joined other Indigenous peoples in pushing against white Americans' belief in their own benevolence and in their power to craft their reputation.

* * *

Cultivating Empire follows Apess's lead both by charting the connections between mission work and the U.S. imperial project and by positioning the United States as an empire that grew out of North America's pasts.[8] As the *Eulogy* suggests, U.S. missionaries' work was not divorced from other developments in the republic. Ideas and policies of race, benevolence, civilization, and removal were intertwined in the early nineteenth-century United States, and each were implicated in the making of the American empire. Perhaps nowhere was this clearer than in the U.S. Civilization Plan, a policy crafted by the first secretary of war Henry Knox and secretary of state Timothy Pickering and carried out by missionaries and U.S. officials alike. One of the plan's goals was to acquire Native peoples' lands, yet many early Euro-Americans contended that that acquisition would take place by educating Native peoples in the ways of Euro-American-style agriculture and in the "domestic arts" (such as spinning and weaving). The advent of agriculture in Indian Country, they argued, would lead Native Americans to require fewer lands—lands that Euro-American settlers could then use for themselves. Settler desire for land, a concern for the honorable or benevolent reputation of the young republic, and the belief that Native peoples misused their abundant lands all encouraged the creation of the plan; fictions bolstered by Euro-Americans' ideas of race and Native peoples' supposed savagery facilitated the plan's acceptance.[9]

Agricultural education was at the heart of civilizing policies, yet other goals—such as the spread of Christian and moral ideals, the adoption of Euro-American patriarchal gender ideologies, and, sometimes, Euro-American forms of literacy—represented white Americans' hope that they could shift Native peoples' social and economic worlds. Missionaries were central to the plan, and members of the Moravian church, along with Presbyterians, Methodists, and, often in the earliest years of the nineteenth century, the Society of Friends (Quakers) worked to realize the plan's goals. Each of these groups brought to their work their own approaches and ideas regarding their faiths. Early on, Knox found particularly able partners in the Quakers thanks to their expertise and historical participation in Indian affairs, and Friends' relationship with the federal government proved both foundational and long-lasting. With federal support and funds from both public and private coffers, Friends and other missionaries performed the work of clearing fields, building agricultural infrastructure, and educating already agriculturally proficient Native people in the ways of Euro-American farming and domestic life. As the first several decades of the nineteenth century wore on, missions increased in number, as did the number of denominations with which the U.S. government worked. Such work was the backbone of the United States' quest to bring so-called "civilization" to Indian Country, and it—along with the ideals that accompanied it—contributed both to the expansion of U.S. territory and to the development of a national economy.

No doubt Apess had, in part, this work in mind when he chastised missionaries for their costly role in the making of Euro-Americans' empires in North America: missionaries during the era of the early American republic were, after all, agents of empire.[10] As with earlier imperial efforts, they could bolster federal authority, form or solidify relationships with Indigenous peoples, act as diplomats, facilitate the further spread of markets and consumerism, and alter the land in ways that Euro-Americans could use to both facilitate their own settlement and argue for Indigenous peoples' removals. Missionaries could do all this while also carrying to the heart of the continent Euro-Americans' ideas of what constituted "civilization," as well as their own ideas of religion and faith. They were individuals who helped make and manage Americans' empire, and their work ultimately contributed to the making of the U.S. imperial state and its economy.[11] Speaking and writing from 1836, Apess perhaps knew this all too well.

* * *

Civilizing missions and the federal government's civilization plan together furthered U.S. imperial development in Indian Country, and they therefore reveal much about the making of that empire. They offer a means to examine the manner and extent to which the U.S. imperial state exercised authority on the edges of the early American empire; they show how U.S. territorial and economic development took place and went hand in hand; they highlight the ways in which benevolence and philanthropy in the early republic were bound up in and reinforced the ideas of emerging racial capitalism (an economic system that had deep roots in Euro-Americans' notions of difference); and, finally, they allow us to explore how Native peoples shaped the American imperial project, the state, and its economy through their politics and efforts to assert authority and maintain sovereignty.[12] *Cultivating Empire* analyzes the history of missions and the U.S. civilization plan in an effort to better understand each of these phenomena and how they reinforced one another. By doing so, it also charts how U.S. missions in Indian Country both borrowed and diverged from earlier imperial precedents in North America.

At the center of this study lie connections between U.S. state formation, the development of capitalism in the new nation, the role of philanthropy in empire-building, and Indigenous authority. Understanding civilizing missions as a particular manifestation of philanthropy—what I call *speculative philanthropy*—offers a means to connect histories of the civilization plan with broader developments in North America and beyond. The term "speculative" is here used in both a territorial and economic sense: by framing philanthropy as speculative, I explicitly link the philanthropic and economic motivations that guided many of the civilization plan's participants. Speculative philanthropy, then, involved both a desire (which could be performative or grounded in a sense of paternalism) to promote the welfare of others as well as a drive to acquire economic, territorial, moral, or spiritual capital.

By understanding agricultural mission work and the civilization plan in the nineteenth century through the lens of speculative philanthropy, such efforts, regardless of motivations, gain grounding in the particular context of the early republic and its culture of speculation—an era when agricultural mission work took place in Indigenous lands that were coveted by settlers, speculators, and U.S. officials alike. Some civilizers and officials explicitly considered the profits that they and the United States more broadly might reap from Natives' lands through "improvement" and removal schemes, and they offered philanthropy and policies that were an economic investment in a future premised upon material changes in the land, agrarian labor, and, often, Indigenous dispossession. Others hoped to secure, through their words and deeds, a reputation for benevolence and the dividends of spiritual and moral capital that accompanied the "civilizing" of Native peoples. In either case, Indigenous authority and local, national, and international politics meant that such investments were never guaranteed to be successful.[13] Examining such work as speculative philanthropy underscores the ways in which white philanthropists and reformers offered their labor and funds as a means to invest in their own future capital—both economic and moral—often at the expense of Indigenous and marginalized peoples. The term allows for a nuanced reading of both benevolence and profit, and it allows us to explore the ways in which the quest for various kinds of profit—be it financial, political, or civilizational—often undergirded philanthropic work (with civilizing missions being one example) in the early republic and its world of emerging capitalism.[14] At the same time, the use of the term "speculative philanthropy" does not necessarily ascribe intentionality—it is impossible to know the motivations of every individual who engaged in acts or rhetoric of philanthropy. Rather, it offers a means to acknowledge some actors' quests to do good and others' overtures to do the same, even as it also shows the consequences of their work and how their efforts nonetheless created and perpetuated conditions of inequality, violence, and marginalization in early America.[15] Thinking with the concept of speculative philanthropy in the specific context of U.S. civilizing missions and policies elucidates, then, the larger processes behind the accumulation of territorial, economic, political, and what historian Christopher Leslie Brown terms "moral capital," as well as the ways in which a culture of speculation and investment permeated U.S. Indian policy.[16]

Both non-state and state actors—and those in between—were implicated in speculative philanthropy. As a result, speculative philanthropy found a place in civilizing missions, the U.S. civilization plan, and U.S. international relations both on the continent and overseas. Baltimore Quaker philanthropists, for example, engaged with the civilization plan for a combination of reasons—they were moved by a sense of benevolence, they sought moral capital and good standing in their communities, they hoped to transform Ohio Country lands and economy in ways that resembled their urban coast homes. State actors, meanwhile, performed the work of civilization for similar reasons, yet they also hoped to elevate the moral reputation of the young republic. They repeatedly argued for the benevolence of the United States in the realm of Indian affairs, investing in the policies of civilization at a time when they competed with Great Britain and other European empires to showcase an enlightened form of empire-building on the world stage. By the 1820s, U.S. officials invoked images of U.S. benevolence in the realm of Indian affairs—often rhetorically positioning missionaries as the vanguards of such work—and they worked to cultivate a reputation of humanitarianism in the world, using such images to do so.

Catholicism and Protestantism had accompanied Europeans' imperial efforts in North America and the Atlantic world, while civilization—a notion that was nonetheless entangled with Protestantism and Christianity—became the dominant creed through which U.S. imperialists justified their empire-building in North America and the world. Though some U.S. missionaries undoubtedly carried their (often) Protestant faith with them, particularly ideas regarding work, many, including Quakers, often positioned civilization as a necessary prerequisite to any religious instruction. The language and ideas of poor relief and charity were likewise key pieces of civilizing work, and civilizing funds often went toward the building of economic infrastructure rather than toward the purchase of Bibles or religious tracts. Such efforts were part and parcel of the world of philanthropy as a result, and the concept of speculative philanthropy facilitates a juxtaposition of the U.S. government's civilization plan alongside the broader reform efforts of the early republic. It offers a productive space for both reconceptualizing the way we understand reform movements in relation to state formation and empire-building and for ensuring that Indian Country occupies a central place in histories of the early nineteenth-century United States.[17]

* * *

Examining the intersections between speculative philanthropy, civilizing missions, and the U.S. civilization plan reveals much about early American empire-building, the development of racial capitalism in the early United States, and how Native peoples and their politics shaped both. To begin with, tracing the development of the civilizing project, missions, and missionaries' connections to the making of American empire illuminates the particular ways the U.S. imperial state grew, functioned, and managed territories on the edges of the imperial republic. The subject of federal state power has long been of interest to historians of the early United States, and often scholars have centered their debates on the size, visibility, and capability of the state.[18] Some historians have begun to center Indian Country in their analyses of such questions, and as a result their work offers rich detail regarding the administrative state in Indian Country, settler colonialism as it intersected with state power, and the importance of the U.S. military in garrisoning state power.[19] The state was an incredibly important presence on the edges of American empire, and underscoring that is imperative. As one scholar puts it, to see the American state "as distinctively 'weak' continues to frustrate a reckoning with American power in the twenty-first century."[20] So, too, does it frustrate any attempt to comprehend the violence that remade the North American continent and claimed Native lives and lands.[21] Yet, by centering civilizing missions as nodes within a burgeoning landscape of U.S. empire—nodes that operated thanks to far-flung and diverse individuals and networks—it becomes apparent that the state, settlers, local officials, and Indigenous actors together combined to create and negotiate the extent and limits of federal authority in Indian Country.[22] The state could be powerful, yet its power did not derive unilaterally from the top.[23]

The early U.S. imperial state, then, was one that grew and operated from a blending of federal, state, and local authority, and that authority was most visible on the empire's edges.[24] It was one that borrowed from precedents set by the British Empire, and, like the British model, it was one wherein a vision for political economy and territorial growth were realized both by coercive efforts and by distant actors who helped build the infrastructure of empire.[25] Though the terms "empire" or "imperial state" might threaten to obscure individual actors' efforts and experiences, highlighting the blended nature of the early American state ensures that individuals remain at the heart of the story. Indeed, the state was built as a result of myriad actors' actions and sometimes-competing impulses, and this becomes evident in an examination of the civilizing project and its consequences in the Ohio Country. The U.S. Indian agent John Johnston, for example, was a pivotal figure in Ohio Country politics because he was able to harness both national and local authority. As a result, he corresponded about and assisted with the civilizing project in the region, participated in local canal politics, managed Indian agencies, corresponded with high-level officials, and was both a face of the imperial state and a familiar individual who could broker day-to-day transactions. Johnston's authority, however, interacted with and was sometimes checked by the politics and desires of other individuals, such as the Miami leader Jean Baptiste Richardville (Pinšiwa)—a man who, among many other things, insisted on receiving a fair price for his people's land. The resulting actions or policies or treaties—and Native peoples' insistence that the U.S. meet treaty obligations—in turn produced, bolstered, or sometimes checked the federal state and U.S. Indian policy. Native people, then, were crucial to the defining of imperial state authority, even as they worked to define their own as well. By paying attention to both U.S. national and local politics—by approaching the history of American empire-building in Indian Country from a simultaneously top-down and bottom-up perspective—it becomes apparent that the growth of the U.S. state and its economy in the Ohio Country took place as a result of Indigenous peoples', settlers', and U.S. officials' negotiated and entangled motivations and endeavors.[26]

Centering the U.S. federal government's partnerships with various individuals and organizations is also key to understanding how the blended early American state operated. The civilization plan was built upon and flourished because of governmental partnerships with missionaries and their societies.

Members of the Society of Friends and other religious societies were non-government individuals who were nonetheless quasi-state actors. Friends and other missionary societies performed diplomatic work alongside U.S. government officials, corresponded with federal and state actors, shared information about local Indigenous politics, and offered their labor in mission spaces. In return, they received financial support and public lands for their missions, as well as explicit endorsements, often from the secretary of war or the president, that facilitated both traveling to mission sites and striking up partnerships with regional Indian agents.

After years of working with Friends and other missionaries, the U.S. government institutionalized its partnership with missionary societies in 1819 with the passage of the Civilization Fund Act, which guaranteed $10,000 annually for missionary endeavors in Indian Country.[27] Another prominent missionary society, the American Board of Commissioners for Foreign Missions (ABCFM), established in 1810, followed the model of agricultural education, and they continued, like the Friends, to work at home and overseas into the twentieth century. The United States' partnership with missionary societies lingered throughout the century: Friends served, for example, as key partners of the Grant administration's "Peace Policy" in Indian Country after the U.S. Civil War.[28] Analyzing the formation of the partnership between the U.S. government and the Society of Friends and other missionary societies is therefore foundational to understanding both the United States' humanitarian work in the nineteenth and twentieth centuries as well as how the early state developed and operated.

* * *

Following the civilizing project and its consequences in the Ohio Country also offers one means to explore how U.S. political and economic development went hand in hand—and how ideas of race became baked into the foundation of that development.[29] Agricultural missions in Indian Country served as nodes that could connect urban manufacturing centers with rural fields and towns as a result of the shipment of wares such as axes and hoes, and they offered a means to encourage Native peoples' consumerism and agricultural labor. In the process, missionaries perpetuated conceptions of Native peoples as other, and offered instruction in very specific kinds of labor: farming, spinning, and weaving. As many scholars have pointed out, in the United States, as elsewhere, the histories of capitalism, race, and imperialism are intertwined.[30] Studying the civilization project offers a means to chart these linkages.

If speculative philanthropy encourages us to understand how religious philanthropy and a culture of profit intersected in the early republic, the *mission complex* offers a means to see the material and economic consequences of civilizing work in Indian Country and, indeed, the world—to see, in other words, a material manifestation of speculative philanthropy on the ground. Understanding the networks of markets and capital that linked missionaries, philanthropists, manufacturers, federal officials, and Indigenous peoples as a mission complex offers a means to examine how the connections between philanthropy and profit operated in Miami and Shawnee Country. The concept of a mission complex highlights the fact that mission work required labor as well as manufactured items such as axes, hoes, and plows, which were most often produced and shipped from the urban coast toward forts and emerging cities like Fort Wayne and Cincinnati, but also from places like Britain as well. The federal government often partnered with members of the Society of Friends for mission work in the Ohio Country, and it offered several Friends salaries and, in at least one instance, public lands for their mission work. Such investments, along with the broader mission complex, ultimately aided in clearing fields and building the markets and infrastructure that eventually dovetailed with the rapid growth of canal and railroad construction in the region.

The mission complex offers a clear way to chart Indian Country's close connection with the rise of capitalism in the United States. The emphasis on agricultural production and the consumption of American manufactures in Indian Country complemented the expansion of the U.S. market economy and further encouraged the intertwined development of both the agricultural and manufacturing sectors of the American economy—an intertwining that men like Tench Coxe and Thomas Jefferson debated in the years of the early republic.[31] Meanwhile, the labor, funds, infrastructure, and emphasis on the commodification of land that accompanied mission work made those Native lands, to Euro-American eyes, even more valuable than they already were, while Native peoples' work to adapt to a changing economy likewise fueled settler desires. Ohio Country lands were, after all, the key to (literally) feeding the markets that knit together the United States, including those that stretched to the southern economy and its regime of slavery. Such perceived value encouraged additional settler greed and led to further calls for Indigenous peoples' removals—removals that cleared the way for the "transportation revolution" that so many scholars point to as playing a crucial role in the "transition to capitalism." Yet many of the most oft-cited histories of this transition, changes in transportation, and "market revolution" fail to explicitly and thoroughly explore how Indigenous dispossession was the foundation—though not an inevitability—of the particular developments they chart.[32] *Cultivating Empire* corrects this oversight. It analyzes speculative philanthropy, the mission complex, settler and speculator greed, and federal support to illuminate how Indigenous dispossession and the development of railroads and canals were intertwined, with that intertwining often dismissed under the guise of benevolence and progress. By doing so, *Cultivating Empire* also adds to the conversation regarding the role of government in nineteenth-century economic policy. While other scholars have shown that government played a role in facilitating the transportation revolution, federal Indian policy and Indigenous dispossession is too often missing from the story of canals and railroads in places like the Ohio Country.[33]

Just as the transportation revolution was not possible without government assistance, the mission complex was not possible without financing. Missionary societies and private donations provided funds for the missions, but that money was accompanied by federal dollars as well—particularly after the passage of the 1819 Civilization Fund Act. The public, and some private, money that financed missions was often raised with merchant capital. Scholarship on early republic customs houses demonstrates clearly that customs were the primary source of revenue for the early federal government; this revenue in turn funded the work of American empire on the continent.[34] What was more, many of the most prominent Friends who contributed their own labor, time, and funds to the early civilizing project often did so thanks to the boons of Atlantic trade.

Many of the most prominent members of the Baltimore Indian Concerns Committee were wealthy men who made their money as a result of their work as traders, merchants, or bankers. Philip E. Thomas—a Quaker and the eventual president of the Baltimore & Ohio Railroad—donated his time and no doubt his money, too, to Friends' civilizing mission work as a prominent member of the Indian Concerns Committee. Thomas's work on that committee was, however, an investment: by supporting the commodification and "improvement" of lands in ways that increased white settlers' greed, civilizing missions ultimately aided in the dispossession of Ohio Country Native peoples, which in turn cleared the path for the building of his B&O Railroad.[35] Thomas's investment was, moreover, also one in power derived from a benevolent reputation and social standing or moral capital: at least one publication memorialized Thomas as, "in the largest sense, a philanthropist."[36]

Thomas's contributions to Friends' civilizing work ultimately paid handsomely, and it anticipated the common practice of funneling private wealth to invest in far-flung infrastructure during the later nineteenth century.[37] Civilizing missions ultimately, then, help illuminate the connections between imperialism and capitalism in the early United States. As Thomas's connection to Friends' civilizing missions suggests, considering philanthropy's role in supporting the civilization project, while also taking into account philanthropy's connection to the world of speculation and emergent capitalism (as well as ideas of race), offers a means to complicate the notion and role of philanthropy in the early republic—and, indeed, in the United States broadly. It opens a space to understand that a desire to do good could coexist with a desire to make profit; it leaves space, too, to see that such work further created and entrenched racial and social hierarchies.

Scholarship on world economies and the transatlantic slave trade has shown that capitalism grew out of older political economies that were built upon assumptions of difference, with the emergence of racial capitalism being, in the words of Robin D. G. Kelley, "dependent on slavery, violence, imperialism, and genocide."[38] In analyzing the actions, politics, and rhetoric that made Indigenous dispossession so profitable for Euro-Americans in North America, *Cultivating Empire* highlights the ways in which speculative philanthropy and Indigenous dispossession were central to the United States' economic development.[39] At the same time, this book's focus on missionaries' and reformers' actions offers a means to see the ways in which larger processes of dispossession and violence both furthered and were built upon inequalities, marginalization, and ideas of difference. By the 1820s and 1830s, a distinct form of "benevolent racism" guided white reformers, and ideas of racial difference informed and were perpetuated by numerous reform projects, including the civilizing missions.[40] If numerous scholars of the new histories of capitalism have revealed how insurers, enslavers, and merchants commodified human beings in their everyday tallies and calculations—and in turn reaped the profits of violence—one aim of this book is to show how reformers assumed, perpetuated, and created ideas of race and difference in their own efforts.[41] It also demonstrates that reformers' work, ideologies, and the discourse of philanthropy informed government policy on the continent and overseas. By doing so, it shows the extent to which such ideas grew to be systemic in early American society and how they continued to be so throughout the nineteenth century and beyond. It is in large part for this reason that *Cultivating Empire* traces the work of reform and religious societies in its analysis of the political, social, and economic history of the early United States: doing so enables us to see the larger and everyday impulses that created and perpetuated the marginalization of people of color in the early republic.

* * *

While Euro-American reformers and state actors brought their ideas of race, economy, and benevolence to their efforts, Indigenous peoples, too, had their own ideas of philanthropy and welfare that likewise influenced the civilizing project. Cherokees' conceptions of social services, for example, offered a means by which they could adapt to other social welfare systems and new social realities produced by Euro-American colonialism, create a hybrid system, and maintain some of their older forms of social welfare.[42] In the Ohio Country, Miamis and Shawnees wove ideas of poverty and distress into their negotiations with Euro-Americans, borrowing from their own ideas of community and reciprocity. Nonetheless, these ideas, like Cherokees' systems of welfare, adapted and changed over time, and Native individuals wove their own notions of poverty and charity into their rhetoric in ways that secured material goods for themselves and their people, shaped the policies of the United States, and reminded the United States of their treaty obligations to sovereign Native nations. Miamis, Wyandots, Delawares, and their neighbors, then, heard the overture of Euro-Americans' speculative philanthropy and shaped it for their own purposes.

Missions offered the U.S. imperial state political footholds in Miami Country and Shawnee Country. They physically transformed Ohio Country landscapes and markets in ways that facilitated the ongoing development of both the American state and its economy, and they enabled missionaries, officials, and settlers alike to claim "philanthropic" intentions—whether heartfelt or not—while investing in their own futures. Yet Native peoples were not passive recipients of "civilization," nor were they reactionaries. Some Native peoples found much meaning in Christianity, while others strategically engaged with missionaries and their civilizing efforts, and still others protested and refused to do the same. The U.S. civilization plan and civilizing missions thus offer a means to trace how Native peoples chose to engage or not engage with the U.S. imperial project as well as how they shaped their own landscapes, communities, and futures. Some Miamis, Shawnees, and their neighbors used missionaries, Indian agents, and the discourse of civilization to their advantage by accepting these and other Euro-Americans' labor as well as infrastructure on their lands. They also used these Euro-Americans to invest in their lands in an effort to gain economic power and remain, and they developed diplomatic partnerships with the U.S. government and its representatives on the ground to do so. Such efforts borrowed from Algonquian notions of diplomacy, reciprocity, and charity but also reflected these peoples' ongoing willingness to engage with—and shape—a changing economy.

Following these developments in the Ohio Country directs the attention of scholars of the early republic toward the heart of the continent and demonstrates that histories examining the development of the U.S. state and American capitalism must consider the ways in which peoples and policies in Indian Country shaped the creation of both. It also allows us to trace Indigenous peoples' *survivance*—a term coined by the Anishinaabe scholar Gerald Vizenor—in order to understand the ways in which their politics shaped their own lives and societies and the American empire itself.[43]

Miami chiefs Little Turtle (Mihšihkinaahkwa) and Richardville, the Shawnee chief Black Hoof, along with myriad individuals each made political decisions that changed and sometimes buoyed their own communities and that shifted, engrained, or sometimes eradicated U.S. Indian policies. When allied Native people gathered at Wapakoneta to discuss removal in 1823, for example, they agreed to send "a deputation of each Tribe . . . to the City of Washington with [Captain] Lewis . . . to state their views and wishes, exchange their lands, and make arrangements to move to and occupy such lands as they may receive in exchange." Captain Lewis was chief of a town wherein Quakers had worked, he had the ear of William Clark, and he was generally well-connected. In a letter to John C. Calhoun, Clark revealed the allied peoples' desires that the government would "give to Indians forming this Council a settlement by which they may exact & enforce their own law and regulations necessary towards the agricultural life, in which they are extremely anxious to exchange that of the hunters; So precarious of the means of Subsistance and so little to be depended on in future."[44] While Clark's pen formed these phrases, the sentiments expressed therein are reflective of the many moments when Native peoples used the rhetoric of civilization and agriculture to achieve political ends. Here, Captain Lewis, who was chief of a town where Quakers established a mission for a time, employed the rhetoric of agriculture and civilization—to "exchange" their lives "of the hunters"—in an effort to secure as best a plot of land west of the Mississippi as they could. He also, however, insisted that they be able to "enforce their own law and regulations"—he insisted on their sovereignty. Such efforts are representative of Native peoples' willingness—and, often, need—to engage in negotiations with the U.S. state. They also reveal why it is vital to highlight these moments when trying to understand how the U.S. imperial state operated: Native peoples' negotiations forced U.S. imperial officials to recalibrate their demands—sometimes in seemingly small ways, from Euro-Americans' perspectives—and they simultaneously bolstered and checked the state's authority by recognizing the state as an entity to which they could petition and by insisting that the U.S. maintain its treaty obligations.

Sometimes, Native peoples traveled to Washington, DC, to be heard; sometimes they penned petitions and encouraged their white allies to present their proposals and requests for them; and many times they used a combination of these strategies to achieve their goals. As in the case of Captain Lewis and his allies, often the rhetoric of civilization accompanied these strategies, signaling the fact that U.S. civilizing policies could both wreak damage on Native communities and provide additional tools with which Native peoples could combat and negotiate American imperialism. While such strategies were not universally adopted or successful—violence nonetheless claimed many Native lives—in some cases, they enabled Native people to secure better lands and to stave off the worst abuses of the federal government and Euro-American settlers. In other cases, they were able to influence the trajectory of U.S. policies and the attitudes of its settlers and representatives.

Following these moments of pushing back against U.S. policies and plans, *Cultivating Empire* aims to reframe the history of the U.S. civilization plan—and U.S. Indian policies more broadly—by focusing on the ways in which Indigenous peoples engaged civilizing agents and, indeed, shaped the very policies that sought their dispossession. By leaning on the scholars who crafted the New Indian History, settler-colonial studies, and Indigenous history, *Cultivating Empire* builds upon and is indebted to a rich lineage of work that similarly places Indian Country at the heart of early North American history.[45] It follows these scholars' lead and insists that policies—and thus policy histories—are not and cannot be merely one-directional: they are shaped both by those who seek to enact them and by those who live with them. The chapters that follow thus contribute to a new reading of U.S. Indian policy—one informed by the Indigenous and local politics of the early nineteenth century—and it analyzes that policy in the context of U.S. imperial state formation and economic change. This survey of the civilization plan, early U.S. Indian policies, and empire aims to center both the stories of Indigenous survivance as well as the history of state and settler violence in Indian Country. In doing so, it explores the ways in which the political economy and the political landscape of what is now the United States developed as a result of the politics of U.S. officials, settlers, capitalist philanthropists, and Indigenous leaders and people.

* * *

The Ohio Country serves as a logical focus for this present study of missionary work, empire, speculative philanthropy, economy, and Indigenous peoples' survivance and politics. Though scholars define the geographic bounds of the region differently, *Cultivating Empire* focuses on the lands and peoples that make up present-day Ohio and Indiana. Because of the frequency with which the Society of Friends cooperated with the U.S. federal government, particularly during the foundational years of the civilizing program, their work also offers a logical case study for much of the book's early analysis. Beginning in the late eighteenth century, members of the Society of Friends established and maintained agricultural missions in what is now New York State and in the Ohio Country: Philadelphia Friends labored in the former, in Haudenosaunee Country; Baltimore Friends, meanwhile, worked in the latter on the lands that Shawnees, Miami and Wabash confederacies, Delawares, Wyandots, and their neighbors called home. As time wore on, other missionary societies received money and assistance from the federal government, and missions and mission schools grew more numerous.

Baltimore Friends established their agricultural missions within the bounds of these modern-day states, at Wapakoneta and Captain Lewis Town (Lewistown) in Ohio and at Dennis's Station (near present-day Huntington) in Indiana, and it was also in the Ohio Country that the federal government established its blueprint for colonization with the Northwest Ordinance of 1787. That document established the procedure for U.S. territorial acquisition and for the translation of "territories" into "states" and "settlers" into "citizens" who possessed the equal rights of their counterparts in other states. It was here, too, that Indigenous dispossession cleared the path for the technological marvels—railroads, canals—that scholars have long associated with the rise of capitalism. An analysis of the region allows us to see how American imperialism facilitated the economic rise of one of the most rapidly changing regions in the early United States—and to see how that rise compared to the ways in which Indigenous dispossession, the civilization plan, and the expansion of slavery intersected with one another in the Old Southwest.[46]

What becomes quickly apparent in an examination of civilizing efforts in the Ohio Country is that any history of mission work in this relatively small region requires an examination of more far-flung locales. Colonial Pennsylvania, early republic Baltimore, and even western New York, Detroit, Missouri, and London factor into the story of American empire in the Ohio Country. For this reason, *Cultivating Empire* begins and ends with an examination of how wider-ranging places and their histories connect with the story that unfolded in Miami and Shawnee Country. Traveling Quakers, U.S. officials, settlers, and Native people created linkages between discrete locales, and such linkages should encourage scholars to understand regional histories in a wider context. While there is much scholarship that pays excellent attention to the Ohio Valley and Great Lakes, one of the aims of *Cultivating Empire* is to encourage further connections between continental and Atlantic—and, indeed, world—historiographical paradigms.[47]

The mission complex was both a product and producer of the American economy and its social relations, and it operated in the Ohio Country and lands beyond. Mission work in what settlers termed the "Old Southwest"—Choctaw Country, Chickasaw Country—followed the same general formula wherein agricultural and trade labor (which likewise required material goods) were bedrocks of mission education. Missions and mission schools in the Southwest could also offer markers of U.S. authority—largely because, in both regions, the U.S. needed markers of authority as it confronted sovereign Indigenous nations and *their* authority. The processes that resulted from settlers' desire for land upon which to build railroads in the Ohio Country shared similarities with settlers' desire to expand slavery in the Old Southwest, yet they also diverged—in no small part because Indigenous and enslaved peoples made these spaces as well.[48]

American missionaries in Liberia, too, endeavored to bring the "gifts" of civilization to free Africans there, and they, too, opened new markets for consumption and linked these markets with the United States. Early Americans themselves understood the situations of Native Americans, African Americans, and laboring peoples as connected and in dialogue with one another: Missionaries compared the civilization plan with the colonization plan that endeavored to send free African Americans to Liberia, while Baltimore Friends perceived Ohio Natives, and explicitly wrote about them, in ways that drew upon their experiences living among the enslaved peoples and wage laborers of the city. Agricultural mission work among Native peoples, then, was bound up in and connected to other ideas and developments of the republic at large. While *Cultivating Empire* takes the Ohio Country and Miami and Shawnee Country as its focus, the story here shares many similarities with other locales—along with crucial differences—that other scholars will undoubtedly continue to chart in histories to come. One goal of this work is to point to these larger imperial aims while simultaneously emphasizing the extent to which Indigenous peoples—as individuals and nations—shaped, negotiated, and therefore produced alterations in those aims on the ground.

The book contains three parts. Part I, Foundations, discusses the history of missionary-imperial cooperation in North America into the 1790s. This section offers a backdrop for understanding the ways in which U.S. Indian policy both borrowed and diverged from early imperial precedents, and it also showcases the vital role that Indigenous authority played in that process. Chapter 1 offers a broad chronological and policy overview that complements Chapter 2's focus on ground-level politicking and relationship-building during the 1790s Northwest Indian War. Taking these chapters together, this section argues that we must understand the imperial state as a blended one that grew out of earlier imperial precedents and that analyzing top-down and bottom-up efforts reveals much regarding how the United States more broadly, Indigenous nations, and missionaries related to one another in the late eighteenth and early nineteenth century.

Part II, Routes, progresses to the early nineteenth century and tracks the development of agricultural mission work in the Ohio Country by following both the development and flow of ideas as well as the movement of material goods, labor, and capital more broadly. This section is particularly concerned with speculative philanthropy and the ideas of race, humanitarianism, profit, and "useful" education that undergirded it, and it centers on the construction and functioning of the mission complex by highlighting the material connections and transformations that took place as a result of mission work in Indian Country. The section keeps its focus upon the Society of Friends yet narrows to examine Baltimore Friends in particular, as it was they who continued to work with the Shawnees, Miamis, and neighboring peoples in the Ohio Country while Philadelphia Friends worked among the Haudenosaunee in what is now New York State.

Part III, Negotiations, explores the consequences of the mission complex as well as its connection to the continuing growth of the American empire and its economy abroad. It also demonstrates, however, that Native peoples shaped that growth by engaging with the politics of speculative philanthropy according to their own logics and in an effort to realize their visions of their futures. Such efforts frustrated U.S. officials, leading one trader and merchant to comment that the Miamis, in particular, were "a damnd rebelious race." Native individuals' use of petitions, meanwhile, enabled them to seek redress for stolen goods and for obligations that the United States government left unfulfilled. These efforts showcase Native peoples' knowledge of U.S. bureaucracy and their ability to rely upon Indian agents like John Johnston to ensure that their petitions were heard, and they highlight the fact that Native individuals recognized the U.S. imperial state as an entity to which they could make claims. Such strategies of survivance and negotiation ensured that the U.S. empire and its policies did not develop solely from the top down, but rather that Native peoples continuously shaped policies with their own politics.

After the passage of the Civilization Fund Act in 1819, the federal government partnered with and offered funding to an increasingly diverse array of religious societies. As ideas of removals became a more explicit piece of official rhetoric and policy by the 1820s, missions and removals increasingly went hand in hand. Missionaries explicitly wove economic considerations into their civilizing projects, and Native peoples' own investments in their lands encouraged settlers to clamor for the removal of Native peoples in the Ohio Country. The 1820s and beyond saw Euro-American population growth in the region, and it ushered in a period of rapid transformation in economic infrastructure—canals and railroads in particular—that rendered, from settlers' perspectives, the presence of Native Americans increasingly intolerable. Missionaries' own rhetoric of humanitarianism and speculative philanthropy ultimately intersected with the transportation revolution and facilitated Indigenous peoples' dispossession.

The book closes with an examination of how missionaries, settlers, and U.S. officials each capitalized on mission work and ideas of humanitarianism to cultivate an image of American benevolence abroad. It shows that the history of speculative philanthropy and the American empire in Indian Country is thus crucial for understanding the role of the U.S. in the world.

Ultimately, then, *Cultivating Empire* illuminates the ways in which philanthropy and reform intersected with the emergence of capitalism and ideas of race, and it demonstrates that Indigenous peoples shaped the contours of the American empire while also struggling, surviving, and, sometimes, thriving. It insists that we cannot understand the development of the U.S. imperial state and its economy without centering Indian Country in that story. Settlers' commodification and accumulation of Indigenous lands enriched the American empire, making possible so many of the technological marvels and human tragedies—namely, the transportation revolution and slavery—that marked the rise of American capitalism. Missionaries established and perpetuated the United States' claim to benevolence on the continent and the world stage, all while exposing philanthropy's inextricable link with emergent capitalism in the United States. At the same time, however, Native peoples and their strategies of survivance ensured that they would continue to negotiate the terms of American empire into the twenty-first century, as they have on the Standing Rock Sioux reservation—resisting the brand of American colonialism that is premised upon extracting profit from the land. *Cultivating Empire*, then, explores the United States' imperial beginnings, while also offering a means to understand the world that we are left with today.

PART I

Foundations

CHAPTER 1

Missionaries and the Making of a New Empire in North America

In 1804, Gerard T. Hopkins, Baltimore Quaker and prominent urban grocer, was far from home. He had recently completed a journey beyond the Appalachian Mountains to the Ohio Country and, more specifically, to the homelands of the Miamis. He no doubt felt both out of place and confident: though he was in unfamiliar surroundings, he believed that he brought with him a great gift. Presenting himself before the powerful chief Little Turtle of the Miamis, he declared that he was "confident that if you will pursue our method in the cultivation of your lands that you will live in much greater ease & plenty and with much less fatigue & toil than attend hunting for a subsistance." He continued to assure the Miamis gathered that their land was "far better than the land the white people cultivate near the great water," and that he and his fellow Quakers were "persuaded that your land will produce double the quantity of any kind of grain, of flax or hemp with the same labour that is necessary near the great-water." Likely feeling assured that his message was sound, his society's plan a good one, Hopkins would soon return to his home in Baltimore, while his colleague Philip Dennis remained behind to open a model farm. Through the labor of Dennis and on a patch of earth near the Wabash River, Baltimore Friends sowed the seeds of their hope: through education, Friends thought, the Miamis might cultivate their vast and fertile lands, and, in the process, they—Native individuals and missionaries alike—might grow as human beings too.[1]

The U.S. federal government explicitly endorsed Hopkins and Dennis's journey. Just several years prior, secretary of war Henry Knox had declared, "Missionaries of excellent moral character should be appointed to reside in their nation, who should be well supplied with all the implements of husbandry and the necessary stock for a farm. These men should be made the instruments to work on the indians [*sic*]."[2] Highlighting the manufactures, land, and labor required for this policy path, Knox offered, in a few lines, the outlines of the U.S. civilization plan. The centerpiece of the plan was agricultural education, and that plan was why Hopkins and Dennis traversed hundreds of miles to reach the Miamis: by teaching the continent's Indigenous peoples to farm, Euro-Americans' thinking went, civilizers could "save" Native peoples from "extinction" by discouraging their supposed overreliance upon game.[3] At the same time, however, civilization's boosters could also ensure that neat plots of private property and farmland would replace large, open hunting spaces to the advantage of land-seeking settler colonizers. Hopkins would not be the only Euro-American to notice that Ohio Country lands were "far better than the land the white people cultivate near the great water." He also did not fail to notice the abundance of crops that were already growing thanks to the skill of Indigenous women. The Ohio Country was, after all, a land of Indigenous prosperity—the product of sustained trade between Native nations and between Native peoples and Atlantic markets.[4] Perhaps what the Quaker underestimated at the time was the extent to which his society's efforts would become inextricable from Indigenous dispossession.

With the institution of the civilization plan, Knox hoped to dispossess the continent's Native people by what he deemed to be cost-effective, efficient, and, according to his rhetoric, honorable means. Knox was a military man who played a key role in the Continental Army during the American Revolution. He was both a trusted leader and a friend of George Washington, who would later appoint him to the post of secretary of war. Knox understood the financial costs of war: the republic was deeply in debt following the American Revolution, and he hoped to avoid costly violence with the continent's sovereign Indigenous nations.[5] Civilization, diplomacy, treaty-making, and gift-giving, the secretary determined, would enable the United States to gain the lands it coveted while also avoiding the expenses of war.

Knox worked alongside both President Washington and secretary of state Timothy Pickering to make the plan reality, and these latter men shared Knox's vision of a strong federal government taking the lead in the republic's Indian affairs: they believed that if the federal government took precedence over the states, dealings with Native nations would be orderly. With the advent of the federally directed civilization plan, they thought, Native peoples would receive both funds and the "gift" of Euro-Americans' civilization in exchange for their lands. Guided by such notions of systematic and paternalistic colonization, Knox, Washington, and Pickering hoped to both reap the financial profits from the sale of Indigenous lands and position the United States as humanitarian on the world stage.[6] Complementing the federal civilization plan would be other federally centered policies such as the Trade and Intercourse Acts and land ordinances that attempted to transform Native lands into territories of the young republic.

President Washington heartily supported the civilization plan, and it was first implemented by both missionaries and Indian agents in Haudenosaunee, Cherokee, and Creek Country. Quaker missionaries established missions in the 1790s among the Oneidas and the Senecas in what is now New York State, while Indian agents Silas Dinsmoor and, most especially, Benjamin Hawkins took the early lead in carrying out the civilizing work among the Cherokees, Creeks, and their neighbors in the Southwest Territory. These civilizing agents encouraged the adoption of private property: they hoped that Senecas and Cherokees each would fence in and cultivate individual plots of crops.[7] Teaching "proper" land use was central to the civilization plan, and the heart of early civilizing spaces was the farm.

Indian agents like Hawkins remained crucial components of the civilization plan, yet, increasingly over time, numerous religious societies would take up the task as well. In Miami Country (in present-day Indiana), for example, Quakers established a simple model farm—dubbed "Little Turtle's Farm School" after the prominent chief Little Turtle. A small mission, the farm school consisted of a farmed plot of land and a dwelling for the missionary, at first Philip Dennis, who modeled Euro-American agricultural practices. Euro-American and Native laborers might add grist and sawmills to mission grounds, as they did, for example, at the Quaker mission among the Shawnees at Wapakoneta (in present-day Ohio). Depending on the desires of missionaries' pupils-to-be and the leadership of the nation wherein they hoped to work, however, missions could be either contained towns where people could choose to settle, or, more often, missionaries offered a model farm and a central set of buildings. Those who wished to emulate the model farm's work in these latter spaces would then do so near their own homes.[8] By the 1820s—after the U.S. federal government institutionalized its subsidies for civilizing work with the Civilization Fund Act—missions grew in number and were often more complex: they ranged from missionary families offering model farms to large-scale manual-labor boarding schools. These latter institutions usually kept a place for the model farm as part of a complex of buildings.[9]

Figure 1. 1804 map of Ohio. Baltimore Friends' earliest missions in the region were in Miami Country near Fort Wayne and among the Shawnees at Wapakoneta in what is now Ohio. Library of Congress, Geography and Map Division.

Thanks to the efforts of numerous scholars, we know much about how these civilizing spaces kindled cultural interaction and negotiation between Native and Euro-American peoples. Yet equally important to consider is how missionaries, civilizing agents, and Native individuals saw and used these spaces as ones that could promote their political and economic interests. So, too, is it important to understand how this plan connected to, built upon, and encouraged other early U.S. imperial policies. How Indigenous peoples interacted with and sometimes manipulated these spaces for their own purposes, why Euro-Americans developed and advocated for civilizing missions and the civilization plan—why they placed so much hope in missionaries—and how missions contributed to the making of American empire and its economy are the central issues that animate this book.

Before we can fully understand the ramifications of Knox's pronouncement and the civilizing project—and before we can fully grasp why Hopkins and Dennis showed up in Miami lands in the first place—it is crucial to note that when Knox and his compatriots conceived of the U.S. civilization plan in 1789, its agriculture-focused missions, and a proposed partnership with missionaries to carry it out, they did not create a wholly novel paradigm of imperialism. The United States instead borrowed from an older imperial script: the Spanish, French, and British Empires also engaged missionaries in their North American imperial schemes, and, in each of these empires, mission spaces centered religion yet also furthered imperial political and economic goals.[10] Missionaries were crucial agents of myriad imperial states in North America, and missions served as crucial political footholds and economic nodes in the Spanish and French Empires, in particular. Even British missionaries who lacked the hierarchical organization of their Catholic counterparts served pivotal political, diplomatic, cultural, and economic roles in the British Empire. In this way, Knox, Pickering, and Washington picked up where other empires had left off: they formulated a civilizing plan that borrowed from the lessons of the continent's imperial past.[11] Like earlier empires, missions in the United States could be spaces of religious and cultural negotiation, and they would be hinges for political and economic change as well.

It is therefore important that we begin our examination of civilizing missions and American empire by touring the ways in which the civilization plan was both old and necessarily innovative. The increasing pressures of settler colonialism—a process wherein settlers work to dissolve Indigenous societies and replace them with their own—shifting geopolitics, technologies, and economies in the late eighteenth and early nineteenth centuries meant that the United States had to adapt earlier imperial blueprints to an evolving world.[12] The civilization plan was one such adaptation, yet so, too, were other imperial policies such as the Northwest Ordinance and the Trade and Intercourse acts.

Knox articulated the civilization plan at the precise moment that the United States both embarked upon the work of constructing its imperial machinery on the continent and worked to build the republic following the American Revolution. He, along with missionaries like Dennis and Hopkins and Native individuals like Chief Little Turtle, helped conceive of missionaries' relationship to the U.S. state while also operating in a world of evolving land ordinances, acts that regulated trade, a new Constitution, and a continent of shifting Indigenous politics. The civilization plan and the various land and trade acts were key policies for an imperial republic that was desperate for private property—land that could mitigate settler violence and that would raise revenue as a result of land sales. Following the longer history of missions in North America, including the roles of Catholic and Protestant missionaries, Quakers, and Native peoples—with particular attention paid to missions' relationships to imperial politics and economies—therefore offers a means to examine the ways in which the emerging U.S. empire and its officers both borrowed and diverged from its Atlantic forebears. Understanding how and why the civilization plan emerged alongside other imperial ordinances and laws, meanwhile, enables us to understand both the limitations of top-down policies and how they worked with the U.S. civilization plan and agents on the ground to construct the scaffolding for empire. Such work offers a means to explore how the U.S. state developed and how it defined what the role of missionaries would be in and on the edges of the continent's newest empire.

* * *

Earlier Spanish, French, and British imperial projects each incorporated missions as part of their political and economic schemes, though the relationships between missions, the missionary impulse, and the imperial state differed in extent and character in each. In the Spanish Empire, for example, Catholic leaders worked in close partnership with the state, sometimes serving as officials, and religion was a central component of policies and practices. Missions and Christian imperialism likewise played roles in altering Indigenous peoples' economic and social lives in these empires, yet such changes could also vary. The existence of such commonalities and differences suggests the extent to which the United States was part of and borrowed from an Atlantic imperial paradigm, though it also displays the extent to which imperial policies—including those of the United States—were the product of both top-down and bottom-up decision-making and contingencies. There was nothing preordained about Spanish, English, French, or U.S. imperial policies, and there was no straight line from these earlier empires to that of the United States. Yet each grew out of the world of European empires. In each case, moreover, was a constant: Indigenous peoples negotiated imperial worlds of all sorts, and many used missions and missionaries as one way to do so. Such would remain the case in the American empire.

As one historian observes, missions "differed across the Spanish Borderlands, as they differed throughout the Americas, and that variety was a function of time, place, and above all, people: those who held the keys to the kingdom, and those who elected to enter Christendom."[13] In short, there was a vast diversity among missions and mission experiences—and many scholars have offered in-depth analyses of missionary endeavors in various empires over time.[14] An overview of missions and their relationships with imperial states and economies here will allow us to explore the imperial lineages and foundations for the ways in which Christianity and notions of civilization likewise permeated U.S. Indian policies. It will encourage us to refrain from seeing 1776 as a total break in North American imperial history, and it will offer a starting point for exploring the ways in which Indigenous peoples negotiated American imperialism in and near civilizing mission spaces, just as they had with Atlantic empires and missions and missionaries prior.

Catholic and Protestant missions developed in dialogue with one another and with African and Indigenous beliefs in the Atlantic world.[15] Catholic Spaniards took the lead when it came to efforts to convert Indigenous souls in the Americas beginning in the fifteenth and sixteenth centuries; their Iberian counterparts, the Portuguese, focused their religious attentions on the kingdoms of Africa. The Spanish Empire's governing structure was hierarchical and organized, with Indigenous lands of North and South America carved up into viceroyalties that viceroys and regional governors oversaw. Despite such organization, individuals throughout the empire played key roles in asserting and maintaining imperial authority, even as individuals—merchants and smugglers involved in illicit trade, for example—also found ways to adapt or evade imperial policies as befit their circumstances and with, sometimes, the tacit support of local bureaucrats.[16]

Spanish religious men often worked alongside conquistadores in the Americas, performing mass baptisms in an effort to, from their perspective, save the souls of Indigenous peoples in the case of death.[17] Meanwhile, the infamous *Requerimiento* encapsulated the intertwining of religious conversion, colonialism, and policy in Spain's empire in the Americas: Spaniards declared the Catholic Church and the pope as the highest power on the earth, required Native peoples to accept Christianity, and demanded their political subjugation as well. The policies, rhetoric, and justification of the Spanish Empire were intimately linked with the idea of converting Indigenous peoples to Christianity, yet the work did not end with conversion. In mission sites and *reducciones*, clergy and settlers alike carried out the work of ensuring that Indigenous peoples lived according to the precepts of Catholicism.

Economy, religion, and power were central to the Spanish imperial project in North America. In New Spain, one of missionaries' crucial roles as agents of empire was participating in and facilitating the extraction of labor from Indigenous peoples. Friars and priests often supported imperial economic schemes, and top-down directives to convert Native peoples to Christianity as part of the *encomienda* (wherein a conquistador received title to land and Indigenous laborers) and *repartimento* (wherein Indigenous communities were required to provide a set amount of labor) systems meant that many clergy, colonial officials, and settlers alike engaged in the process of Christianization and conversion. Such processes went hand in hand with the silver mining and infrastructure projects championed and desired by the imperial state and its officials.

By the eighteenth century in what is now California, Franciscans resettled Indigenous peoples in order to seize their labor for the missions' agricultural needs, and they simultaneously worked to inculcate Christian doctrine.[18] In the process, they enacted a regime of violence: One scholar notes that of eighty-one thousand Indigenous people baptized between 1769 and 1834, sixty thousand perished.[19] Indigenous peoples who lived at mission sites often worked to produce goods that were then sold to the military, with some of the profits infused into the operations of the mission itself.[20] Such projects produced varying results: death and survivance were both found within mission spaces. On the one hand, missions offered some Indigenous peoples a way to sustain themselves, their identity, and their authority in the context of violent imperialism—even as many individuals, on the other hand, were unable to do the same.[21] The economics of these sites also meant that missions were nodes in Californian economies: they were sites where Indigenous labor both sustained and took Indigenous lives, even as they fed imperial actors and markets. Missions in the Spanish Empire—though they differed both from locale to locale and over time—were intricately connected with developing and sustaining European ways of economy, exchange, and profit, and they were sites of both survivance and imperial violence.

Catholic missionaries' efforts in New Spain often promoted their imperial state's political and economic interests, and they did so in New France as well. French Jesuits were, according to one scholar, "enthusiastic, enterprising empire-builders for the Bourbon state": Jesuit missionaries used their contacts among Indigenous polities to broker alliances, wade into conflicts in support of the imperial cause, and facilitate trade. They did this all while working to convert Native peoples' lives and lands according to the norms of European economy, society, and politics: they transformed Indigenous "villages into secure, economically productive centers of trade and military preparedness."[22] What was more, the Jesuits' *Relations*—famous for their ethnographic detail—were not merely a recording and promotion of their religious efforts but also documents that championed the cause of the French Empire. Jesuits in New France were, in other words, crucial agents of empire.[23]

The political, economic, and religious consequences of Jesuits' Catholicism in New France were far-reaching. In the *Pays d'en Haut* of the Great Lakes region, religion and economy went hand in hand in the fur-trading heart of the French Empire in North America. Yet Indigenous peoples did not simply receive Catholicism, and they did not fail to recognize Catholicism's potential as a powerful tool for navigating the world of French imperialism. As the French journeyed into lands that were firmly Indigenous, Indigenous women—the Anishinaabeg among other peoples—wielded great power in their interactions with French men.[24] Jesuit Black Robes sought the souls of the converted and promoted empire, but the importance of Catholicism also had to do with the fact that it functioned as a glue that linked networks of Indigenous families and women by religion. These women and their families leveraged their power, their networks, and knowledge of their country to become the linchpins of the profitable fur trade. While such efforts did not necessarily negate any belief in Catholicism itself, Indigenous women were at the center of the French imperial and Indigenous economies in part by virtue of their ability to wield their adopted religion in the pursuit of survival, prosperity, and endurance. As such, Indigenous women in the *Pays d'en Haut* ensured their authority remained into the era of French imperialism and beyond.[25]

Protestants in North America lacked the hierarchical structure that facilitated and ordered so much of their Catholic counterparts' work in the Spanish and French Empires.[26] As a result, they lagged behind in pursuing missionary activity among Indigenous peoples. John Eliot's "praying towns" in what is now Massachusetts were an exception, though even that experiment flagged over time.[27] A key difference between such Protestant work and that of the Spaniards and French, then, was the fact that Protestants of the English and then British Empire took much longer to realize their stated goal of converting North America's Indigenous inhabitants to their faith.[28] In part this was because of theological differences: Protestants often expected a foundation of learning before baptism, whereas Catholics proceeded on the road to conversion by first administering the sacrament of baptism.[29] This Protestant approach to missionary work would not disappear: when considering their civilizing missions in the United States, Protestants debated whether Native peoples should be offered instruction in the Bible or in Euro-American society and culture—civilization in their eyes—first.[30] Yet even this debate was possible only after Protestants "learned to be missionaries."[31] Before the later portion of the eighteenth century, Catholics' baptismal work accompanied and facilitated their state's imperialism, while Protestants' words, claims, and promises furthered the British imperial project in North America.[32]

Protestants living in the British Empire were also a more diverse lot theologically—while Spain could conceivably unite its subjects with Catholicism, the Church of England did not offer a similar means to unite all Protestants. Within British colonies in North America, Anglicans, Congregationalists, Baptists, Moravians, Quakers, and others all proceeded with their religious lives differently, in different locales, and among different peoples.[33] The Society for the Propagation of the Gospel in Foreign Parts (SPG)—the missionary arm of the Anglican Church—for example, undertook mission work in the eighteenth century, with efforts focused on enslaved peoples in the Caribbean, Indigenous peoples in what became New England, as well as on British settlers. They funded their work using a corporation model.[34] Moravians, meanwhile, hailed from Central Europe yet endeavored to proselytize among their fellow European Pennsylvanians. When that proved to be less fruitful than they hoped, they focused more of their attentions on establishing missions among Delawares in Pennsylvania and among a variety of peoples of North Carolina and the Caribbean. Moravians, too, confronted the problem of money and solved it by building an economy at Bethlehem, Pennsylvania, that connected with the robust Atlantic trade.[35] These are but two of the many Protestant approaches to mission work in the Atlantic world.[36]

Despite their differences, Protestants in the British Empire nonetheless infused their religion and what mission work they undertook in the Caribbean and on the continent with ideas of race, and they, like their Catholic counterparts, were also implicated in the economies and politics of the British Empire. In the Caribbean, Protestant missionaries articulated an idea of "Christian slavery" that contended that enslaved peoples would work harder with Christianity. Over time, the SPG grew to accommodate slavery in the Caribbean as well as in the wider Atlantic world.[37] In North Carolina, Moravians' missions benefited from the labor of enslaved people, rendering their own missions inextricably linked with the economy of slavery.[38] Such efforts were bound up in ideas of race and the other. While Moravians welcomed European Moravians into their fold, they nonetheless framed Indigenous peoples such as the Delawares in Pennsylvania as outsiders, requiring Moravians to physically journey to them.[39] Ideas of savagery and the heathen were crucial to Protestants' efforts among Indigenous peoples, and they would prove enduring. The prolific writer and Methodist William Apess would go on to lament his own lesser place in the eyes of his fellow Protestants in his *Eulogy on King Philip* in the 1830s.[40]

Missions played crucial roles in the politics and economies of European empires, yet throughout each of these contexts a constant existed: Missions and lands near missions were largely Indigenous spaces, and within them Native individuals and imperial officials and missionaries negotiated authority on a regular basis. Individuals touched by Christian imperialism likewise maintained the authority to negotiate with settlers, imperial officials, and policies, sometimes using Christianity to do so. In sixteenth- and seventeenth-century Pueblo Country, for example, Pueblos alternatively resisted and selectively adopted Spanish missionaries' Christianity. In the case of some Pueblos, Christianity added to their already robust faith and religious practices; for others, it was something with which they wanted nothing to do. The Pueblo Revolt in 1680 was but one especially violent episode of Pueblo men and women rejecting Spanish influence, but it was not the only one nor was it the only means Pueblos used to push back against Spaniards' efforts. Pueblo women found their authority undermined by the patriarchal influence of the Spaniards, yet Pueblos found ways to quietly maintain their religious beliefs and practices in their kivas and villages—including those that centered fertility in human reproduction and in the harvest.[41] Resistance could be both violent and clandestine.

Among those Indigenous peoples who lived with the English and French Empires in their midst, the choices were similar. Among the Wampanoags of what is now Massachusetts, many engaged in a "religious translation" that encouraged individual Wampanoags and their networks to make sense of, selectively incorporate, and reject aspects of Christianity according to their own logics. Elements that complemented their understanding of the world could easily be incorporated; other aspects were left behind.[42] Wampanoags encountering the missionary Thomas Mayhew Jr., for example, came to understand Mayhew's *God* and *Satan* through their own ideas of *Mannit* and *Cheepi*—a great spirit and a "god of the dead."[43] What was more, sometimes Indigenous peoples chose to spread the message of Christianity themselves and become missionaries, and such was the case across empires and time.[44] Still other individuals, such as Kateri Tekakwitha, adopted much of the Catholicism found at the mission community at Kahnawake.[45] Indeed, Indigenous peoples did not merely react to missions and missionaries: they incorporated them into their worlds and landscapes, choosing to engage with or reject them as befit their circumstances, beliefs, needs, and desires.[46] Despite the violence and trauma that accompanied colonization and epidemic disease, Native people regularly asserted the power to decide their religious beliefs and their religious and political allegiances.

This remained the case into the era of the American empire, into the boarding school era, and beyond. Missions, mission schools, communities near which missionaries resided, and boarding schools alike could be spaces of empire—with missionaries taking on crucial roles as the vanguards of empire in myriad contexts—as well as places of negotiation and Indigenous authority.[47] The memory and historical narratives of these mission spaces, and the ways in which Indigenous peoples continue to live with each, continue to be sites of both contestation and authority today as Indigenous educators and activists work to reclaim the histories of the past as well as make educational spaces their own.[48]

* * *

Historian Emily Conroy-Krutz's conception of "Christian imperialism" highlights the linkages that existed between U.S. and British missionaries in the early nineteenth-century world.[49] U.S. missionaries borrowed from their

British counterparts, and they also inherited the lessons learned by their Protestant forebears they had Eliot's example for forming a corporation to raise monies; they could look to the SPG for ideas regarding both revenue raising and organization; and some had their own experience as well. Moravians, for example, worked among Delawares, enslaved peoples, among others in North America, and had additional experience establishing missions in the Caribbean as well.

As with other religious societies, Quakers, too, had their own British pasts to reference when considering their late eighteenth- and nineteenth-century work in Indian Country. Quakers in Pennsylvania did not establish missions in the colony, but they did act as go-betweens and diplomats.[50] They partnered with several Delaware leaders, most notably Chief Teedyuscung, and with them, they sought to establish peace between the colony and the Delawares during the Seven Years' War in Pennsylvania.[51] Friends' Friendly Association was key to their efforts in the colony, and it helped to establish a precedent for engaging in Indian affairs as a society and as private individuals. The association raised funds for the purchase of presents that would be distributed during conferences with Delawares, and Friends also attended numerous councils and treaties between 1756 and 1758, with the most significant being the treaties at Easton. The Delaware leader Teedyuscung, in particular, embraced Friends' willingness to pursue peace, and he used that to his and his compatriots' advantage. He professed that he was glad that they were "willing to renew the old, good understanding, and that you call to mind the first treaties of friendship made by Onas, our great friend. . . . We take hold of these treaties with both our hands, and desire you will do the same, that a true friendship may be re-established."[52] By invoking the memory of Onas—the Iroquoian name for William Penn, the Quaker founder of Pennsylvania colony—Teedyuscung encouraged diplomacy and negotiation, he asserted the Delawares as possessing the power to pursue and encourage peace, and he connected the past to his present.

Friends attended the treaties at Easton in an unofficial capacity that frustrated the colonial government's efforts to unilaterally deal with the Delawares. Friends endeavored to steer politics by circumventing the colony's official political process. Some Delawares, undoubtedly aware of the divisions between the Quaker Party and the Proprietary Party in the colony, used Friends to gather information and to act as go-betweens on their behalf.[53] At one point, when several Delawares were left "inquisitive about the Governor's coming" to Easton to meet with them, they were left satisfied once Israel

Pemberton, a leading figure in the Friendly Association, gave them assurances.[54] Friends' account here is, of course, likely a bit biased, yet it highlights the ways in which Friends could play political roles, navigating negotiations between Indigenous nations and individuals and colonial governments. Friends were effective go-betweens during the Seven Years' War, and they gained a wealth of experience that they would pass onto other members over the years. The Friends' meetings and committees took copious notes and preserved their histories well, and they preserved the knowledge of their diplomatic efforts during the Seven Years' War both through individuals' oral retellings and through diaries and meeting minutes.

Just as Friends preserved and transmitted their experiences, many of the lessons learned by missionaries' pasts were consumed in print by religious individuals after them. By the late eighteenth and early nineteenth century, there was a wealth of knowledge available to missionaries and religious individuals in North America. David Brainerd's memoir, published in 1742, for example, grew in influence into the nineteenth century. That memoir joined other tracts and narratives as printing grew more advanced and literacy rates rose, and together they influenced subsequent generations of missionary Christians.[55] Yet even before mass printing was possible, Euro-Americans read and knew of other religious individuals' exploits in Indian Country. Writings that portrayed Spaniards as brutes unrivaled by any other imperialists—later known as the Black Legend—was one source of knowledge regarding religious conversion efforts in New Spain, while Jesuit's own *Relations* added to individuals' memoirs to create a current of information, inspiration, and ideas regarding mission work and Indigenous peoples.[56]

As numerous scholars point out, early nineteenth-century missionaries and reformers were also the consumers of an eighteenth-century print culture that shifted ideas regarding humanitarianism, pain, and sensibility. Works by Adam Smith, David Hume, and others changed individuals' toleration for the suffering of others, and it spurred more reformers to undertake work that would alleviate it.[57] Changing ideas regarding humanitarianism and philanthropy combined with the lessons learned from past missionary endeavors, and together they ushered in new approaches to mission work.

Political, economic, and technological change also ensured that missionary efforts transformed over time. Roads, turnpikes, canals, and railroads grew to crisscross the region, connecting the more urban U.S. coast with the heart of the continent and in turn rendering that continent smaller—in the imaginary and, gradually as technology and infrastructure developed, in the time it took to traverse it. Travelers' diaries, textbooks, reports from Indian Country, and letters from loved ones also combined to alter the continent in the imaginations of many late eighteenth- and early nineteenth-century Euro-Americans who saw in the lands taken from Indigenous peoples the prospect of prosperity and property ownership.[58] As will be seen, these changes, particularly the material changes in the land and in the infrastructure of travel and commerce, encouraged missionary Americans to conceive of their work in Indian Country in ways that diverged from past precedents. Whereas, for example, British missionaries employed rhetoric of pity to solicit donations and create a community of Britons, such rhetoric shifted with a changing economic and political landscape in North America after the American Revolution.[59] Agricultural education, labor, "usefulness," and profit would become central to missionaries' projects as a result of both the yeoman ideals of Jefferson's imperial republic and due to the continually developing world of speculation and racial capitalism taking root in and on the edges of the American empire in North America.

Despite these changes, from the 1780s through to the middle of the nineteenth century, the contested nature of the continent's geopolitics remained a constant as did Indigenous power. Anishinaabewaki in the upper Great Lakes, for example, remained a world wherein Native authority reigned, even as other locales grew more hotly contested.[60] The Ohio Country was one such contested location, with Shawnee and Miami presence manifest to midcentury (with some citizens remaining there to this day), even as Euro-American officials and settlers worked to erase that reality often.

As with earlier imperial efforts, U.S. missions remained important locations in contested spaces, and missionaries remained vital imperial agents who facilitated the U.S. federal government's political and economic aims. And, also like their counterparts in other empires, they were not universally successful. Some Miamis and Shawnees, for example, saw missionaries as viable partners in negotiating a changing political landscape; others expressed little interest in the messages that missionaries brought to their lands. A changing continent and economy, the endurance of Native authority, and a new government also ensured that Quakers, Moravians, and their colleagues from other denominations had to improvise, adjust, and listen to the Indigenous peoples, government officials, and settlers among and with whom they hoped to work. Missions and the spaces near them were increasingly linked with the market economy of the U.S. urban coast and with the port of New Orleans as time wore on even if market linkages were not, of course, new.[61]

* * *

As with Europeans' imperial ventures in North America, U.S. officials would strive to strengthen United States authority through a combination of top-down policy pronouncements and individual efforts—including those of missionaries. Just as the Spanish Empire created an elaborate schema for hierarchical governance, early national men like Washington, Knox, and Pickering constructed policies that made imperial expansion in Indian Country seem remarkably simple. The Northwest Ordinance and the 1790 Trade and Intercourse Act, in particular, were key means by which the upper echelons of the U.S. state endeavored to build their empire and assert the power of the federal government in Indian Country, and these acts complemented the civilization plan. The intensification of settler colonialism in the trans-Appalachian region, however, meant that Euro-Americans' pursuit of the "elimination of the Native" intensified during the nineteenth century.[62] Warfare and treaty-making was one way to pursue elimination, civilizing—eradicating Indigenous lifeways—was another. In the Ohio Country, Euro-Americans would employ both tactics, spurring the relationship between missions and the imperial state to develop as a result of both top-down and bottom-up efforts as they had in centuries past. This time, however, there would be an emphasis on eradicating Native peoples' own understanding of property held in common while instituting Euro-Americans' notions of private property.

When Knox articulated the civilization plan in the last year of the 1780s, he did so both at a time of great change and as U.S. officials worked to establish political authority on the continent and overseas. These officials had to work to gain authority while simultaneously building the machinery of their nation and empire. The 1787 Northwest Ordinance was a defining piece of legislation that offered a top-down blueprint for U.S. imperial expansion in North America. At its most basic level, the ordinance provided a procedure for territories' incorporation into the United States as states, and it sketched a plan for their government.[63] The U.S. Congress appointed territorial governors and secretaries, and territorial officials were to "adopt and publish in the district such laws of the original States, criminal and civil, as may be necessary and best suited to the circumstances of the district, and report them to Congress from time to time."[64] It was a practical system, and it was also a clear assertion of federal power over states and territories.

Congressional power over the territories meant that subsequent states and territories must adopt laws, procedures, and rights of "the original States" that were "not repugnant to the principles and articles" of the ordinance created by the federal government.[65] It was, in essence, a plan for self-replication across the continent. What was more, the legislation required "an oath or affirmation of fidelity and of office; the Governor before the President of Congress, and all other officers before the Governor."[66] The territories thus had their own governments, laws, courts, even a representative in Congress, but all were subject to congressional approval or to the approval of a congressional appointee. Lastly, the ordinance explicitly banned slavery in the Northwest Territory revealing that the federal government claimed the power to limit the extension of slavery and to define the property rights of individuals living beyond the bounds of the original state. Of course, such a pronouncement did not wholly limit slavery in the region; white settlers continued to enslave Native, African, and African-descended peoples in the territory—as had European settlers before them—regardless of the ordinance.[67] Nonetheless, power flowed from the center outward and the Northwest Ordinance should be interpreted as a watershed moment in defining the federal state's powers.[68]

The Northwest Ordinance aimed to answer many questions regarding how the United States would increase its territory, and it also offered some guidance for conducting U.S. Indian affairs. U.S. officials heatedly debated many issues during the early national period—including how to handle relations with Indigenous nations—yet one of the things that individuals like Alexander Hamilton and James Madison could agree upon was this: the government under the Articles of Confederation was too weak to adequately deal with the threat posed by Indigenous nations who fought to maintain their homelands. Despite this similarity, Madison argued that the federal government should be prominent in Indian affairs out of a paternalistic approach—one that would "protect and restrain Indians and states alike"—whereas Hamilton advocated for the creation of a fiscal-military state that would position the military to defeat the Native peoples that stood in the way of the republic's unfettered imperial expansion.[69] Though divergent in their visions of federal action, both men saw a role for the federal government—with the individual states enjoying less authority—in Indian Country.

Imbuing the federal government with much power, the Northwest Ordinance laid out a policy prescription for Indian affairs in the Northwest

Territory: it declared that "the utmost good faith shall always be observed towards the Indians; their lands and property shall never be taken from them without their consent; and, in their property, rights, and liberty, they shall never be invaded or disturbed, unless in just and lawful wars authorized by Congress."[70] Despite this veil of niceties—framing colonization through the lens of consent—the ordinance presumed Euro-American colonization in the region, and it also presumed future land sales. The language of "just and lawful wars" also offered much power to Congress, for it was they who would determine when a war was "just and lawful." The ordinance presumed to dispossess Indigenous peoples first through land sales, or, in the words of the ordinance, through "their consent," and such language was very much in line with the vision of "honorable," federally directed imperial expansion that men like Knox, Pickering, and Washington would come to prize. Yet, with its language of "just and lawful war," the declaration would also mark the beginning of a violent process of U.S. colonialism.[71]

Despite its methodical, straightforward sheen, the ordinance had limitations: its orderly road map for acquiring lands did not prove a reliable guide in large part because Native peoples had their own ideas regarding the lands in question. Native peoples possessed ideas of property ownership, and they were both similar and dissimilar from those held by Euro-American officials and settlers. They understood property as a communal resource, they understood and delineated use rights, and, often, they understood ownership to lie with women.[72] It was women, after all, that performed the work of farming, linking them with the land.[73] Yet, from the perspective of Euro-Americans, it was from Native *men* that U.S. officials needed to purchase commodified plots of land. If Native peoples' property could "never be taken from them without their consent," then the United States needed to translate and transform Native peoples' own ideas regarding property rights into ones of commodified private property so that they could be rendered purchasable by the federal government. Such quantifiable purchases would promise peaceful dealings with Native peoples, and it would facilitate the acquisition of Indigenous peoples' lands through formal treaties negotiated by the federal state. In doing so, however, the U.S. government would need to erase Native peoples' claims to and conceptions of the land as held in common—as a "dish with one spoon" and as a resource to be used by many and often owned by women.[74]

Like the Northwest Ordinance, the 1790 Trade and Intercourse Act (and the successive acts that renewed and strengthened the original) contributed to the U.S. effort to assert federal authority in the Ohio Country. The act endeavored to control U.S. citizens' ability to buy and sell goods in Indian Country, and it prohibited American citizens or individual U.S. states from buying Native lands, reserving that privilege for the federal government instead. It ultimately attempted to bolster the power of the U.S. state in its dealings in Indian Country, even as it aligned with Knox and Washington's hopes for orderly imperialism.[75] The act was renewed in 1793 and, in that iteration, Congress included funding for the civilization program—$20,000 for teaching agriculture and the "civilized arts." Such funding was included at the precise moment that the United States was embroiled in a war against Allied Indian Nations in the Ohio Country—likely in part due to a recognition of the fact that war was costly and additional methods of engaging Native nations were necessary. It offered a clear recognition, in other words, that the empire needed non-government actors to support the work of imperial expansion. This latter version of the act laid the groundwork for the further institutionalization of civilizing work in 1819 when Congress passed the Civilization Fund Act.[76]

While the Northwest Ordinance and the Trade and Intercourse Acts could make imperial expansion seem secure on paper, Congress's inclusion of civilizing funds in 1793 suggests a messier reality. Individuals needed to perform the hard work of shoring up U.S. imperial power, and such work cost money. As earlier empires found, authority over a paper empire was a thing that needed to be gained. The military was one way in which the young imperial republic could carve out zones of authority in places such as the Ohio Country, while U.S. Indian factory stores, agencies, and missions would come to do so as well in the first several decades of the nineteenth century.[77] At the heart, from the perspective of the imperial state, was a need to embody authority on the edges of empire, and such a need was the product of continued Indigenous sovereignty and presence.

* * *

Two key groups of individuals would work to embody U.S. authority on the ground during the nineteenth century: U.S. Indian agents and missionaries. By the later years of the eighteenth century, both groups heeded the Washington administration's call to civilize the continent's Indigenous peoples, and members of the Society of Friends were among the earliest religious individuals to collaborate on the plan with the federal government. Yet Friends made both logical and unexpected partners: Quakers possessed both a long history of diplomacy in Indian Country and relationships with Indigenous individuals, but they had also endured political backlash during the American Revolution due to their pacifist beliefs. The Quaker Israel Pemberton of Philadelphia, for example, was a knowledgeable leader in Indian affairs in Pennsylvania colony, yet Patriots banished him to Virginia when he refused to swear an oath to the emerging republic. That Friends worked alongside the new federal government by the 1790s was a complicated development, indeed.

In the years leading up to and during the American Revolution, Friends experienced what some scholars have described as a period of "turning inward."[78] While they did not wholly retreat from the world around them, they did seek to minimize their involvement with government affairs. During the decades that followed the emergence of the United States, Friends similarly traded in their political authority in colonial legislatures for the work of reform. Abolition, Indian affairs, and temperance became focal points of Quaker activism during the first half of the nineteenth century, yet their reform efforts were not an abdication of power. Social authority that was built upon a cultivated reputation of benevolence—what historian Christopher Leslie Brown aptly calls "moral capital"—became Friends' currency of choice.[79] Friends' participation in the civilization plan was thus borne from multiple impulses: some Friends thought that they had a moral duty to help the continent's Indigenous peoples, others thought they had a spiritual duty to do so, and still others hoped to emerge as social leaders in their communities—and some, no doubt, engaged in the work of civilization for a combination of reasons. Yet the drive to accumulate moral, spiritual, social, and, in some cases, financial capital meant that Friends were willing to lend their society's substantial expertise in Indian affairs to the federal government. Civilizing work became a means of obtaining moral capital while also affording an opportunity to claim some distance from governmental affairs.

Friends' earliest missions were among the Oneidas and Senecas in Haudenosaunee Country. The mission among the Oneidas was short lived, yet immensely important in offering a foundation for future missionary endeavors in Indian Country during the nineteenth century. Philadelphia Friends took the lead at the Oneida mission site after an Oneida delegation visited Philadelphia in 1790 and after Secretary of State Pickering and President Washington specifically entreated Friends to take on a leading role in the civilization program after the Treaty of Canandaigua in 1794.[80]

The task at hand was clear, at least to Euro-American missionaries and policymakers: Friends should teach agriculture and the "mechanical arts" rather than spending time proselytizing or teaching theology. This was a departure from missionary efforts of the past, yet it reflected the changing economic and political goals of the American empire: "benevolent" imperial expansion that emphasized basic morality and labor was the desired outcome. Training in farming and other mechanic arts were nearly universal components of civilizing mission education regardless of form, and English reading and writing, as well as other subjects, could accompany these programs—though they did not always. Some religious denominations, particularly the Moravians, emphasized theology in their instruction; many, however, preferred to leave such learning for after Native peoples had, in their estimation, reached the appropriate level of civilization to receive religious instruction.

As Baltimore Friends in the Ohio Country would just a few years later, Philadelphia Friends adopted the model farm approach to mission work in Oneida Country; Friends hoped that by learning plow agriculture, Oneidas would be mesmerized by the material comforts enjoyed by Euro-Americans and convert their systems of agriculture and economy accordingly.[81] Of course, as numerous scholars have pointed out, what Quakers were really asking Oneidas to do was to take a step backward in terms of their engagement with markets. Oneidas had traded extensively with other Indigenous peoples and with Euro-Americans, yet Friends encouraged subsistence and, as we will see, more limited market engagement.[82]

Philadelphia Friends included English instruction at their mission, formally opening a school in Oneida Country in 1796. The school was, however, short lived. As many as thirty students enrolled at the school, yet Oneidas' desire to maintain their own patterns of living meant that they fit attendance around their everyday hunting, agricultural, and market activities.[83] Such engagement was emblematic of Oneidas' approach to the mission: they engaged as much or as little as they desired and as both benefited them and would allow them to maintain their own practices.

The Quaker mission among the Oneidas—and, eventually, among the Senecas, Miamis, Shawnees, and others—thus departed from past missions' overtly theological goals, yet a clear constant remained: Native peoples continued to engage with missions and missionaries selectively, adopting elements in which they could see a clear benefit and pushing aside those they could not. Oneidas valued Quakers as diplomats, intermediaries with the federal government, and as a buffer between themselves and white settlers who threatened their lands.[84] Oneidas also valued the material benefits that Quakers brought—cleared acres of land, agricultural implements, a barn, and a house.[85] In this, Oneidas were not unique: Miamis, Shawnees, and their neighbors in the Ohio Country, too, would value Friends for similar items in addition to the value that Friends added as diplomats and go-betweens.

Though Philadelphia Quakers' mission among the Oneidas would eventually close by 1800, they continued to work with Oneidas to protect Oneida lands from settlers and speculators. Yet, even in this, a foundation for Quakers' future work among Indigenous peoples would form. Quakers supported Oneidas' land claims into the 1820s and 1830s, yet they pointed to evidence of Oneidas' civilization to do so—evidence that, as we will see, served to embolden settler desires for land.[86] Philadelphia Friends' Oneida mission was a testing ground for what was possible—and, crucially, for what was not. And other early initiatives would be so likewise. Just after the close of the Oneida mission, the Presbyterian Gideon Blackburn would attempt, and ultimately fail, to offer instruction to Cherokees with support of federal funds, while Moravians would open a school in Georgia that enjoyed minimal success.[87] At the same time, Baltimore Quakers would begin their missionary efforts on a farm—with Philip Dennis and a small plot of cultivated earth in the Miami homeland. There, too, Friends would find both successes and failures that were nonetheless crucial for defining how missionaries would partner with the U.S. state and how Native people would engage with both. U.S. officials, Indian agents, and missionaries could articulate their plans for imperial expansion, and they could do their best to realize their goals on the ground, yet their ideas and hopes were time and again melded by those they engaged in Indian Country.

* * *

The years that saw the adoption of the U.S. civilization plan were ones wherein changing economy and technology, the pressures of settler colonialism, and the emergence of republican governance led the United States to partner with missionary societies in ways that befit the moment. That partnership grew on a foundation of earlier missionary-imperial state endeavors in North America. Notions of civilization—ranking certain peoples as more "barbaric" or "savage"—were not new: empires both ancient and contemporary used such ideas to identify outsiders.[88] Missionaries served as key vanguards of empire in Spanish and French imperial contexts in North America, and the United States followed suit. Yet the U.S. government's emphasis on labor, basic morality, and the commodification of land at the expense of converting souls and teaching complex theology would define a distinctive missionary partnership in nineteenth-century North America. Philadelphia and Baltimore Friends agreed with such an approach: labor could combat the sin of idleness, and they foregrounded education in simple morals. Other missionaries would offer a spectrum of religious education in U.S. missions in Indian Country—ranging from basic Christian tenets such as the downfall of man and his redemption through Christ to more complicated ideas such as predestination—yet U.S. officials like Pickering would routinely applaud Friends' approach to education and civilization.[89]

Though Friends' relationship with the U.S. state was foundational, it was no mistake that Philadelphia Quakers began their mission work among the Oneidas in earnest after 1794 and that Baltimore Friends first considered their own mission work in 1795–96. Before Friends could embark on their labor in either Haudenosaunee or Miami lands, allied nations of the Ohio Country and beyond would ensure that the civilizing scheme dreamed up by Pickering, Knox, and Washington in the late 1780s and early 1790s would not be implemented in the Northwest Territory for several years. In large part, this was because policy pronouncements like the Northwest Ordinance did not render the Ohio Country an empty land, and it failed to account for the strength of Native authority. Nor did the Trade and Intercourse Acts deliver lands belonging to and beloved by Indigenous peoples to the United States with a mere flick of a pen. White settler colonists, too, were not stymied with paper decrees. As a result, throughout the 1780s and 1790s, tensions between white settlers and Indigenous nations mounted, and war came to the Ohio Country.

When Knox spoke of the civilization plan in 1789, enlisting missionaries to be the "instruments to work on the Indians," he articulated Americans' desires for the "west," and he offered an implicit acknowledgment that the U.S. federal government needed help: top-down policy pronouncements were insufficient. That need increased dramatically as the war that Knox had so hoped to avoid descended on the Ohio Country in 1790. When Friends opened their mission among the Oneidas, they did so after engaging Oneida leaders, yet they had also received specific encouragement from President Washington and secretary of state Timothy Pickering. Baltimore Friends, too, received support from both Washington and Pickering in the mid-1790s. When the prominent Philadelphia Quaker Henry Drinker informed Pickering that several Baltimore Friends planned to journey to the Ohio Country "for the purpose of learning their situation and disposition and thence to judge of the practicability of introducing among them the simplest and most useful arts of civil Life," Pickering was pleased. The secretary of state sent the news onto Arthur St. Clair, the governor of the Northwest Territory. Pickering informed the governor that the "approbation of the Presedent has been asked and obtained," and he went on to suggest that St. Clair should offer "the delegation all the protection & countenance to which their respectable characters and philanthrophic [*sic*] views entitle them."[90] As Pickering's correspondence suggests, the Washington administration endorsed Friends' earliest civilizing mission efforts, and Friends would receive government support as a result.

Pickering entreated Friends to assist the federal government for many reasons. Friends' reluctance to engage in Bible instruction dovetailed with the vision of education that Knox, Pickering, and Washington supported in Indian Country. What was more, if Catholics' hierarchical structures facilitated their mission work in earlier centuries, Friends' own hierarchies—their meeting and committee systems—meant that they could efficiently correspond with the secretary of war and state, raise funds for the work of civilization that would complement federal dollars, and call upon both members' relationships with Native individuals and knowledge of diplomatic protocols.

This last item—Friends' history of engaging with Native leaders and their subsequent knowledge of diplomacy in Indian Country—was crucial. As war broke out in the Ohio Country, Friends took up the roles of go-betweens and diplomats, rubbing elbows with key U.S. officials during negotiations and in army encampments. They would further develop their relationships with both Native leaders and several key officials in the U.S. government as a result. Such work marked a key moment in the emergence of a tripartite relationship between the United States, Indigenous nations, and missionaries—one that would echo those of earlier centuries and imperial contexts. The negotiated development of such a relationship—sometimes smooth and sometimes a bit awkward and fraught—took time, and the work involved would be on full display at a wartime dinner table in Haudenosaunee Country in 1791.

CHAPTER 2

Resurrecting the "Chain of Friendship"

The International Politics of Intercultural Diplomacy

Before Quakers' mission among the Oneidas and before Pickering could smile at the prospect of Baltimore Friends journeying to the Ohio Country to establish a farm school, war would erupt in the Ohio Country. That war would, for several years, force the Washington administration to recalibrate its Indian policies. Rather than begin civilizing work in the region immediately, the Society of Friends would first embark on the work of diplomacy. Such diplomacy, a collaborative effort between federal officials and missionary diplomats who possessed a reputation for peace, was a necessity for a young republic confronting Native nations' allied efforts to push against U.S. territorial aspirations in the region. Friends' diplomatic efforts, in particular, both linked them with their own history of mediating negotiations between Delawares and colonists in Pennsylvania, and it would lay the groundwork for a partnership between themselves and the federal government that was built upon familiarity and practicality.

During the first years of the 1790s, Quaker John Parrish and several other Friends participated in a series of treaty negotiations between the U.S. government, the Haudenosaunee, and several of the allied nations of the Ohio Country. During one of these occasions, in particular, the complicated nature of international politics was on full display. In the heat of June 1791, Parrish dined in western New York with the future U.S. secretary of state Timothy Pickering, then a colonel and a U.S. commissioner to the Haudenosaunee (Six Nations). They were joined by an interpreter and "12 or 15 Sachems and head wariors of the Six Nations." Conversation was friendly, and the food, in Parrish's opinion, somewhat too lavish given both his Quaker taste for simplicity and the fact that a war was on. After several servers cleared the table,

Parrish solicited the group's interpreter to aid him in offering the diners a speech on behalf of the Philadelphia Society of Friends. Parrish informed the Haudenosaunee men that he was of the "peaceable people called Quakers," and that he and his brethren had come "with a design to see our Bretheren the Indians and take them by the hand and brighten the Chane of friendship agreeably to the Custom of their friends our Ancestors." He explained that "the People called Quakers came into this country with Wm Penn a bout 108 Years ago and in consequence of which lived together a bout 70 Years in uninterrupted Peace & fellowship." In his opinion, "if the Indians desire[d] to perpetuate the same friendly disposition . . . a peace of still longer continuance may be the happy consequence of the Presant Treaty." Toward the end of this speechmaking, however, another U.S. commissioner interrupted him and insisted that "there was none but men of Peace presant." Parrish later reflected that the statement "occationed me to stop shorter than otherwise I should have done."[1]

The commissioner was not, however, the only individual put off by the speech: Parrish's words irritated at least one Oneida diner that evening as well. Shortly after Parrish spoke, the Oneida chief Good Peter informed him that "we ware now in a free freindly conversation between Brothers it was not the business of the Treaty we ware not at the Council Fire."[2] Parrish violated diplomatic protocol by talking business over a meal, and, by rebuking the Quaker, Good Peter aimed to ensure that the men adhered to the diplomatic norms and procedures of his nation.[3] By interjecting as he did, Good Peter made plain that Native leaders held the upper hand, that they would dictate the terms of diplomacy.

While at first glance the awkwardness of the dinner is readily apparent, less obvious is the extent to which the episode illuminates the delicate negotiation of power that characterized the dinner and, more generally, the nature of Native-U.S. relations in the region during the 1790s. This negotiation would leave a lasting mark on U.S. Indian policy. It would encourage the ongoing development of relationships between U.S. officials, Native people, and missionaries that would linger into the nineteenth century and undergird the U.S. civilization plan, and it would ensure that missionaries retained a role in the imperial history of North America. Perhaps most of all, however, it ensured that the success of the U.S. project was anything but inevitable.

The early 1790s were years of tumult in the Ohio Country. The Washington administration had articulated its plans for civilizing Native people, yet politics and violence ensured that those plans would not be implemented in the region for several years. Instead of teaching agriculture, the United States found itself embroiled in a war that it was losing. The Northwest Indian War was, in 1791, tilting in favor of the allied Native nations of the Ohio Country. Just several months prior to the June dinner, in October 1790, the United States suffered defeat at the Battle of the Maumee. A few months later, the United States would lose again at the Battle of the Wabash. On the minds of all diners was likely a clear reality: The United States could lose to the Miami chief Little Turtle and his allies. The dinner was thus a diplomatic gathering of utmost importance—and Indigenous leaders such as Good Peter had the upper hand. Though Pickering may have momentarily regretted Parrish's presence that evening, the dinner table affair offers a glimpse of just how much the U.S. government needed help from quasi-state actors like go-between missionaries. The United States needed individuals who could facilitate the work of peace—even if those individuals erred from time to time.

Despite the imbalance of power among those gathered, each diner brought ambitions, goals, and at least a partial awareness of their counterparts' relative positions and power to influence the course of the present war. John Parrish mustered the reputation of his society's long history of diplomacy among Native nations in an effort to intervene and work for peace. The U.S. commissioner who interrupted Parrish sought to both negotiate a peace and remind the Quaker of his subordinate place in the hierarchy of official U.S. diplomats. Good Peter, meanwhile, aimed to assert the power to conduct diplomacy according to Oneida norms and on Native nations' terms.

That the dinner—and diplomacy in the region more generally—took place on Native peoples' terms offers important context for two central questions: Why was Parrish, a member of a religious society, present among official U.S. diplomats and powerful Native leaders at that dinner in June 1791? Why were other missionaries, such as the Moravian John Heckewelder, involved in diplomacy? The answers lay, in part, in U.S. officials' work to shift Indian policies away from one of overt aggression and toward one of land acquisition via diplomacy, gift-giving, and negotiation. The United States did not desire war with Native nations—the new nation was short on cash and military personnel, and men like secretary of war Henry Knox understood diplomacy to be cheaper than war.[4] Yet the Society of Friends' history of diplomacy among and alliance with the Haudenosaunee and the Lenni Lenapes (Delawares) in Pennsylvania also offers an explanation for Parrish's presence among some of the most powerful men in eastern North America that night. Several Indigenous nations knew of Friends' reputation for diplomacy: Friends' efforts to mitigate the most deleterious effects of Euro-Americans' settler greed in Pennsylvania colony decades before served to position Quakers—as well as other missionaries like Heckewelder who also had diplomatic credentials—as desirable allies. Some Native leaders' willingness to work with Quakers and select other missionaries, however, meant that Friends in turn made useful partners of the U.S. government. Quakers, pacifist and historically sympathetic to Native complaints, served as logical go-betweens as, in many ways, they embodied the possibility of peace—calumet pipes in human form.

Go-betweens like Parrish were useful to Native leaders and U.S. officials alike. Parrish, Heckewelder, and the Quakers who traveled with Parrish were key to U.S. diplomatic efforts in the region given the fragile condition of the burgeoning U.S. state. Federal officials like Pickering relied upon middling or low-level officials and, in the case of the June dinner, a non-governmental organization, the Society of Friends, to get the work of nation-building, land acquisition, and diplomacy done. With Native power manifest, the U.S. government appealed to Indigenous diplomatic protocol and preferences to both avert defeat and maintain hope that they could secure Ohio Country lands.

Native leaders, meanwhile, likely saw men like Parrish and Heckewelder as both buffers between themselves and the United States and as allies of peace and, possibly, their cause. The Society of Friends possessed a reputation for peace-making—they were known throughout Haudenosaunee Country and in the Ohio Country—and they also possessed a history of advocating against war. The memory of William Penn, but also individual relationships cultivated during the Seven Years' War in Pennsylvania, did much to convince Indigenous leaders of Friends' usefulness, and rhetorical images of Penn were present in Native leaders' and Quakers' speeches alike. Friends thus facilitated the work of the U.S. government, but their presence also underscored that government's need to accommodate Indigenous authority. They would speak against the U.S. government's and settlers' worst abuses—the alcohol trade and land encroachments, for instance—and they could work toward an uneasy peace by listening to both sides.

Welcoming the Quaker Parrish to the diplomatic table was thus no mere happenstance and it was no small gesture. Parrish's presence was a powerful symbol of Native authority and strength, and it represented the U.S. government's recognition of that authority. In the early 1790s, Native nations' power forced the United States to recognize Native sovereignty in the dinners and pipe-smoking affairs that characterized U.S. diplomacy with Indigenous nations and they ultimately reinforced and further defined a partnership between the federal government and members of societies like the Society of Friends.[5] Native nations, their authority intact as evidenced by Parrish's presence, ensured that they both checked and shaped the United States' imperial ambitions in the Ohio Country. They also ensured that men like Parrish—imperfect as he was—would find a seat alongside powerful leaders like Good Peter and the Seneca Red Jacket and emerging power players like Timothy Pickering. Delicate relationships between imperial officials, Native leaders and individuals, and these go-betweens would prove to be the grease that turned the wheels of diplomacy in eastern North America. These relationships would also, however, ensure that missionaries continued to act as diplomats and go-betweens in their future endeavors in Indian Country.

If Chapter 1's survey of missionary-imperial state cooperation, federal civilizing ideas, and top-down policies illuminated in broad terms how and why the civilization project began, we shall now turn to a closer examination of on-the-ground work—the small moments such as that awkward dinner—that undergirded U.S.-Indigenous relations at the conclusion of the eighteenth century. The detailed work of diplomacy produced and supported relationships among Native nations, missionary go-betweens, the United States, and various individuals, and following the formation and trajectory of

Figure 2. The Seneca chief Red Jacket, also known as Sagoyewatha. National Portrait Gallery, Smithsonian Institution.

Figure 3. Timothy Pickering: Indian commissioner, eventual secretary of state, and an architect of the civilization plan. National Portrait Gallery, Smithsonian Institution; gift of Mr. and Mrs. Paul Mellon.

these relationships enables us to view from the bottom-up how and why they formed, endured, and facilitated an ongoing negotiation of power over time.

* * *

Regardless of the language found in the Northwest Ordinance and various Trade and Intercourse Acts, the United States could not claim uncontested control of the early 1790s Ohio Country: Though Knox had hoped to avoid war and pursue dispossession efforts through the U.S. civilization plan, international politics ensured that the U.S. government would instead need to appeal to the authority of other nations. Native power and presence remained manifest in the region, and Indigenous politics therefore dictated diplomatic protocols. Miamis, Shawnees, Stockbridges, Senecas, and Mohawks each pursued their own diverse political agendas. The British, too, maintained an important presence in the region, enabling Native nations to apply even greater political pressure to the United States. As a result, U.S. officials had to court an array of international leaders and nations, particularly as conflict broke out in the Northwest Indian War.[6]

In the early 1790s, then, two realities dictated U.S.-Native relations. The first was that the government of the young United States struggled to assert authority on the North American continent and on the world stage. Eager to become "among the powers of the earth," officials sought to both project U.S. power to others and confront the fact that the new U.S. state was small, its precise form and extent yet to be determined.[7] This meant that officials on the edges of empire—consuls, diplomats, military men, and missionaries—possessed the power to not only represent the new U.S. empire but also determine how that empire would function on the ground.[8] By necessity, then, the early U.S. imperial state operated as a result of local, national, and regional power—a blended state that balanced top-level decision-making with on-the-ground actions. U.S. Indian policy was subsequently a product of official direction and local negotiation and diplomacy.

This blended and emerging state power combined with Native nations' own power to produce a second reality that characterized early U.S.-Native relations: Native peoples retained the authority to push against U.S. hegemony on the edges of the U.S. empire. The Treaty of Paris ending the American Revolution attempted to obliterate Natives' claims to Ohio Valley and southeastern lands, but it ultimately failed in its aim. Native peoples scoffed at the idea that the British could turn over Natives' lands to the Americans in defeat after the American Revolution, as the 1783 treaty stipulated. In the south, for example, the Creeks effectively played Spanish interests off American, and, for a time, maintained their lands in the region. Alexander McGillivray, a Creek with Scottish heritage, was crucial to that effort, and he, like the Shawnee Blue Jacket and Miami Little Turtle in the Ohio Country, maintained connections with European officials to do so.[9]

Ohio Native nations likewise resisted attempts by Americans to claim Ohio lands, and they were willing to match settlers' violence when necessary.[10] The remaining French and British presence was part of that effort: though defeated in the American Revolution, the British did not disappear from the Ohio Country and French individuals remained as well. Native nations there continued to use European officials in ways that would prevent the United States from asserting robust authority for a time. Such interactions facilitated Native nations' efforts to work for a future that emerged on their terms—with their people remaining on their lands—and it also encouraged Secretary of War Knox to pursue diplomacy as a key part of policy in the Ohio Country.[11] The civilization plan would have to wait.

In the 1790s, then, the landscape of the Ohio Country was in flux.[12] U.S. settlers squatted on lands, angering Indigenous people and the U.S. federal government alike. At the same time, Miamis, whose ancestral lands were centered at Kekionga, worked to assert their authority north of the Ohio

River, even as they welcomed Shawnee and Lenape refugees—people fleeing U.S. settlement and settler violence—to their lands. Miami towns were thus increasingly areas of intercultural and international exchange; Miamis emphasized, however, that the lands upon which all lived were Miami lands.[13] Despite this hierarchy within Miami Country, Miamis' allies and neighbors respected the authority of Kekionga. When, in 1789, the United States worked to gauge Native peoples' attitudes toward both the republic in general and American settlers who were squatting in the region, Weas, Piankashaws, and others told the Americans to talk to the leaders at Kekionga.[14] The Miamis, under the leadership of Le Gris, Little Turtle, and Jean Baptiste Richardville, held immense power and they worked to ensure that trade remained open and diplomacy was productive. During this period, then, the Miamis amassed a great deal of power, and they stood poised to threaten U.S. ambitions.[15]

Miamis, Shawnees, and others' relationships with particular individuals were equally as important as their nations' interactions with empires, if not more so, and diplomacy revolved around reciprocity and exchange that was built upon a foundation of familiarity. Trade often took precedence over imperial loyalties, and the Miamis, for example, played both sides during the American Revolution.[16] During the violence of the 1790s, Miamis drew upon their connections with some among the French—neighbors who became kin via the social world of the fur trade—and they used them to ensure that the Americans enjoyed few victories early on.[17] Miami women were crucial to that effort, as it was Native women who often formed kin relationships with French men.[18] Miamis also, however, had allies in the Shawnees—with Blue Jacket, in particular, a key pro-war leader among the Shawnees. Blue Jacket's town near the Glaize on the Maumee River was, like Kekionga, intercultural, and Blue Jacket, like the leaders at Kekionga, maintained relationships with British and French individuals.[19] He used these individuals together with the force of his fellow Shawnees and neighboring Lenapes to fight alongside Miamis, Cherokees, Creeks, and some among the Six Nations during the Northwest Indian War. The forces arrayed against Americans in the 1790s represented myriad nations, and they used relationships with each other and outsiders to pursue their goal of restricting U.S. imperial expansion. Missionary men like Parrish and Heckewelder could draw upon their own relationships with Native leaders in ways that would align with Native nations' own diplomatic norms and, in turn, bolster their ability to negotiate in the region.

Importantly, by the 1790s, Indigenous *men* were often on the forefront of Native diplomacy. This was part of a larger shift in gender roles that began in the eighteenth century and would accelerate in the nineteenth. Prior to the 1790s, Indigenous women played major roles in politics and diplomacy throughout Native America. In many cases, nations were matrilineal and matrifocal, with men ascending to leadership roles through their mother's line. In diplomacy, women often spoke freely, their voices and advice valued. By the 1790s, however, already much had changed. At a conference at the Glaize in 1792, for example, one historian notes that "women were present but not consulted."[20] Molly Brandt, the sister of the powerful Mohawk diplomat Joseph Brandt, noted that there were too few women present at that gathering, and she mentioned as much when she encountered another diplomat, the Mohican Hendrick Aupaumut.[21] Historians have noted that U.S. colonialism would continue to erode Indigenous women's authority in diplomacy and politics in favor of replacing it with a focus on domestic labor. This shift would continue throughout the nineteenth century as civilizing mission work continued the work of realigning Native peoples' gender ideologies. Replacing Native women's roles in diplomacy with a focus on domestic labor aligned with Euro-American ideas of civilization and an emerging U.S. economy that prized and rewarded particular forms of white masculinity.

As the encounter between Hendrick Aupaumut and Molly Brandt, a Mohawk, suggests, Miamis and Shawnees were not the only ones to employ relationships with individuals and empires during this time of war.[22] The Haudenosaunee (Six Nations), whose ancestral lands were in western New York, took part in the war but adopted a policy of pursuing peace, often working with the United States to do so.[23] Molly Brandt, for example, was working to do just that, albeit by remaining in the shadows more than she would have liked.

Much of John Parrish's diplomacy took place among representatives from the Six Nations as the United States saw the confederacy as playing a key role in ending the Ohio Country war, yet his journals reveal much regarding the diplomatic workings of the broader conflict. The Haudenosaunee maintained close ties with the British Empire and its representatives after the American Revolution in an effort to pursue their own ends. The Seneca diplomat Red Jacket, for example, reminded Timothy Pickering of just this point in 1791. When Pickering asked Red Jacket why the Senecas sought alliance with the British, the Seneca man informed the colonel that "the British are our Anchant friends, they live near us when we treat with them they make use of Wampum which we understand they give us good advice. . . . They make use of waighting when they speake to us." Red Jacket went on to explain that "not one man among us can read," and therefore if the United States violated Natives' customs of wampum-giving and speechmaking, "then we are oblige to go to our Kneghbours the British to get them explaind us."[24] Here Red Jacket made it clear that the Haudenosaunee allied with the British as a result of custom and proximity, as well as because American officials had not always conducted diplomacy according to Native norms. He also underscored the consequences that would befall the United States if officials did not adhere to Native protocols: Red Jacket would go to the British.

Red Jacket's speech to Pickering reveals much about his own perceived power and that of his nation, as well as the state of international affairs in the Ohio Country and Great Lakes regions. The Seneca man continued to explain, "We desire you to appoint an agent for Indian Affairs to whom we may go to [tell] every thing that happens to us and from whom we may hear what concerns us as this used to be in old times."[25] In responding to Pickering's query regarding the Six Nations' relationship with the British, then, Red Jacket ultimately made an appeal. He recognized the extent to which Pickering and the United States needed the friendship of the Six Nations, and he used that knowledge to acquire an Indian agent go-between. Such an individual would also serve as an ambassador between his nation and the United States. Though Red Jacket was no doubt aware that the United States commanded formidable power, he nonetheless also understood that the Haudenosaunee had the upper hand.

In noting the ancient customs of wampum as well as his request for an Indian agent, Red Jacket emphasized that the meeting between the United States and the Senecas was one between two nations with diverse traditions. By insisting upon "Anchant" customs like the use of wampum belts in diplomacy, Red Jacket indicated his preferences regarding protocol but also emphasized his own conception of Senecas' sovereignty and authority to dictate the modes of diplomacy. As Pickering understood by the 1790s, acknowledging and courting Native authority and protocols could produce a number of advantages in both the political and military realms. Because of this, the United States grew to adopt, for a time, the British Empire's policy of respecting Native customs of speechmaking, gift-giving, and other traditions in the realm of Indian affairs. U.S. officials understood that appeals to Native traditions, along with the recognition that Native nations commanded the power to require such appeals, fostered productive diplomatic relations. By the 1790s, men like Pickering recognized that appeals to Native authority and protocols were, simply put, smart international relations. Enlisting Friends as unofficial diplomats who possessed knowledge of these protocols and, more importantly, a friendly reputation was part and parcel of this approach.

While the Northwest Indian War's various combatants endeavored to accomplish diplomatic goals, other individuals likewise hoped to secure advantage for themselves or for their nation. The volatile moment involved individuals from myriad nations, and each sought to negotiate the terms of American and Indigenous power on the continent. The Mohican Hendrick Aupaumut, for example, became a useful ally of the United States during the war, but he simultaneously acted on behalf of his people. In 1791, Aupaumut visited Ohio Native nations "having agreed with the great men of the United States to take a Tour with their Message of peace." Some among the Haudenosaunee leaders opposed his trip, yet still he went. To his mind, "if the western nations could be rightly informed of the desires of the United States—they would comply for peace." Such information, he argued, would be delivered best by "an Indian to whom they look upon as a true friend." Like the Quaker John Parrish had at the June dinner, Aupaumut relied upon a peaceful past to make claims to power in a violent present. His nation, the Mohicans, possessed a reputation for peace-making, and in describing the kinship relationships between the Mohicans, Miamis, Shawnees, Delawares, and others, he explained that "it was the business of our fathers to go around the Towns of these nations to renew the agreements between them—And tell them many things which they discover in among the White people in the east."[26]

Aupaumut's travels through the contested Ohio Country as a diplomatic messenger, along with his presence at the 1792 conference at the Glaize, reveal his close ties with the United States, but also his own political motivations. The Mohican informed Delawares: "since the British & Amaricans lay down their hatchets—then my Nation was forgotten. We never had had invitation to set in Council with the white people.—not as the 5 Nations & you are greatly regarded by the white people but last winter was the first time I had invitation from the great man of the United States . . . according to that invitation I went and after we arrived at Philadelphia—I find that the business was for the wellfare of all nations—and then I was asked whether I would carry a Message of peace to you, here."[27] Aupaumut's statement appealed to Delawares' sense of themselves—they were, after all, "greatly regarded by the white people"—but it also belied his desire to give the United States reason to remember the Mohicans. Lamenting that his "Nation was forgotten" after the American Revolution, Aupaumut undertook the work of peace that was central to his nation's historical identity, and he allied himself with the U.S.

government. His motives were born of a desire for peace but also for political authority.[28]

Aupaumut hoped that the alliance with the United States would offer the Mohican nation advantage, yet he also hoped that he could secure a place in the region for his people. Though he was a partner of the U.S. government, he did not shy from expressing his frustration with U.S. policies and with settlers' unchecked movements. He pointed to Euro-Americans' previous treaties with the region's nations, and expressed that Americans unlawfully took lands. Meanwhile, Aupaumut's messages to Native nations at councils frequently invoked ideas of kinship and the idea that lands might be shared. Ultimately, he hoped to use his journey to the region and his work as a diplomat to advance peace and to curry favor with Miamis, Shawnees, and Delawares who had previously offered Aupaumut's people a place alongside them in the Ohio Country. Aupaumut was thus working for and speaking to all sides of the international conflict: he ardently hoped that peace in the region would secure the interests of all parties.[29]

Aupaumut's work and motivations reveal the international nature of 1790s diplomacy. Like Friends, Aupaumut's diplomacy aligned with the desires of U.S. officials, and the U.S. government recruited him for its purposes, but he undertook his mission for the Mohicans. Indian Country, like the United States, was not a united place; rather, it was fractured by alliances and viewpoints. The Native "western nations" so often mentioned en masse in U.S. government correspondence were conflicted. Some wished to broker peace with the United States but remained firm that no further land sessions should be made. The Pan-Indian union of nations, meanwhile, fought for their lands under the leadership of the Miami Little Turtle and the Shawnee Blue Jacket. "Back nations," as Aupaumut called them, disliked the Shawnees and "wished to see the Shawannese [on] one side by themselves . . . and have washed their kittles [*sic*] to boil the Shawannese so as to have Good broth."[30] There were other views too. The Haudenosaunee engaged the United States, Britain, Shawnees, Delawares, and others of the allied Ohio Nations in talks, sometimes to broker peace, other times to push for war, but always with the political future of their people in mind.

The international politics unfolding during the Northwest Indian War occasioned Native polities to negotiate according to their own diplomatic protocols, yet the United States was not powerless. Native leaders sometimes presented themselves as sovereigns that were intelligible according to Euro-American diplomatic standards. During his time as a diplomat, Parrish observed diplomatic pageantry that suggested both U.S. and Indigenous polities' power. The Quaker's observations were also, of course, shaped by his own conception of both. Prior to the treaty proceedings in 1791, for example, Parrish witnessed three to four hundred Senecas marching into Colonel Pickering's encampment. The "wariers . . . came in Indian file with their Rifles on their sholders and drew themselves up in a line by the [colonel's] Tent and gave him 2 Sallutes by the discharge of their guns, which the Colonel received as a mark of respect."[31] Not only was this a show of Seneca military power, but Pickering's reception of their army, along with the Seneca salutes, suggests that the Senecas, in the eyes of both Pickering and Parrish who interpreted the events, were engaging with the Euro-Americans' own framework of state-backed military power.

On yet another occasion of a Seneca military parade, "about 50 Indians" formed "a line near the Coln." and "sent and fired 3 sallutes & informed that their was as many more on their way."[32] The marching indicated that the Seneca Nation possessed military capabilities, even if it was not, at the moment, hostile; the assurances that more warriors were available conveyed a claim to power as well as a subtle threat. The Senecas' military showing demonstrated that they possessed the power of arms, men, and respect, and it served to translate Native sovereignty into a performative diplomatic space that was easily understood by U.S. officials. Such a show facilitated Senecas' ability to minimize their cultural differences while also asserting their place among the many nations that the United States government recognized as sovereign. The meeting of two sovereign polities—each foreign to the other—created such spaces, and they were representative of each power's attempt to find a common performative language that would render one intelligible to the other.[33]

These elaborate spaces of diplomacy further complicated U.S. officials' perceptions of Native leaders and Native nations' political standing. For John Parrish, Native leaders were the equivalents of the most prominent European statesmen. Parrish described the Shawnee Blue Jacket's "person and appearence" in 1793 as "much like the great man such as an Admiral or General."[34] When, in 1791, moreover, the Seneca Red Jacket spoke to Pickering and others of the U.S. diplomatic entourage, Parrish reflected that the chief's "appearance and maner his eliquence and person I concluded would out no inconsiderable figure on the flore of a British Parliment or an American Congress[.] I do not remember have seen any states man make a more magisterial appearence."[35] The Quaker understood Red Jacket as belonging to the realms of diplomacy and international politics, while Pickering, who received the Seneca statesmen in the company of Parrish and an interpreter, legitimated the Seneca's claim to authority by engaging in his nation's diplomatic traditions of speechmaking. Parrish's presence, a consequence of Pickering's appeal to Six Nations' alliances and protocols, likewise underscored the power of the Six Nations; Colonel Pickering encouraged the Quaker's participation in the meeting and thereby recognized the legitimacy of the Senecas and their diplomatic networks. These were the international politics that combined with U.S. imperial ambitions to produce the political landscape of 1790s North America, and this was the context that brought Parrish to that diplomatic dinner in June 1791.

* * *

Against this backdrop of Indigenous power, men of friendly reputation like John Parrish and his fellow Quakers—William Hartshorne, Joseph Moore, William Savery, and others—became indispensable to U.S. hopes for peace with Native nations. Friends' reputation for pacifism and diplomacy, their hierarchical organization, and their diplomatic experience—including relationships they cultivated over years—all contributed to their value as go-betweens from both Native and federal perspectives. Such value would outlive the Northwest Indian War: the War Department would occasionally call upon Friends to act as missionaries in the first part of the nineteenth century as well.[36] Individual Friends, just like Aupaumut and others, had their own goals and ambitions, and they found ways to carry out their agendas while working alongside U.S. officials.[37] In particular, many Friends hoped to secure a lasting peace between the United States and Native nations as well as garner political and moral capital. Their efforts also served their religious aims: they hoped to create a godly society on Earth through peaceful relations and labor. Diplomacy, too, could dovetail with their religious goals—particularly with their pacifism—by pursuing peace, but also via what one scholar dubs "peace through conversation."[38] Such an approach made them ideal partners for both the U.S. and Native polities.

Some Native peoples grew to value Friends as go-betweens for many reasons, including their commitment to peace and pacifism and their reputation. The U.S. federal government, meanwhile, partnered with the Society out of a combination of necessity, wariness, and practicality. In part, the complicated nature of Quakers' relationship with the federal government was a consequence of Friends' activist tendencies; they had a history of intervening in government affairs in order to advocate for Native nations. When violence escalated in the 1790s Ohio Country, Friends wrote a memorial to President Washington, the Senate, and the House of Representatives indicating that they were "deeply affected with the distressed situation of the frontier inhabitants," and that they "desire[d] a solid and careful enquiry may be made into the cause." In that memorial, they claimed it had been their "uniform care to admonish and caution our members against settling on lands which have not been fairly purchas'd of the original owner." They went on to insinuate that the government should do the same with its citizens, and they promised that "as far as our influence extends, we mean to maintain this our ancient testimony inviolate, which from experience has been found effectual to the preservation of peace with the natives, who with great hospitality, cherished and assisted our forefathers in their early settlement of this country."[39] With this message, Friends reminded the federal government of their previous history with Native peoples on the continent, encouraged officials to work toward peace, and, in turn, asserted their ability to promote peace. They also, however, carefully trod the line between support for Native peoples and the United States, which facilitated their work as go-betweens in Indian Country.

Though the Society of Friends in Philadelphia engaged in the national politics of Indian affairs and war through their petitions, from the perspective of the debt-ridden federal government, Friends' most valuable work took place on an individual basis in Indian Country. Henry Knox encouraged missionaries to partner with the federal government and promote "civilization" in 1789, yet in the Ohio Country, diplomacy was needed before the work of civilization could take place. Here, Friends (along with some other missionaries) made logical partners. One consequence of the Quakers' already-extensive dealings in Indian Country—as well as the constant migrations of Native communities and individuals during the latter half of the eighteenth century—was that knowledge of Friends and their friendships with Native peoples circulated throughout eastern North America by the 1790s.[40] In 1793 Detroit, for example, John Parrish encountered several local traders who informed him that "our cuming will be usefull as a number of the tribes have a Knowledge of friends of whom they have a faverable oppinion from their haveing nothing to do with the sheding of Blood and their honest deeling with them in the first setling [of] the Country." A Shawnee in western New York likewise knew of Friends' past work in Indian Country, as did "18 Onados [Oneidas]" who visited the Quaker and several other Friends in 1793. Friends conversed with these latter Oneidas "to mutual Sattisfaction" akin to "a time of brighting the Chain of friend-ship which they exprest their gladness to find that the fire which was kindled by our fore fathers was not quite gone out."[41]

Such encounters reveal that Friends had garnered a reputation among Native peoples, and their repute proved useful in furthering friendly interpersonal and diplomatic networks. Many other religious-minded men, conversely, could be negatively lumped together. In 1751, for example, the renowned Presbyterian missionary David Brainerd wrote, "[the Indians] understood that the white people were contriving a method to deprive them of their country in those parts" and "that I was sent on purpose to accomplish that design."[42] Of course, Parrish and other Friends no doubt glorified their friendly reputations in their writings, but their consistent ability to interact with Native leaders and their countrymen, coupled with some other missionaries' comparatively few successes during the 1790s, suggests that they did, in fact, possess a special reputation for diplomacy among Native nations.

The Society of Friends' hierarchical organization added to their reputation as an attractive partner for the U.S. federal government. Yearly meetings at Philadelphia, Baltimore, and London oversaw more local quarterly and monthly meetings, which, in turn, supervised individual meetings that consisted of local Friends. These various committees appointed clerks with whom federal officials and Native peoples alike could communicate, in consultation with the committee. Those clerks could also call upon volunteer committee members for various tasks among Indian nations—including travel, diplomacy, and, eventually, mission work and its requisite reconnaissance. Like the Society for the Propagation of the Gospel in Foreign Parts (SPG), the Society of Friends thus offered a relatively efficient means to coordinate communication, diplomacy, and labor in Indian Country. Friends' organization, however, underscored their somewhat ambiguous status vis-*à*-vis the United States. The Society of Friends operated as a non-governmental society that nonetheless possessed the efficiency, funds, and labor necessary to effectively offer the United States diplomatic—and later mission—support in Indian Country. Friends' organizational model was shared by later missionary societies: the American Board of Commissioners for Foreign Missions (ABCFM), established in 1810, adopted a similarly hierarchical structure.

Friends' organizational efficiency, along with their reputation for usefulness and past diplomacy, aided them in the 1790s Ohio Country. It was not unusual for Quakers traveling through western New York or the Ohio Country to encounter Haudenosaunee, Delaware, or Shawnee individuals with whom they or a member of their society had already formed friendships. Near Detroit in 1793, for example, John Parrish crossed paths with a Nanticoke, John White, who lived among the Christian Indians under the tutelage of the Moravian missionary John Heckewelder. White, who had visited Philadelphia on several occasions prior to encountering Parrish in Detroit, exchanged pleasantries with the Friends and asked after several other members of the society, including John Pemberton, Robert Parrish, and Isaac Zane—all men who had been involved with Indian affairs prior to the crisis of the 1790s. Thomas King, one of the "neighbouring Indians" Parrish encountered during his travels to western New York, likewise "inquired perticularly after his freinds [*sic*] Isaac Zane & Israel Pemberton." Such memories of Israel Pemberton and others were the consequence of Friends' efforts among the western nations and, in particular, members of the Delaware nation during the Seven Years' War in Pennsylvania. When Parrish encountered a Shawnee in Detroit, he later noted in his journal that the Shawnee knew "as most of the Shawneys do a good deel a bout friends, as well as the Delawares."[43] The Delawares were among Friends' closest—if not the closest—of their Native allies, and they were central to the creation of Quakers' reputation in Indian Country.

Like the Shawnee who possessed knowledge of both Friends and Delawares, Wyandots (who had close relations with Delawares in Ohio and Indiana) also possessed knowledge of the Society of Friends. By the 1790s, moreover, one Wyandot linked the Society with the U.S. federal government. Just prior to treaty proceedings in 1793, Parrish "received a visit from a Wyondot Chief" who had an interest in reaching an eventual "accomedation between their people and those of the U. States." The man "said he remembered the old friendship that subsisted in time past that they had still a large Belt in possession as I understood him from Pennsylvania."[44] For this leader, the Pennsylvanian colonial past—Friends' past—lived on in the present and had the power to shape the relations between his nation and the United States; he understood Friends as diplomatic extensions of the U.S. federal government—people with whom he desired a friendly, working relationship.

Memories of Pennsylvania's past and Friends' work with the Delawares became a useful means of building and spreading Friends' reputation for peaceful negotiation with Native peoples. Those memories also, however, served as powerful diplomatic tools. Just as Parrish did at the 1791 dinner table, Native and Quaker diplomats often invoked rhetoric of a "chain of friendship" in their messages between one another. The diplomatic chain metaphor originally structured relations between the Haudenosaunee of what is now New

Figure 4. Peace medal depicting a Quaker holding a peace pipe with a Native man. These medals were distributed by members of the Friendly Association for Regaining and Preserving Peace with the Indians by Pacific Measures as tokens of friendship and amity during the eighteenth century. Such material items likewise contributed to the crafting—and remembering—of Friends' reputation for diplomacy. Yale University Art Gallery.

York State and the British Empire in North America.[45] Yet this image of the chain—sometimes rusty after a period of neglect, sometimes silver, sometimes gold—lingered into the era of the United States, and it became a crucial piece of a mutually intelligible language for both Friends and Native peoples. The Oneida Good Peter, for example, asserted the power of the Six Nations by using the chain metaphor to assert a Haudenosaunee diplomatic agenda. At a 1791 meeting between the Six Nations and the United States he remarked, "it is the voice of the 6 nations that the chain of friendship be made Bright, we dont intend to sell any more of our lands."[46] Here, Good Peter invoked history to resurrect both past alliances but also former Haudenosaunee power—power that was threatened by the growth of United States authority. Such rhetoric was crucial to the ongoing development of cultural and political spaces within which Native polities and some Americans could converse in metaphor.

Diplomats such as Parrish and Good Peter and political leaders such as the Wyandot Tarhe used the chain metaphor to articulate and achieve their own political objectives, and in doing so they also invoked a binding political relationship. This continued even after the Northwest Indian War. Tarhe, for example, informed Philadelphia Friends in a 1799 letter that they "told us at that time when we met together . . . that you then formed a Chain of Frienship: You said it was not a Chain of Iron, but that it was a chain of precious metal, a chain of silver, which would never get rusty. . . . We have no records or place of security for our Speeches as you have—nor can we write as you do. . . . But if you examine your old Books and papers you will there find written all that passed between your Forefathers and ours."[47] By 1799, after the birth of the Baltimore Yearly Meeting, Baltimore and Philadelphia Friends divided philanthropic work among Native peoples into separate jurisdictions presumably for the sake of ease and efficiency of resource use. Relations with Wyandots and Shawnees, Delawares, and others in the Ohio Country were in the hands of the Baltimore Yearly Meeting of the Society of Friends; Philadelphia Friends handled relations in New York. When Tarhe offered his speech to the Philadelphia Friends he was either unaware that his lands fell under the philanthropic jurisdiction of the Baltimore Yearly Meeting, or he failed to care. The Wyandot's business concerned the Society of Friends writ large and he, for the time being, associated Friends with Pennsylvania; in his mind, it was to that group that his memory-infused language was intelligible.

What was more, in a calculated diplomatic stroke, Tarhe emphasized his relations with Philadelphia Friends' former allies, the Delawares. He informed Friends that his people were "much pleased to hear that you still hold in remembrance our nephew the Delaware nation, The promises and obligations made between your grandfathers and ours included our two Nations (Wy andots [*sic*] and Delawares) in the Chain of friendship and brotherly love, concidering us as one and the same people, which . . . pray, that the great Spirit will never permit to be divided."[48] Tarhe's message may have referred to a time when the Delaware Teedyuscung presented himself as a leader of the Delawares and of a political confederation that he referred to as the "Ten Nations" during the Seven Years' War.[49] That coalition may have included some Wyandots among those confederated nations, yet the Wyandots were not present at Penn's treaty in 1682. Indeed, for most other purposes and despite the intercultural nature of Ohio Country Indian villages by the late eighteenth century, Delawares and Wyandots would still have insisted on their separate identities. Tarhe thus proved himself a master politician: Quakers had allied themselves with Delawares in the past and, by resurrecting the chain of friendship metaphor and asserting his people's political alliance and fictive kinship with the Delawares, the Wyandot hoped to capitalize on that partnership and ensure that his people would not confront United States officials alone.

As evidenced by Tarhe's overtures, the reputation and malleability of the Society of Friends and its members—along with some Native leaders' willingness to use them as go-betweens—contributed to Friends' value as a government partner, and it did so before, during, and after the Northwest Indian War. So did, however, Friends' years of diplomatic experience in Indian Country. Indeed, Friends' experience meant that Parrish's misstep at the 1791 dinner table was a rather rare occurrence, and it was likely the product of his religious society's changing role in official U.S. diplomacy. Relative to many other Euro-Americans, Quakers understood the importance of Native nations' protocols, and they willingly undertook the sometimes tedious work of cultivating partnerships with the various Native nations that they encountered. Friends' copious meeting minutes, epistles, and publications ensured that knowledge of diplomatic protocols and Native alliance networks survived within the meeting. Since men of varying ages served on Friends' committees, the committee system likewise ensured that knowledge passed from one generation to the next became an essential foundation for Friends' diplomatic work in Indian Country.[50] Thus, though Parrish blundered in June 1791, Friends were, on the whole, reliably educated diplomats in Indian Country. That the United States sought Friends' expertise and knowledge illuminates both Native authority and the fact that the United States recognized that authority in their political relations.

Of course, it is important to note that Friends were not the only missionaries to work with the United States in diplomacy during the conflict. Several Moravians, in particular, proved equally adept in conducting Indian affairs. John Heckewelder and David Zeisberger, like Friends, attended treaty councils and often discussed Indian affairs with colonial and then U.S. officials, and both their treaty attendance and mission work offered them ample opportunity to gain intimate knowledge of their pupils. Heckewelder's and Zeisberger's journals offer detailed ethnographic information, and they reveal their ability to cultivate close ties with Native peoples.[51] After receiving an invitation from Henry Knox, Heckewelder partnered with Rufus Putnam—a man chosen by Washington to lead a U.S. delegation in the Ohio Country—and together they hoped to pursue peaceful negotiation with the region's Indigenous polities.[52] Together, Putnam, Heckewelder, and their delegation negotiated a peace treaty at Vincennes that both established a boundary line for U.S. settlement and freed Native female captives. While doing so, the U.S. delegation was careful to know and follow Native diplomatic protocols—a trait that would prove important to U.S. diplomats more generally in the region. Despite their initial success, however, the treaty ultimately failed to sway Congress.[53] Nonetheless, Heckewelder's partnership with official U.S. representatives showcases the extent to which the federal government deemed missionaries of several sorts as essential to its international diplomacy in the region.[54]

* * *

For all these reasons, Friends, along with other missionary go-betweens, made for useful partners of the U.S. government in the 1790s. Yet it was not enough to possess the right allies in the business of diplomacy. The *work* of diplomacy required pre-existing relationships, knowledge, skill, and the ability to remedy any missteps made along the way. This was a world where the United States played by Native diplomatic scripts, and where personal relationships, gift-giving, and a knowledge of various Indigenous diplomatic protocols mattered a great deal. Friends' past experiences facilitated their diplomatic efforts in the 1790s, while past interpersonal encounters could similarly facilitate ongoing relationships. Such knowledge, experience, and connections were crucial to U.S. diplomacy in Indian Country, and it underscores the extent to which Indigenous authority shaped the contours of U.S. diplomacy.

For Friends' part, their relationships with Native individuals were a consequence and a facilitator of their diplomatic roles. Such relationships had sometimes formed when delegations of Native leaders visited Philadelphia or met Friends during treaty councils. These trips continued into the nineteenth century and ensured that relationships remained well-oiled.[55] When Parrish visited the Tuscaroras in 1793, for example, he was pleased to find that "divers of the inhabitants came in and seemed pleased to see us, and what made our Visit more agreeable one of the Chiefs I know who had been several times at my house."[56] While a general history of past diplomatic efforts could be important in the 1790s, so, too, could personal relationships.

Friends' connections with various Native leaders also blossomed as a result of Friends' open curiosity. During Parrish's 1793 voyage from western New York to Detroit "a bord the Schooner Dunmore," he observed that there were "representitives of 5 different Indian Nations on Bord, some Mohocks Mossesogers, Mohickins, Kighugers, & Stockbridge." The Quaker likely gleaned such particular information through word of mouth, but also from the onboard exchange of pleasantries. Captain John, one of the Mohawks aboard the *Dunmore*, made the effort to visit Parrish in his Detroit lodgings after their journey together and "exprest his sattisfaction in his acquaintance with us and wished we could make it in our way to return by the Bay of Canty that we might see him at his [own] house that he might make us welcome."

Never one to miss an opportunity to develop closer ties with a new contact, Parrish "red to him Friends missage to the Indians which he much approv'd of" whereupon Captain John "said he would communicate the substance to the Indians at their council where he expected to set out for next day."[57] What began as a casual, chance acquaintance aboard a schooner quickly developed into the interpersonal foundations for diplomacy.

Sometimes, however, Friends' attempts to cultivate their international networks failed due to unforeseen circumstances. In such moments, Friends would need to find other means of establishing or polishing a relationship. When Zebulon Heston, a Friend traveling with Parrish to the eastern Ohio Country fell ill along the way, for example, Parrish settled for sending a letter to the Shawnees and Wyandots rather than paying them a personal visit. He wrote, "we should have been glad to have come and seen you . . . but one of us Zebulon Heston . . . being far advanced in age & in a poor State of helth & our horses forspent, we are not [at] liberty to go any further then . . . Newcommers Town." He then conveyed his affection for the nations and reminded them that Friends "had no other motive meaning then your good and the Peace of our own minds we seek nothing that is yours, but you unto God."[58] Episodes such as this reveal not only Friends' persistence but that they were aware of the importance of their connections and of the diplomatic protocols common to many Native nations. Failing to pay a promised visit to an ally could have devastating consequences in Indian Country, and thus a letter was required to ensure that relations remained strong. Through years of alliance and observation, Friends knew how to maintain relationships with Native nations.

Friends cultivated knowledge through experience, and their time spent acquiring such knowledge throughout the eighteenth century added to their pre-existing relationships with individuals in Indian Country. This increased Friends' value to the U.S. federal government by the 1790s. Indeed, the Society of Friends' relationships with various Native nations could facilitate traveling Friends' intelligence-gathering work. Before setting out for Detroit, Parrish reflected that "we should be likely to have an opertunity to see a number of Indians and such others that might give us some necessary inteligence to facilitate the Business we are ingaged in." Once in Detroit, the Quaker did, indeed, gather intelligence "which was not the most favourable," and he then wrote to various commissioners working with Colonel Thomas McKee near Grand Rapids "informing them the Inteligence we had received since we came heare."[59] By the 1790s, Friends were crucial links between Native nations and the United States; by using their own interpersonal networks to promote peace, they facilitated U.S. diplomatic reconnaissance and constructed a valuable international information network that linked Philadelphia, western New York, the Ohio Country, and the Great Lakes.

By the 1790s, Quakers such as John Parrish had acquired years of experience and knowledge of Native diplomatic protocols. Yet mistakes could still happen, as Parrish experienced in 1791. Failure to abide by Natives' rules of alliance-making could make things awkward, if not dangerous, during treaties with various nations, and such a reality was not new. In 1761 Pennsylvania, for example, one Quaker woman described a particularly uncomfortable interaction that was the product of Friends' ignorance. A Delaware leader, Papoonan, informed the Quakers that "God had been so kind to them" so as to ensure "that his young men had success in hunting & killed a great many Deer," and the resulting skins he wished Friends "to accept as a token of his love." Unaccustomed to Native politics of gift-giving and consequently caught off guard, one Friend explained that "as Providence had favoured us with abundance, he thought we ought rather to be helpfull to them, & excused friends from receiving their presents." Papoonan, appearing noticeably "uneasy" then, again encouraged Friends to accept the skins, "that this was their practice, of their forefathers, therefore they had brought those skins, & again requested friends would accept of them." Sensing their mistake, the Quakers quickly replied that they "desired him not to take it amiss, that we did not at once receive them." Two days later Papoonan, still "uneasy," visited Friends' lodgings to revive the issue, whereupon the Quakers explained "that we were sorry that any thing that was said respecting their presents should give him uneasiness."[60] Friends were savvy enough to learn from their mistake, and immediately set about repairing their relationship with the Delaware leader. The ability to learn, adapt, and remedy missteps were crucial to any diplomat's skill set.

Native nations' politics and protocols shaped missionaries' abilities to work with their peoples, and diplomatic blunders could render relationships between missionaries and Native nations untenable. In 1802, Joseph Patterson, a Presbyterian missionary near Chillicothe in the Ohio Country, experienced great frustration when a group of Shawnees refused his primers, books, and preaching. A man unknown to the chiefs there, Patterson "went to the chiefs who were assembled, and . . . informed them of the design of my mission, and that tomorrow was our day of worship, and signified my intention of [preaching] to any who would attend." Rather than offering Patterson statements of friendship and invitation as Friends often received, the

Shawnees "answered roughly that they would hear nothing from me till the great council determined, nor should any of their people." These Shawnees ultimately decided that Patterson should go home.[61]

Patterson blamed his failure upon his interpreter's lack of commitment, the Shawnees' being too "alarmed and confused" to engage him in formal speech at the chiefs' council, the ill effects of alcohol among the Indians, and, perhaps closer to the truth, his own inability to speak their language. Missing from this laundry list of excuses, however, is the fact that Patterson arrived at the Shawnees' town lacking the foundations for meaningful relations with its inhabitants. Though he frequently commented in his journals that the Shawnees offered him food and lodging—gifts that suggest their willingness to bring Patterson into their network of alliances—Patterson was ultimately too hardheaded to realize that mission work required patience as well as a willingness to engage Native nations and their leaders on their own political terms. Waltzing into the chiefs' council without first laying the groundwork for meaningful conversation did not produce faithful converts, and such episodes reveal the great tenuousness of diplomacy in early America. British and then U.S. relationships with Native peoples were fragile, and they required constant—and experienced—cultivation; Friends, with their history of experience in Indian Country, thus became useful in nurturing U.S. relations with Native nations.

As Patterson's experience among the Shawnees suggests, because of Native nations' political authority, gifts, like personal relationships and knowledge of protocols, were also essential to diplomatic relations and in the smaller exchanges between Native and non-Native individuals. U.S. officials and their partners drew upon their experience and earlier empires' modes of gift-giving practices in their own efforts to engage with Native peoples. Gifts ranged from small to lavish and included food, clothing, and an assortment of smaller items such as needles or tobacco. John Parrish in 1791, for example, offered his friend and fellow diplomat Hendrick Aupaumut and two of his companions "a flag hankerchef which was received with gratitude."[62] The gift of a flag symbolized Parrish's association with the United States, and it cemented his status as a partner and representative of that polity. Such items were political symbols, and they were also the material markers of reciprocity, the tangible symbols of interpersonal relationships. It was significant that the failed Presbyterian missionary Joseph Patterson arrived at the Shawnee chiefs' council with nothing but primers when they had already offered him generous lodging and several meals. Gifts were the means by which friendships developed, but, as in the case of Patterson or the Quakers in 1761 Pennsylvania, they could also stifle budding relationships.[63]

Food was also central to Native politics of gift-giving, and successful diplomats engaged in the rituals of food diplomacy. Knowing these rules, in 1793 Detroit Parrish offered "the Moravian Indians that came to us" several items to "releive their presant necessities," including "a bout 27 Bushels of corn & a bout 400 of flower." He followed this offering with a letter—"in couraging them to persevere in a life of Sivilization and Christian fortitude"—to carry with them back to their Moravian community.[64] Though these Moravian Delawares were already "converted," Parrish wasted no time in maintaining his networks with them since his society had already had extensive dealings with the Moravian Delawares during and after the Seven Years' War in Pennsylvania. In the turbulent years of the later eighteenth century, all friendly alliances were crucial, and Friends' overtures paid off. The Delawares later sent Parrish a letter extending "hearty thanks" for the "Provisions to the Amount of one hundred dollars, which we acknowledge as a testimoney of your former Love and friendship toward us."[65]

In 1790, moreover, the Delaware Captain White Eyes "sent a message to request" that Parrish and other Friends "would make him a visit." Upon arrival, they found that not only had the Delaware "had the logs cut that was fell a cross the road . . . out of the way" for their coming, but that he "had a Calf killed" whereupon they enjoyed several items "rost and boiled & were entertained with much kindness & hospitality." Immediately after dinner, Friends and White Eyes "smoked our pipes together," and Parrish reflected that "it was like a time of brightening the chain and renewing of friendship agreable to the Easton of our forefathers."[66]

White Eyes, an old friend and political ally of the Quakers in Pennsylvania, made a point to solicit Parrish's company and offer him gifts of sustenance, but this encounter extended beyond the bounds of mere friendship. When in his journal he connected the dinner and subsequent sharing of tobacco with the "Easton of our forefathers," Parrish revealed that the meeting was simultaneously personal and diplomatic. That was not an unusual experience in the eighteenth century. The lines between friendship and official diplomacy often blurred because effective diplomacy was impossible without friendship. Indeed, as Parrish's 1791 blunder at Pickering's dinner table reveals, even experienced diplomats stumbled from time to time precisely because friendship and diplomacy were so intermingled.

Such instances of gift-exchange long characterized both Native-non-Native interpersonal relationships as well as, more broadly, diplomacy in colonial America, and they remained at the center of U.S.-Native relations throughout the nineteenth century. When he was not at the dinner table of Colonel Pickering or attending the treaty deliberations at Newtown in western New York in 1791, John Parrish spoke with locals and distributed gifts among the Senecas who camped nearby. He offered Senecas "600 seames of thread with 300 nedles to the women & girls" and "about 100 fish hooks & some lines to the men & boys which highly delighted them for which they gave many thanks."[67] The gendered prescriptions here were obvious and aligned with Euro-American ideas of a gendered economy more generally: women were to perform domestic activities such as sewing, while men fished. Several days later, Colonel Pickering and the interpreters likewise attempted to distribute "the publick Present." The Senecas were the recipients of private and public gifts, but because Parrish was allied with Pickering and the U.S. government, all the gifts supported the United States' goal of maintaining friendly diplomatic relations with the Six Nations.[68] With help from the Society of Friends and its members, then, the United States government continued the British imperial tradition of appealing to the various nations on Natives' terms.

The power of Friends' diplomatic past, together with their relationships with the many Indian nations they encountered during their experiences in Indian Country, meant that, by 1791, events such as John Parrish's dinner with Colonel Pickering and others were relatively commonplace. The Quaker dined with Pickering on several occasions, often with Native men in attendance as well. He shared another meal after his plunder, for example, with the colonel, an interpreter, and the Seneca Red Jacket "& several other Indians" in 1791.[69] Members of Native nations, however, were not always in attendance. In 1793 Detroit, Parrish dined with Colonel England and "a company of well-behaved genteelmen mostly officers" and "with the Officers at their Mess" on another occasion.[70] Men like Parrish, then, were important diplomats among Native and non-Native men, but they also worked to maintain their relationships with their American connections.

Such dinners among Quakers and U.S. army men involved, however, more than mere pleasantries: Parrish was often privy to official government information. At one meal, he learned that the United States interrupted a council between Britain's ally, the Mohawk Joseph Brant, and various representatives from regional Native nations, while another evening's talk was "on the Subject of war & the Slave trade."[71] Dinners and informal conversations rendered Parrish not only useful to Pickering among Native leaders, but they also sowed the seeds of trust between the Quakers and the U.S. government. Not long after dining with Colonel England in Detroit, for example, Parrish found himself in "the Garden of Coln. England a beautifull airy Place where we spent some time in Looking over Some papers relative to Indian Affairs."[72] Friends' relationships with top U.S. officials gave them intimate knowledge of official policy, and they served to blur the lines between their roles as private citizens concerned with peace and as official United States diplomats.

Indeed, those lines were so blurred that Parrish himself often struggled to define whether he was a private citizen or an official U.S. diplomat. He informed the Seneca Red Jacket that he, along with his fellow Quaker companion, was "here in a privit [*sic*] capacity." He continued to explain that "we had nothing to do with Government affairs, but we ware heartly united with the Commissioners for promoting the work of Peace." He then again felt it necessary to state that "although we ware in a private capacity yet it was a matter of much concern that we had obtained the concurrence of our Bretheren at home . . . & like wise our proceeding was approved of by the Presedent of the U. States."[73] In a single message to Red Jacket, then, Parrish twice informed the Seneca that he was there on private business, and twice informed him that his work was done in conjunction with the official leadership of the United States. Parrish's status relative to the U.S. government was blurred.

Parrish often contemplated the nature of his relationship with the federal government. He attended treaties in a self-described "privit capacity," yet he kept his journal of events with the awareness that they were "disigned for publick Views."[74] This understanding of public and private underscored the Society of Friends' work as a non-governmental organization: the Society's papers were not officially policed by the government—the Society of Friends was "private"—but Parrish's papers were intended for public consumption by other Friends. Parrish and the Society of Friends understood their role as a spiritual one of promoting peace and uplift among Native peoples, but also as one wherein Parrish and the Society acted as liaisons between the federal government and the broader U.S. citizenry. Parrish, by calling explicit attention to his presence in a "privit capacity," revealed the ambiguous—if increasingly important—relationship between the Society of Friends and the U.S. government. Friends' non-military status also underscored the emerging qualifications for diplomats.

It was in the function as liaisons between government and citizens that Parrish took the most liberties in his writing. The issue of alcohol, in particular, occasioned Parrish to question whether he had the authority to confront Colonel Pickering and the U.S. commissioners with his concerns for Native leaders' sobriety. The Quaker, deciding it most appropriate to address the issue in a letter to Pickering, insisted that he "came heare from a apprehention of duty and with the Concurrence of our friends of Philada. to attend the Treaty without any intention to Interfeer or meddle with the publick business." Continuing on in his letter, however, he reflected that, "as Subjects of the United States equally concernd in it[s] wellfare with our fellow Sitizens," he had a duty to ensure that the treaty was conducted "to the general benifit of the white Inhabitants and the good of the Indians."[75]

The Quaker, also, however, included his opinions of the government's official policy toward Native nations. Though he was usually pleased with Colonel Pickering's efforts, he did not shy from offering scathing criticism of federal Indian policy. He wrote, for example, that "many People it may be said Lement the steps that was taken by Goverment after the war Ceased with Great Brittan that insted of singly attending to the Establishing a Peace (with the Natives) measure ware persued to procure Large & extensive tracts into their Country, and making them believe they ware a conquered People and that all their Lands in reallity was the Property of the United States, which only tended to raise their resentment and become a [?] Enemey." As the word "believe" reveals, Parrish undertook his work for reasons of perceived benevolence, but also because of a fundamental political disagreement: he did not buy into the imperial fiction that Native peoples "ware a conquered People."[76] Though he and other Quakers worked alongside the U.S. government during the war and after, that did not necessarily mean that their views aligned perfectly with that of the state. The fact that Parrish was included in the United States' diplomatic efforts underscores the correctness of his position: Indigenous sovereignty rendered him necessary.

* * *

Native nations' memories of diplomatic friendship with Friends shaped the character of U.S. efforts by ensuring that some of the nation's leading philanthropists aided state officials in their empire-building project in North America. They compelled the United States to develop a brand of empire that relied, in many ways, upon the reputation-cultivating and labor-intensive diplomacy, mission, and educational work of missionaries. In this, the United States followed in the footsteps of earlier European empires in North America.

Understanding the partnership between the United States and the Society of Friends during the 1790s obliges us to consider together the breadth of Native sovereignty during the era of the early republic and both the limits of U.S. state power and the ways in which that power grew during the same period. Parrish's presence at the 1791 dinner table reveals that the federal government cultivated its diplomatic apparatus in order to effectively treat with Native nations, and that missionaries played a defining role in the development of that diplomatic order. As U.S. officials well knew, among the Shawnees, Delawares, and others, there existed a division between the power of "civil" leaders and "war" leaders. Prior to the meeting of a treaty council, the Shawnee Blue Jacket informed Pickering and Parrish as much when he stated that if "he was presant he had no voice in the Council he was of the war department . . . he said he had heard of the Quakers and had come on purpose to see us and he believed a peace would take place but he had no voice in the Civil department." Such a statement reminded the U.S. commissioners that diplomacy needed to take place on and according to Native peoples' terms. For Pickering and Parrish, both their experience and knowledge of Indigenous diplomacy, as well as their understanding that they did not hold the upper hand, informed their understandings of diplomacy and war with Native nations: U.S.-Native diplomacy required both war and civil chiefs.[77]

U.S. diplomatic relations with Native nations required knowledge regarding Native protocols of gift-giving and alliance networks but also savvy human symbols of peace—missionaries. These essentials were premised upon both Native polities' sovereign and, for U.S. officials, ambiguous diplomatic status with the United States. Partnering with a society like the Society of Friends offered the United States the ability to cultivate peace and authority through Friends' interpersonal networks, but it also offered opportunities to exert influence in Indian Country via unofficial means. Friends' diplomatic work continued into the nineteenth century, but in the Ohio Country—and in western New York and the Southwest as well—it was coupled with agricultural mission work.

After the defeat of the allied Indian nations at the Battle of Fallen Timbers in 1794, the United States Senate ratified the Treaty of Greenville in an effort to assert authority over the Ohio Country's Native populations. The treaty established a boundary line between the United States and Indian Country in the region; it also ushered in a renewed effort to "civilize" Native peoples. Friends were, by 1795, reliable partners of the U.S. War Department, and they took the lead in these civilizing efforts with the support of none other than John Parrish's dinner mate, Timothy Pickering. Philadelphia Friends would begin their mission among the Oneidas at precisely the moment that the United States emerged victorious. Baltimore Friends, too, would receive Pickering and Washington's blessing in 1795–96 as they considered embarking on their own mission efforts. Warfare gave way to redoubled efforts to obtain land via "peaceful" means. 1795 thus marked a change in Ohio Country U.S.-Indian relations, but it did not bring with it the disappearance of the region's Native American inhabitants. With the Society of Friends at their side, U.S. officials like Knox and Pickering would begin the work of implementing their vision of spreading civilization and securing private property in the Ohio Country and throughout eastern North America.

PART II

Routes

CHAPTER 3

Becoming Useful

Speculative Philanthropy, Civilization, and Educational Reform

The knowledge, experience, and relationships gleaned from missionary and diplomatic pasts offered a foundation for civilizing missions in the Ohio Country, and so, too, did emerging ideas that flowed to and from the Atlantic world, Baltimore, and Indian Country. Indeed, to fully understand the social and intellectual underpinnings of U.S. civilizing missions as they developed during the first decades of the nineteenth century, we must first stop at a school in the Southwark borough of London. It was based on a school there that in 1807 the influential British Quaker reformer Joseph Lancaster implored London's moral leaders to aid children who experienced poverty by offering them education. Such children, he wrote, "brought up in ignorance, and amidst the contagion of bad example, are in imminent danger of ruin; and too many of them, it is to be feared, instead of being useful members of the community, will become the burden and pests of Society."[1] These young pupils were supposedly in danger of becoming useless either because of the parents' "extreme indigence . . . their intemperance and vice, or [because of] a blind indifference to the best interests of their offspring."[2] These children were potentially diseased—exposed to a "contagion"—Lancaster claimed, and they were thus in danger of being both useless and a threat to the health of Britain. Lancaster proposed to educate them in order to remedy the dire situation in which they found themselves. The studies he prescribed often involved education deemed practical for a life of labor.

Yet Lancaster could not do all the work himself. Public leaders, he argued, could further ameliorate the situation by contributing to reform efforts that would make these children "useful." "It becomes the duty of the public," Lancaster wrote, "and of individuals, who have the power, to assist them in the discharge of this important obligation."[3] Philanthropy in the realm of education was thus an "obligation" and a necessary activity for those who had "the power" to assist. If such people offered their aid, they could rid their polity of a potent disease—poverty—by making children who experienced poverty "useful." Philanthropy, like education, was a public good.

Lancaster's ideas both traversed the Atlantic and borrowed from a transatlantic discourse of "usefulness" that informed reform efforts in Great Britain and the early American republic. Publishers circulated Lancaster's thoughts on schooling, and those ideas in turn undergirded a number of reform schools in the republic. Euro-American reformers employed Lancaster's methods in Cherokee Country and elsewhere on the continent, particularly after 1819, while, earlier on, ideas regarding "usefulness" permeated Friends' and their fellow missionaries'—as well as federal officials'—ideas regarding the civilization plan in Indian Country.[4] In 1801, for example, the secretary of war Henry Dearborn, building upon the relationships formed between Friends and U.S. officials in the earliest years of the republic, thanked Friends for their work among Native peoples in western New York and expressed his hope "that by a Steady and persevereing application of the means provided by the Government of the United States, powerfully aided by the constant exertions of your Society, the Savage tribes will ultimately form a useful part of the great family of the United States."[5]

While pervasive, ideas regarding one's usefulness were grounded in hierarchical socioeconomic and race-based ideas that differed depending on the individual. Such ideas resonated with Friends' approach to civilizing mission work—and with Protestants' tendency to offer education in "civilization" before complex theology in their U.S. missionary efforts more generally—and it also linked Native peoples with a race- and class-based hierarchy of educational prescriptions offered in both Lancaster's schools and in a number of reform schools throughout the republic. A Shawnee woman's usefulness was very different from that of a Euro-American Quaker woman, which was very different from those pupils at Lancaster's schools: the first could be useful through spinning and remaining in the home, the second through social reform work or by educating her children, if she had them, to be virtuous republicans, while the third would be useful by learning the basics of reading and to labor.

These ideas meant that unlike their pupils, but very much like their wealthy London counterparts, elite white Quaker men living in urban Baltimore could be useful by engaging in philanthropy that would help others realize their inherent usefulness. Such men often possessed the power—and, importantly, the time and the resources—to engage in social reform.[6] One such man, Elisha Tyson, would find his usefulness by moving to Baltimore in order to fulfill his "desire to be useful to his fellow human beings."[7] He ultimately served on a number of committees of reform simultaneously within his Quaker meeting, and he journeyed to the Ohio Country to assist in laying the groundwork for Friends' agricultural mission work there. For Quaker men navigating the world of emerging capitalism, philanthropy became a primary means by which they could maintain a role in politics, gather moral capital, balance individual profit with their faith's tenets of simplicity and public good, and, importantly, perform and showcase for others their usefulness.[8]

Ideas of usefulness and Friends' reform efforts alike were grounded in a social hierarchy, but also in a culture of speculation premised upon the investment in and acquisition of economic, political, and social capital. Friends bought properties and participated in manufacturing in an effort to grow their wealth near Baltimore, while their participation in the civilization plan, educational reform, and poor relief offered similar opportunities to invest in their political, social, and spiritual futures, a "settled" and physically altered frontier, and an increasingly trained, if temporary, agricultural laboring class (or, in urban spaces, an industrial laboring class). Friends' philanthropy and their work as part of the broader civilizing plan—a form of educational reform that focused on agricultural instruction—was therefore intertwined with economic change and with Euro-Americans' notions of economic growth. It was part and parcel of an economy built on speculation—it was *speculative philanthropy*: philanthropic work that was part of an effort, even if performative, to do good as well as part of an effort to invest in one's own interests.

Speculative philanthropy allows us to see the quest for profit (moral, political, spiritual, and economic) that accompanied Friends' civilizing efforts in the early nineteenth-century world of emerging capitalism, and it also offers a means to understand the financial underpinnings of philanthropic reform efforts more broadly. "Philanthropy" during this period simply meant "love of humanity," yet elite settler-civilizers mobilized that idea in the service of political and economic investment and profit-minded projects, often employing the discourse of usefulness and poor relief to do so.[9] Engaging in speculative philanthropy ensured that one could practice social reform as well as invest in one's own economic, political, and moral capital. Such a practice guided many of the civilization plan's proponents and reformers more generally. It would also, as Chapters 6 and 7 will detail, guide U.S. officials' efforts and policies as well. Speculative philanthropy thus underpinned both individuals' and the federal state's reform-minded efforts in cities, Indian Country, and, ultimately, the world.

Analyzing individuals' speculative philanthropy enables us to see how ideologies of difference were produced and reproduced by myriad individuals, philanthropists included. Those who engaged in speculative philanthropy—regardless of their various motivations—offered a form of reform that ultimately did little to overturn the systems of power that inspired their philanthropy in the first place. Rather, their efforts often perpetuated those systems of power by feeding and replicating the developing socioeconomic and racial hierarchies of the early republic through discourse and deed. Reformers offered prescriptions for labor that grew out of their assumptions regarding others' usefulness, even as that labor in turn reinforced both their pupils' and reformers' own statuses. Reformers thus engaged in a form of philanthropy borne out of early American economic development, and, along the way, they linked religion and profit even more tightly in the early nineteenth century.

Baltimore Friends' civilizing efforts in the Ohio Country, in particular, were both part of broader reform culture and a form of speculative philanthropy, and they must therefore be understood within the context of Baltimore and the early republic's changing racialized, socioeconomic world as well as alongside other reform efforts—such as Lancaster's charity schooling—that likewise engaged with the ideas of usefulness. Friends' ideas regarding race, gender, class, and labor traveled between their urban home and the Ohio Country, and that movement served to further entrench these ideas in both spaces. Placing Friends' agricultural civilizing work in the context of the republic's broader humanitarian, poor relief, and reform culture is therefore essential for understanding the ways in which the consequences of reform both cultivated and maintained the racial and socioeconomic hierarchies of the early republic. Such work also enables us to understand the ways in which both the republic's emerging economy and social reform contributed to the development of Euro-Americans' empire in North America.

* * *

Myriad beliefs and impulses—ideas regarding education, burgeoning humanitarianism, religion—undergirded early republican reform, and these ideas would eventually travel to Indian Country along with the reformers who carried them. Ideas regarding education writ large, for example, colored the character of civilizing work and its emphasis on agricultural instruction. For some individuals, Baltimore Quakers among them, a belief that ignorance lay at the root of the nation's inequality and moral degeneracy constituted the philosophical core of their benevolence. Men like Thomas Jefferson, Benjamin Rush, and Noah Webster emphasized the utility of education in creating a moral citizenry, and they conceived of educational plans that were relatively expansive.[10] An educated citizenry, they contended, would ensure that the best representatives served the federal government, and it would in turn safeguard the health and stability of the republic writ large. Debates over education were thus no simple matter: at stake was the nation's political future as well as its moral future, and universal education was viewed as a public good.

"Useful" knowledge was a key component of those debates, and it was a phrase employed often by educational reformers who engaged Native peoples, Euro-American women, men, and free African Americans alike. Politicians debated, for example, whether a military education was "useful" for a successful and morally upright life, and prominent men of Baltimore formed an association in an effort to define and attain "useful knowledge."[11] The definition of "useful knowledge" was not, however, universal: it meant different things for different people. While usefulness was often tied to notions of the nation's future and morality, it was also in dialogue with fears about the nation's potential corruption: "failures," including those who experienced the conditions of poverty, appeared to be a threat to the moral health of the republic—a corruptible force that could render the body politic diseased.[12] Friends' agricultural education missions in Indian Country were, meanwhile, an effort to rescue "poor Indians" from the vagrancies of a destitute life, and they supposedly offered Native peoples a tool—"useful knowledge"—for combating poverty and what reformers deemed to be a chief cause of that poverty, ignorance.

Combining with these ideas regarding education was a movement toward notions of humanitarianism, born out of the age of Enlightenment and emerging conceptions of sensibility in the early republic. Novels such as the British work *Clarissa* instilled within many middling and elite white Americans a sense of duty toward those who struggled to make ends meet. Education thus became a means by which philanthropists could do their part to help their fellow citizens—as well as Native peoples and enslaved Africans—while garnering their own "moral capital" in a very public manner. What was more, many thought that acts of humanitarianism would also contribute to the betterment of the young republic as a whole.[13]

While ideas regarding education and humanitarianism shaped both Friends' and other reformers' efforts, leading Baltimore Friends also engaged in reform for reasons that varied depending upon the individual. Religion, a sense of duty or benevolent impulse, economic motivations, as well as a quest to accumulate moral capital each combined to encourage Baltimore Friends' reform work in their urban home and in Indian Country. Their agricultural education initiatives in the Ohio Country were deeply connected with their religious principles. Friends saw in the materiality of the world an opportunity to labor toward godly perfection, and they looked in dismay upon those who "suffered the plantation of God to be as a field uncultivated, and a desert."[14] Through agricultural labor, many reformers thought, they could eradicate the sin of idleness. That educational reform was widely viewed as an integral component of the republic's health and an investment in its future maintenance, moreover, made it an appealing way for Friends to publicly engage with questions of national importance while also adhering to their religious tenets.

Such engagement was even more appealing after the American Revolution when many Friends traded in their political work for that of reform.[15] There had long existed tensions between Quaker merchants' economic dealings and their faith, and these tensions continued into the era of the early republic as Friends became enmeshed in the republic's world of speculation and profit.[16] Reform increasingly became a means by which Friends' reconciled their self-interest and their faith, and it enabled them to showcase their power to fulfill their obligation to aid those who seemingly failed to achieve the promise of prosperity that was supposed to characterize a moral republic. In this, Friends were not alone. One historian, for example, demonstrates that for many white men, participation in civic organizations provided a means to garner and exercise political power in extra-governmental ways.[17] For Friends, reform efforts such as civilization, education, poor relief, and abolition became a crucial means by which they could be active, vocal, and visible participants in the questions that loomed at the center of national politics. By having a clearly defined problem—ignorance and thus vice and poverty—Friends could fulfill a duty—publicly—in ways that would showcase and expand their own power.

Religion and the drive for spiritual and moral capital undergirded many reformers' efforts, yet so, too, did ideas of labor and race. Educational reform in the name of "useful knowledge" and "usefulness" was deeply connected with ideas of labor, laziness, and vice. Like other reformers, Baltimore Friends' philanthropy was shaped in large part by their experiences navigating the socioeconomic world of their urban home. Baltimore was one of the early republic's most diverse cities, and it boasted a robust and evolving economy. Walking through Fells Point or down Market Street, Friends encountered stevedores, seamstresses, enslaved peoples, and street sweeps—all of whom labored for the wages that provided basic sustenance and shelter or, in the case of enslaved peoples, lined the pockets of those who claimed ownership of their labor. Friends witnessed both demographic and economic growth on an unprecedented scale: between 1790 and 1830, Baltimore's population grew by 497 percent. Much of that growing populace provided labor that transformed eighteenth-century Baltimore Town into the thriving metropolitan Baltimore whose harbor was one of the most important ports in the United States.[18] That harbor attracted the United States' rural population, refugees from Saint Domingue, and other travelers, all of whom made the city diverse and its harbor the second-most popular destination for immigrants arriving from Europe, after New York City. What was more, Baltimore boasted the largest African American population in the United States by 1820, and with "two of every five people of color in the city . . . enslaved," this made for complicated race, class, and labor relations.[19]

Baltimore nurtured a robust economic hierarchy, and this was simultaneously a product of and a contributor to educational reform's hierarchical nature. An analysis of class in the early nineteenth-century city reveals in stark terms the material conditions of poverty that accompanied economic change. The city, straddling the worlds of both North and South, was integrated—and becoming more so on a daily basis—with an economy that was reliant upon both enslaved and waged labor. Baltimore's labor hierarchy was uncertain—particularly at the bottom. Wageworkers sought out and answered ads seeking labor for hire, and some managed to string together enough opportunities that enabled them to survive on their own or to survive with the assistance of public services. Employers' needs, however, added to the challenge of finding and maintaining work. They often hired and fired workers depending upon both seasonal and daily business needs.[20] It was an employers' market, and it meant that there was a growing sense of difference between laborers and their employers. Friends, in many ways, occupied central positions in this developing economy that left wageworkers "scraping by" in the otherwise thriving city. Members of the Society of Friends employed free African-descended individuals in their homes and many became prominent merchants and businessmen. Like their Philadelphia counterparts, they manumitted enslaved peoples relatively late. The Maryland Yearly Meeting (which later became the Baltimore Yearly Meeting) did not threaten to disown Friends for enslaving until 1777, three years after Philadelphia took such action.[21]

This stratified socioeconomic world was a central facet of the republic's developing economy, and that hierarchy infiltrated most aspects of daily life in both subtle and obvious ways. Friends' reform work was in part a product of their experiences with the labor market in Baltimore, and that engagement had profound consequences for their efforts in the city as well as in the Ohio Country. Ideas of usefulness in urban spaces—cultivated by reformers partially as the result of class-based stereotypes and ideas of race—rendered educational reform efforts hierarchical and oftentimes vocational. The proposed Baltimore School of Industry, for example, endeavored to provide Baltimore's poor technical training that would enable them to earn a wage in the developing city. The school's proponents hoped to provide struggling individuals with a place to live while teaching them skills to bolster their ability to earn a living.[22] The school never opened its doors, but it was nonetheless symbolic of Baltimore leaders' efforts to find a place for wage laborers at the bottom of the emerging economy. The implicit philosophy undergirding the School of Industry and other similar efforts was that certain individuals were impoverished because of a lack of industry, knowledge, and, often, morality. Such institutions, however, provided education for work only and did not equip workers with the knowledge to advance above earning a living wage.[23] Likewise, Quakers' earliest agricultural missions did not provide Ohio Natives with basic literacy or numeracy skills, and they thus relegated Native people to the bottom of the U.S. socioeconomic hierarchy. Later efforts to educate Native peoples in Euro-American mission and boarding schools would offer literacy and numeracy education, yet agricultural work would remain a crucial piece of these schooling efforts.[24] Baltimore Friends' reform efforts were in part a consequence of the society and place in which they lived, and such was the case for reformers more generally.

Baltimoreans' reform efforts shared similarities to those of their counterparts elsewhere.[25] Early nineteenth-century Philadelphia charity school reformers—many of them Quakers—provided more than vocational training but nonetheless provided an education tailored for pupils who were not among the affluent Euro-American inhabitants of the United States. Friends' Philadelphia Adelphi School—a school intended primarily for African American children—used the Lancasterian method of instruction wherein older students taught younger students in order to cut costs. In contrast to other

Quaker schools, the school's overseers did not endeavor to teach Quaker doctrine, but rather basic spiritual concepts.[26] Indeed, Adelphi School reformers believed these children required no more than the "laws of morality, the obligations of virtue and the more obvious truths according to the Bible."[27] Anything beyond that, they contended, would "not be doing justice to the motives and views of the association."[28] These reformers believed that all youths of Philadelphia should receive education, but also insisted that laboring-class students required "the more obvious" version.

Quakers' place within a robust social and economic hierarchy reveals the extent to which ideas of difference formed a part of their daily lives. Though Friends made up a tiny fraction of Baltimore's inhabitants, many occupied powerful positions in the city's social and political circles and were active entrepreneurs. Prosperous Friends on Baltimore Yearly Meeting's Committee on Indian Concerns, like other wealthy members of Baltimore's religious denominations, occupied the leadership positions in their meetings.[29] Philip E. Thomas (the eventual president of the B&O Railroad), and Elisha Tyson and Elias Ellicott (prominent businessmen in Baltimore's flour industry), for example, were highly visible members of the Committee on Indian Concerns during the first decades of both the committee's existence and its work among Indigenous peoples.[30] The Ellicotts as a family used their relationships with one another to both contribute to and assist in each other's business projects.[31] These men benefited mightily from others' labor, and, though their faith demanded that they embrace simplicity, they showcased their success in a number of ways. Their philanthropy was speculative. They hoped that their efforts would offer them a means to balance their economic ventures with philanthropic acts that would cultivate their reputation as moral and social leaders.

Urban educational reform, poor relief, and civilizing agricultural education became ways by which elite Quakers could exhibit their status and usefulness as well as gain political power. One's visibility within the meeting corresponded with the extent to which one engaged in its public outreach, and participation on committees translated into a form of moral capital that elevated one's status not only within the meeting but in the city as well.[32] Because philanthropy required time, however, it was often the wealthiest Friends who participated most extensively in meeting causes by serving as committee clerks and conducting correspondence with the federal government. It was also these individuals who garnered the most moral and thus political capital fit for Quakers who openly avoided the more obvious political posts.[33] Elite Friends' quest to pursue their own usefulness both linked their speculative philanthropy with that discourse and encouraged them to define others' utility.

Social hierarchy—a notion that seventeenth- and eighteenth-century Friends openly disavowed—infused the core of Baltimore Friends' reform philosophy by the early nineteenth century. Friends' philanthropic work offered a means to participate in public-facing work that aimed to ameliorate others' conditions, yet it did little to address the systems of power that rendered such work necessary. The "benevolence" with which Friends approached their work among Ohio Native peoples was built on an assumption of difference: Native Americans, like wage workers, were in need of assistance not merely because they were supposedly "savage," but because Friends deemed them impoverished and susceptible to immorality.

* * *

Thanks to Friends' experiences in urban spaces, assumptions regarding working-class Baltimoreans traveled to the Ohio Country and influenced their ideas regarding Native peoples and their supposed poverty. In 1796, several Baltimore Friends went to the Ohio "for the purpose of learning [Natives'] situation" and "to judge of the practicability of introducing among them the simplest and most useful arts of civil Life."[34] These traveling Friends carried with them—as they would on subsequent trips and in their correspondences—their religious tenets, assumptions regarding Native peoples' potential, and the ideas regarding race and class that they cultivated as a result of their experiences living in urban Baltimore. As their use of the phrase "useful arts" suggests, they also carried with them the discourse of "usefulness." Before embarking on their journey, for example, Friends noted that their work would bring "religious Instruction, Knowlege of Agriculture and useful Mechanic Arts" to Native peoples. They did their early Ohio Country work, however, without offering complementary instruction in the skills of reading, writing, or numeracy—skills many Euro-Americans deemed "useful" for others and taught as part of a transition toward "practical" education by the late eighteenth century.[35] Such an approach pleased John Parrish's former partner in Indian Country, Timothy Pickering. Pickering relayed President Washington's approval of their journey and applauded Friends' actions since, in his view, "most attempts at civilising the Indians . . . have been preposterous—We have aimed at teaching Religion & the Sciences before we have taught them the simple and essential labours of civil life."[36] Federal officials understood labor as a necessary precursor to further education, and the civilization plan—and Friends' efforts—sought to make that idea a reality on the ground with useful education.

By limiting "useful" pursuits for Native people to agriculture and the "mechanical arts," Friends defined the limits, from their perspective, of Native Americans' utility, and they connected their work among Ohio Natives to the early republic's broader discourse surrounding notions of "usefulness," morality, and education.[37] Baltimore Friends thus included Native peoples in the discourse regarding usefulness, education, and the public good, but they excluded them from the republic proper. In 1807, for example, civilizing agent and Quaker William Kirk proclaimed that his civilizing efforts possessed the power to transform Ohio Country Native peoples into "peasible good citizens on our fronteers" who would "become a strength to our Government."[38] While his words revealed that he envisioned a nation that might one day include Native peoples as "good citizens," they also revealed that that day was not yet at hand. Moreover, even as Kirk courted the idea of Native peoples as "citizens," he was sure to imagine them "on our fronteers"—on the edges of empire as a buffer between the United States, Great Britain, and other Native peoples, or as subject citizens who would remain beyond the metropole proper. By emphasizing Natives' *potential* for transformation, Kirk ultimately excluded them from the nation, while he also contributed to the process of defining the young republic's citizenry and the American empire's subjects.

Baltimore Quakers' agricultural reform work in part grew out of an assumption that Native peoples and laboring people shared much in common. Those Friends who traveled to Shawnee or Miami Country soon saw that the problems that they believed bedeviled wage workers in Baltimore also plagued Native Americans. The Baltimore committee and its traveling representatives often took pains, for example, to contrast Native peoples' supposed poverty with the richness of the lands. Friends wrote that Ohio's Native peoples "suffered all the miseries of extreme poverty, in a country, which, from its great fertility, would, with but little cultivation, abundantly supply them with all the necessaries of life."[39] Gerard T. Hopkins, Elisha Tyson, William Kirk, and other Baltimore Friends who traveled to the Ohio Country attributed this dissonance to Native peoples' "laziness." Elisha Tyson wrote in 1808, "here is a proof of Indian industry, William Kirk last built a house and cleared a corn field for this old Indian. The field is entirely neglected though the land is excellent. A part is grown up with spear or bluegrass so that it would mow."[40] In a similar vein, another Baltimore Friend explained to

Miamis living near Fort Wayne: "Brethren There are some amongst us who are not industrious and will not work; these cannot earn the comforts for themselves which industrious people do: but are often in great distress and poverty so that we clearly see it is by industry that a comfortable living must be obtained."[41] That this Friend compared his audience to "some amongst us" further reveals the extent to which Friends' experiences in Baltimore informed their observations of Native peoples.

Ohio Country Indigenous peoples were impoverished, Quakers claimed, not only because of their supposed lack of industry but because of their predilection toward drinking. Alcohol consumption, these Quaker men believed, distracted the region's Native peoples from properly employing their lands. Baltimore Friends contended that if the region's "traders could not be restrained from furnishing them with this destructive article, in exchange for their skins and furrs, they would not be easily persuaded, to turn their minds toward agriculture and the useful arts."[42] The distracting qualities of alcohol paralleled what Friends saw as one of the primary reasons why urban laborers struggled to care for their families. Friends informed the Shawnee Captain Lewis that "spirituous Liquors not only corrupts the minds of those who drink it, but it also occasions great poverty & distress in the families of those men who get drunk because it destroys their reason and disqualifies them for work, it has this effect upon the white people who drink it and it will have the same effect upon you."[43] Indeed, Friends' concerns over alcohol were so pronounced that they lobbied the Ohio legislature in 1808 to prohibit the sale and trade of alcohol to Natives.[44]

The forms of education offered by the missions and by urban institutions alike, then, created and reinforced assessments regarding both laborers' and Indigenous peoples' potential as well as their morality, and these assessments were grounded in ideas of race and class, in particular. Even those schools (particularly those founded after the War of 1812) that prepared Native peoples for careers beyond agriculture—in medicine, mission work, teaching, interpreting—maintained agricultural education as a key to their curriculum and to the functioning of the mission space.[45] By emphasizing the acquisition of certain skills—often physically labor-intensive ones—reformers, in turn, simultaneously entrenched a racial and social hierarchy. Reformers' educational prescriptions reinforced pupils' status; they became a means by which reformers "othered" wage laborers, Native Americans, African Americans, and their children alike. Universal education, in other words, had its limits.

Ideas of education and "usefulness" thus aided in the creation and entrenchment of ideas of race and class, and they also contributed to evolving and intersectional ideas regarding gender. After the revolution, wealthy and middling white "republican mothers" required education so as to cultivate good male citizens. In the urban United States, at the precise moment when ideas of work and home grew increasingly distinct, men were expected to be the primary providers in the visible labor market, while women, ideally, remained at home to raise, educate, and care for children as well as perform the essential duties of running a household. Such a labor arrangement was both heavily contingent upon as well as a means to perform class; as numerous studies have shown, women engaged the labor market in different ways depending on race and class.[46]

Scholars have made clear that women's work contributed to the early republic's economy by enabling men to leave the home, yet the prevailing assumption by the nineteenth century was that women relied upon men for their well-being.[47] Those women who worked outside of the home were among those who experienced poverty in the urban republic. Stereotypical images of Native women, too—the notion of the "squaw drudge," for example—followed this prescription (though race, of course, played a key role here as well), as Euro-American observers noted that Native women's work in agricultural fields was a mark of Native peoples' "savagery" *en masse.*[48] When Friends, U.S. officials, and other Euro-Americans encouraged Native men to pick up the axe and plow, they reordered gender roles to reflect their own ideas of a "proper" gender and labor order.

Friends' efforts to alter Native peoples' conceptions of labor through agricultural education were in line with government officials' efforts to transform Native peoples' gendered relationships. Agriculture, reformers contended, was a manly pursuit, and, indeed, by encouraging Native people to adopt the plow in particular, they advocated for a technology that, for many Native women and their families, would necessitate men to take over agricultural work due to the tool's weight.[49] Quakers, famously "non-conformist" in the social and theological sense, thus emphasized in rhetoric and practice, like many of their fellow nineteenth-century Americans, that the proper place for Native women was in the home. As Gerard Hopkins explained to Miamis and Potawatomis in 1804, "brothers the white people in order to get their land cultivated find it necessary that their young men should be employed in it and not their women. Women are less than men They are not as strong as men. They are not as able to endure fatigue and toil as men. It is the business of our women to be employed in our houses. to keep them clean to sew knit—spin—and weave . . . for themselves and families to make clothes for the men and the rest of their families to keep the clothing of their families clean and to take care of their children."[50]

The seamstresses and poor women of Baltimore were largely responsible for the making of clothes, spinning, and weaving with which Quakers were familiar and to which they referred in this passage. Many of their wives, while often occupied in the home, took part in Baltimore Friends' public reform culture and even served on the Committee on Indian Concerns by 1815—no doubt to perform their own usefulness as white women.[51] Moreover, Friends' belief in the Inner Light ensured that Quaker women enjoyed spiritual equality and constituted a significant portion of the Society of Friends' ministry. Baltimore Friends claimed to be exceptional (and, in many aspects, were) when it came to their views of women in society, yet these Friends wrote and uttered the line "women are less than men" in their message to Miamis and Potawatomis. Such a statement may be attributable to a number of factors—in terms of the strength required for plow agriculture, for example. Even that idea of strength, however, showcases the assumptions that formed these men's worldviews. The sentiment was yet another indication of the extent to which Friends incorporated ideas of difference into their "benevolent" work. Many Friends encouraged white elite or "middling" women to take on public leadership roles and, by the forties, some of these women pushed to expand female claims to citizenship by fighting for the right to vote. Others—including white women who lacked understanding of Indigenous societies and failed to adequately include Native women and their perspectives in their efforts—encouraged Native women to remain in the home.[52] Importantly, these ideas were no doubt interwoven with the assumption that men owned the land. A reordering of gendered labor roles dovetailed with Euro-Americans' assumption that men were the individuals with whom Euro-Americans needed to pursue when purchasing lands.

Quakers' agricultural efforts in Indian Country, like urban educational reform efforts, thus emphasized the acquisition of particular kinds of knowledge and "habits of industry" for particular people, and, as with other forms of poor relief and educational reform, they similarly framed the "Indian problem" as a moral problem. Complicating this further, however, was Friends' notion that Natives' failures were not solely their fault. In 1796, the Committee on Indian Concerns wrote, "The distresses and difficulties which these poor people labour under we believe may in a great degree be attributed to their propensity to the use of Spiritous Liquors introduced among them by Traders and Evil-minded men . . . and through this their attachment to this debasing and destructive Enjine of Satan, they are left destitute and miserable, their morals corrupted . . . their mind embittered against the white people."[53] Here, Friends made clear that it was also corrupt Euro-Americans who were responsible for Indians' "poverty." Instead of setting a moral example, traders "corrupted" Native peoples in much the same way that the New York Free School's "indigent" parents corrupted their children. This, again, contributed to the notion that there were those within and on the edges of the United States—some white men—who actively spread the disease of vice. One Friend wrote that some Americans' "mannor of living contributes to produce ferosety being continually engaged in hunting savage beasts. . . . These people live between the law & the Indians, & as settlement cultivation & law extends further, The wild game & the Indians retreat, these people keep thier possition & follow the game & the Indians, & in thier commerce with the latter have borrowed all thier Vicess, & neglected thier Virtues."[54] According to this Friend, these settlers were not "poor Indians" but they were not truly American "citizens" either. Instead, they lived "between the law & the Indians," a consequence of their whiteness, "ferosety," and lack of proper virtue and occupation. They needed to cease "hunting savage beasts," learn the proper ways of settlement and cultivation, and, instead of keeping "thier possition," and they needed to learn to live within the law and become civilized for the good of the republic. Here, too, then, this discourse of poverty, morality, and vice was in dialogue with that used in urban spaces.

That traders and settlers spread the contagion of vice in lands on the edges of empire was equally disturbing as the problems plaguing the republic's cities. From Friends' point of view, both had the power to affect the nation's future; Native peoples did possess, after all, the potential for becoming "good citizens." Framing Native Americans' problems in this way thus was in part a neat way of pinpointing the problems plaguing the republic. It meant that Friends could combat Natives' problems—and those facing the republic—by sharing with them their "useful knowledge" of farming, and, through farming, virtue. With knowledge and virtue, the Ohio Country and its inhabitants would become a healthy portion of the growing republic. Such a clear problem meant that a solution was relatively simple: those who had "the power" to do so should assist "in the discharge of this important obligation."[55]

Philanthropy—including poor relief and educational reform—became an obligation, a public good, and a means to both publicly showcase one's power and accumulate more.

* * *

Just as ideas of race, gender, and class shaped how reformers perceived Indigenous peoples and non-elites' status and usefulness, so, too, did they influence both the perceptions and efforts of elite Quaker men. John Tyson enshrined Baltimore Friend Elisha Tyson's reform efforts in print with the publication of *Life of Elisha Tyson, the Philanthropist*. Elisha's life and the publication that memorializes that life showcases plainly the connections between usefulness and speculative philanthropy as well as between Baltimore and the Ohio Country. Elisha Tyson served on the Baltimore Yearly Meeting's Committee on Indian Concerns as early as 1803 and contributed to the attempt to found the Baltimore School (and later, House) of Industry for the urban poor in 1804. He also found time to travel to the Ohio Country in 1808 to visit Friends' agricultural missions then underway as well as to actively pursue abolitionist politics until his death in 1824.[56] Tyson's philanthropic exploits garnered him a position of prestige within the meeting, and it also provided ample material for the memorial penned by John Tyson after his death. That his efforts became enshrined in print meant that a wide audience of Friends—and others—knew of his charitable work, and the act of publishing also suggests that some Friends *wanted* their community to know about his work.[57] That desire, to have acts of philanthropy noticed, suggests the degree to which those acts were linked with not only economic speculation but speculation in moral and political capital. Acts of philanthropy were investments in political clout and, in Elisha Tyson's case, a posthumous legacy.

John Tyson opens his tribute to Elisha Tyson by stating as much. Elisha Tyson's reform efforts were apparently a subject of debate and scrutiny in Baltimore social circles. John Tyson wrote that his book aimed to "do away the false impressions which [Elisha Tyson's] enemies have made upon the minds of many of this community. The motives which led him to make so many sacrifices in the cause of humanity, have been misrepresented. The means he employed, and the mode he adopted, in furtherance of his benevolent designs, have been vilely traduced."[58] While it is not certain what charges Baltimoreans lodged against Elisha Tyson's efforts, when John discusses why Elisha moved to Maryland from the state of Pennsylvania, he is careful to say that "at the time of his removal, there was nothing to a young man seeking his fortune, inviting in Maryland."[59] Profit, he implied, could not have been Elisha's aim. Rather, "the desire to be useful to his fellow human beings, was the predominating motive that led him to change his residence."[60] Even here, in dismissing any economic motivations, the discourse of usefulness positioned Elisha Tyson as an elite white man whose usefulness was not linked with manual labor, but to the aid of others. What is more, John Tyson was clearly concerned with cultivating a particular image of Elisha and his philanthropy. The very act of publishing to dispel rumors reveals that Elisha Tyson's philanthropy was meant to be publicly consumed and noticed.

Rhetoric of adoration suffuses much of *The Philanthropist*, and, throughout, John Tyson fuses ideas of philanthropy with notions of masculinity that had abounded during the post-Revolutionary era, the time during which Elisha worked. On the subject of Elisha's journey to the Ohio Country to meet with Potawatomis, Miamis, and their neighbors, John writes, "as though the theatre of his native state, and one class of men [enslaved peoples], were not large enough for the comprehensiveness of his charity, we see him in the wilds of the west, climbing mountains—traversing wildernesses—daring the rapid torrent—and plunging through the deep and expansive morass, to seek out the untutored children of the forest, and teach them the arts of civilization and peace."[61] Here was Elisha Tyson—a man in his sixties by the time of his trip to the Ohio—"plunging through the deep and expansive morass" (a notion dripping with sexual overtones), climbing mountains, and escaping Maryland because it was "not large enough" for his charity. During the eighteenth century, in particular, philanthropic reform was a means to showcase one's enlightened masculinity in the city of Philadelphia, and John Tyson's text and Elisha Tyson's acts did the same for the nineteenth century.[62] Such rhetoric further suggests that John Tyson hoped to cultivate a particular image for Elisha, an image that was for public consumption, and one that was meant to promote the deceased man's philanthropic manliness.

While the bulk of John Tyson's work pertains to Elisha Tyson's role as an abolitionist, one chapter on the Friends' agricultural education work reveals that both Tyson the philanthropist and Tyson the author believed that Friends were correct in limiting their educational efforts to labor-based tutoring. Other missionaries, John wrote, attempted "to christianize the Indians by sending missionaries among them," while Friends "attempted solely to civilize them; thinking it most proper that christianity should follow in the train of civilization." The author went on to write that "experience has proved the correctness of the course. Christianity is not calculated for *barbarous* nations, nor has the attempt to disseminate its principles among them ever been successful."[63] Elisha Tyson, nonetheless referred to as a missionary several times in John Tyson's text, instead offered Native peoples in the Ohio Country advice on how to stay on their lands, and "he recommended to them the practice of agriculture, as a substitute for hunting."[64] John Tyson continued to note that Elisha "advised them to mark out their lands, and ask advice of the agents established by the society of Friends among them, with respect to their cultivation. They stood ready, not only with their advice, but with their assistance—they were furnished for their use with all the necessary implements of husbandry—with beasts of the plow also, and beasts of burden."[65]

This description suggests a number of things. First, it aligns with the government's ideas of "civilization" that was grounded in agricultural education, and it confirms that many Baltimore Friends, too, put aside outright religious instruction out of a belief that civilization was required first. Second, it suggests that this Friend, John Tyson, continued to see the value in such a project in 1824 when he published his text. Third, it showcases the economic underpinning of the civilization plan and the ways in which Elisha Tyson and his fellow missionaries (as well as John Tyson) wholly embraced that underpinning. Marking out Natives' lands was a material means by which government agents and Friends alike encouraged the commodification of those lands. Telling Native peoples that they should do so in order to remain moreover suggests that Friends, at first, did not intend to facilitate Native peoples' removals, though John Tyson may likely have had, by 1824, the idea of removals in his mind when writing—they were, after all, taking place in the Ohio Country. Nonetheless, dismissing the idea of removal in his text suggests that agricultural education was a means by which Friends encouraged Native people to labor on those lands in ways that would, from Euro-Americans' perspectives, render "empty lands" cultivated. Friends' work would thus "civilize" people and lands.

* * *

Elisha Tyson's efforts and Quaker reformers' readiness to provide Native peoples only agricultural instruction reveals that by the early nineteenth century, Friends embraced an economic and social hierarchy built upon assumptions of Natives' ignorance and material difference. At an earlier point in their history, Friends once refused to show deference when addressing their supposed social superiors, and men like George Fox and William Penn took pains to comment upon Native peoples' similarities with non-Natives—though, of course, men like Penn were not averse to taking Indigenous lands. By the early nineteenth century, however, Friends' educational and reform movements embraced the recognition of a clear difference between Native Americans and African Americans, and the poor more generally, on the one hand and everyone else on the other. Ohio Country Native Americans needed to heed the instructions of Friends in order to learn to raise food that could ensure their survival; the urban poor were to go to the School of Industry in order to learn to earn a living wage; elite white men were to showcase their own usefulness by offering what aid they chose to give; all were to learn to take their place in the developing economy. The most prominent members of the Baltimore Society of Friends were fully entrenched in the new political economy of the early republic, and their benevolence reveals the ways in which they became simultaneously part of and contributors to a culture built around assumptions of inequality and difference. Those assumptions supported their own quests for profit and moral capital, and they rendered their philanthropy a speculative affair. With philanthropic projects that aimed to develop lands and train laborers, Friends' own economic ventures could grow in tandem with their reputations for benevolence.

Traveling Friends carried ideas and visions of their home in Baltimore with them on their journeys, and their experiences in that growing metropolis influenced their observations of Native peoples, their dreams for the Ohio lands, and, ultimately, U.S. Indian policy. Baltimore was a thriving city, however, because of its position as an urban center through which goods moved: it connected the agrarian lands of rural Maryland with a thriving harbor. Baltimore Friends understood the importance of economic infrastructure in the development of lands; their own flour and textile successes were built upon economic projects akin to those just beginning in the Ohio Country. They also understood, however, the importance of workers and consumers in building cities. Their reform work, then, could build a moral, industrious nation and a powerful empire, and, as the next chapter will show, it could transform a vast country into a place resembling home, one farm at a time.

CHAPTER 4

The Mission Complex

The Material Consequences of Civilizing Work

Speculative philanthropy offered a key impetus for civilizing work, and just as ideas regarding race, poverty, and civilization could travel from Baltimore to the Ohio Country, so, too, did material goods and settlers' economic hopes make the journey to the heart of the continent. In the aftermath of the 1790s Northwest Indian War and the resulting 1795 Treaty of Greenville—after John Parrish finally left the diplomatic dinner table behind—the United States confronted the problem of how to transform Ohio Country lands into both private property and territories aligned with the imperial state. Knox's civilization plan seemingly presented a solution: the plan's emphasis on bringing agricultural education to Indian Country encouraged Euro-American settlers and "civilizers" to transform the region's Native inhabitants into "useful" people who conformed to the republic's idealized socioeconomic order, and it also facilitated the commodification of Natives' lands. Agricultural missions could transform peoples, but they could also transform landscapes, mobilize capital, and support a national effort to build a "great and united empire" through commerce by both requiring goods and labor and promoting socioeconomic "conversion." With federal direction and investment, missionaries like the Friends, Indian agents, blacksmiths, merchants, and manufacturers contributed their work and wares toward civilizing missions. In turn, they linked urban and rural economies and produced agricultural goods, laborers, markets, and, so officials hoped, increasingly marketable and taxable land. When the U.S. federal government recruited and paid missionaries for their efforts to civilize Native peoples, then, it employed them as imperial agents in a *mission complex* that further linked the economies of Indian Country with those of New Orleans, the urban U.S. coast, and the world.[1]

Ohio Country lands were situated in the heart of the continent; the soils were rich, and those soils served as a crossroads between the Atlantic coast and the Mississippi River that flowed southward to the port of New Orleans. Many Euro-American settlers generally proclaimed Native peoples to be "backward peoples" who left these rich lands uncultivated, and these settlers thus perpetuated a logic of colonialism that was premised upon rescuing fertile lands from their supposedly inattentive owners and putting those lands to "proper" use.[2] Euro-Americans coveted these rich lands, and they surveyed regional maps and physical landscapes with an eye both toward replicating their Atlantic coast homes and toward dreams of speculation and profit. Agricultural missions in Indian Country supported these visions. Clearing fields, planting crops, constructing mills—these tasks aimed to transform Indian Country physically and in Euro-Americans' imaginations, and they were central to missionaries' civilizing goals: with the civilization program, supposed "unoccupied," "wild" spaces became cultivated ones, and dangerous frontiers became settlements on the edge of empire.

The mission complex facilitated this transformation of Native peoples' lands; it created networks of markets and capital that offered one means of reordering the social, cultural, political, and economic geographies of both Indian Country (and beyond) and the U.S. metropole. It was created and shaped by the particular contexts of speculative philanthropy, settler colonialism, and emerging capitalism. Missions, boarding schools, and the civilization plan more generally were connected with nineteenth-century paternalistic notions of "benevolence," and they were hinges for economic growth. Agricultural missions fostered an imperial market system under the guise of benevolence, even as they became the visible markers of the U.S. imperial state. The mission complex expanded the influence and power of the United States in the Ohio Country through mission work and economic development by linking missionaries, humanitarians, manufacturers, federal employees, and Indigenous peoples through networks of markets and capital.

As part of agricultural education, individuals—often Euro-American missionaries and laborers—cleared fields and built infrastructure such as mills and roads. As Chapter 6 will show, such work facilitated the construction of the railroads and canals that would eventually crisscross the region and foster the republic's transportation revolution.[3] What was more, agricultural missions required manufactured items such as hoes and plows, and U.S. War Department officials arranged for these to be shipped from the urban coast to the heart of the continent. Such shipping networks required labor, and so, too, did agricultural education itself. Settler-instructors encouraged Native Americans to pursue their "usefulness" and in turn endeavored to transform Native peoples into settlers' ideal notions of agricultural producers and consumers and, if temporarily, an agrarian working class. Viewing the intersections between missions, markets, and the physical transformation of lands as a mission complex enables us to situate two central facets of U.S. colonialism—civilizing plans and mission work—within the social, political, and economic strategies that advanced U.S. colonialism on the continent and in the world.

Both federal and local power made the mission complex possible. In the Ohio Country, this project provided a cost-efficient means of imperial economic development, and it reveals the federal state's importance as a pivotal actor in the developing U.S. market economy and its social relations. Yet the mission complex also offered additional opportunities for Native peoples to manipulate U.S. economic development and its accompanying socioeconomic ideas for their own purposes, even as it transformed landscapes and bolstered the United States' ability to reap the rewards of expanding agricultural markets in lands that remained in Natives' hands. The mission complex could spark and further political debates: some Shawnees, for example, welcomed Quaker missionaries and declined to raise arms against the U.S. during the War of 1812. Other Shawnees did not and preferred to join Tecumseh and allied nations in a fight against U.S. empire and settler colonialism. Some Miamis, meanwhile, turned their backs on Quaker missions, some seemed more willing to engage them, still others preferred to focus on the fight to preserve their homelands. Viewpoints and strategies varied, and they meant that U.S. policies would not be—could not be—strictly enacted from the top down.

Thus, while important, the federal state did not have complete power over on-the-ground actions. Federal funds combined with private to render the mission complex possible, and officials, such as local Indian agents, as well as Native leaders and people, influenced the trajectory and functioning of the government's project and the development of markets. Understanding state power in the Ohio Country as a blended phenomenon—a combining of federal, local, and individual efforts and ideas—is therefore pivotal to grasping the ways in which myriad actors cultivated the U.S. empire on the continent. Attention to the mission complex as a component and consequence of blended state power adds to our already rich understanding of market expansion, in addition to economic and political change in the early republic. It underscores the need to analyze the ways in which federal power—along with the actions and ideas of U.S. regional officials, settlers, capitalist philanthropists, and Native peoples—shaped the development of the United States' continental empire and its economy.

* * *

The Friends who undertook the journey from Baltimore to the heart of the continent envisioned lands transformed by farms and Euro-American population growth. Even as traveling Quakers closed their eyes to Miami and Potawatomi corn fields when embarking on their missions to teach agriculture, Friends saw with clarity rural areas' potential to become like the more familiar urban coast. They made references, for example, to the small villages they encountered during their travels to the Ohio Country, and they projected upon them their own prospective visions. One traveler, for example, described a place on the eastern shore of a river in Virginia, as containing only three houses but quickly added that "thier was a time when the cittys of London & philadelphia did not contain more, & I see no reason which it may not grow as large as them or any place, if it do not it is neither for want of room or Materials."[4] Another Friend proclaimed, "Many difficulties attend new settlers—though the soil in most places is luxuriant beyond the conception of those who live in our eastern Counties, yet the labour of clearing is great and the pinching times they experience before they can get much returns ought to be weightily attended to."[5] Life in the "west," Friends contended, was difficult at first, but they could develop that wide expanse through which they traveled in a way that would resemble life near home.

When Friends traveled to the Ohio Country at the turn of the nineteenth century, however, they did not find Euro-American urban population centers, but rather they ventured into a world created by the region's Native communities, British and French inhabitants, and other Euro-American settlers. Native peoples had cultivated the earth and created wide-ranging trade networks long before any Euro-American ventured into the region. Yet even when European peoples entered Indigenous peoples' domain, the regional economies then formed were built upon the rules of neighborly reciprocity and the politics of collective economic advantage: they drew upon the labor practices embraced by regional Native peoples for their utility in efficiently clearing lands and harvesting crops. Euro-American settler families adopted these practices and similarly sent members to community events such as logrollings in order to assist new arrivals in the difficult work of clearing and building on land. The civilization plan in the Ohio Country likewise borrowed and built upon the region's cultural labor relations: it brought together Quakers, U.S. officials, settlers, and members of Native communities to transform the landscape, and it thus modeled, at first, existing economic practices.[6]

Friends used their government connections, cultivated over time, to gather information regarding travel and communication before embarking on their journeys to the Ohio Country. Secretary of war Henry Dearborn responded to Friend Isaac Tyson's 1808 query regarding his Ohio destination and informed him that the government had "no messenger going to Fort Wayne, but the trail for that Quarter leaves the City every Sunday & Thursday. No Post Office being established at Fort Wayne, you will have to direct to that place by the way of Staunton, Ohio."[7] The secretary's response revealed that Tyson would experience a deprivation of government facilities during his travels, but that there was enough administrative support to make an organized departure possible. Regional Indian agents as well as local inhabitants would provide crucial support for missionaries' travels, and their collective efforts reveal the importance of both local and national authority and knowledge. Friends were more fortunate than most early Americans by virtue of their relationships with government officials, Native leaders, and Quaker settlers who established towns in the Ohio lands, and they used them to gather information that facilitated their journeys.

En route to their Ohio missions, Baltimore Friends passed through a region marked by layers of economic development. Mounds—remnants of the Mississippian cultures of the Mississippi and Ohio valleys—dotted their path and caused befuddlement as some struggled to ascertain whether they were the residue of an old European colony or rather built by northward roaming Indigenous peoples from "Mixico" fleeing civil war. Surely "northern Indians," as one Friend wrote, did not build them.[8] Nor did the region's Native peoples, so Friends thought, produce the abundant fields of corn that appeared so impressive. By the time Baltimore Quaker Gerard T. Hopkins passed through the eastern portion of the upper Ohio Valley in 1804, however, regional travel was in the process of adding another layer of change to the lands already altered by millennia of economic development, centuries of fur trading, and imperial conflicts. Friends' journeys, like those of others, bolstered the economic development of a number of Quaker and non-Quaker towns between Baltimore and Ohio or Indiana by feeding local economies that profited from an increasing stream of provision-seeking and migrating travelers.

The Ohio River was the primary artery westward, and towns such as Wheeling and Marietta reaped the profits by offering wares, boatmen, and guides. One Friend traveling near the Scioto River, for example, remarked that "the people in the town endevour to suply them & make them pay well for it."[9] Though traveling Friends made up a small percentage of travelers, their federally sanctioned travel contributed to the small-town profits that in turn encouraged both migration to and settlement in the region. Robust legal settlement had the potential to generate federal revenues and expand emerging markets, and federal officials endeavored to divide the Ohio lands into townships and expedite their sale for such purposes. At the turn of the century, however, land sales were slow; settler migration to the region proved insufficient to produce relief for the debt-ridden federal government. With squatters filling the region, the government failed to reap its desired revenues even after the 1787 Ordinance opened the lands to large speculation. Congress initiated a system of credit with the Frontier Land Bill in 1800 in an effort to attract smaller purchasers, but such a scheme likewise failed to open the lands to small buyers who too frequently failed to pay off their debts.[10]

Government officials, hopeful that migrating settlers would buy and fill the lands, conceptualized plans for the lands even if revenues, because of loan defaults, were less than expected. Governor Harrison's 1802 scheme for Jeffersonville near the Ohio River in Indiana Territory, for example, resembled a checkerboard with open lots adjacent to those that were to be occupied. President Jefferson found Harrison's idea "handsome, & pleasant," believing "it to be the best means of preserving the cities of America from the scourge of the yellow fever which being peculiar to our country must be derived from . . . our cloudless skies, [for] . . . Ventilation is indispensably necessary." Jefferson envisioned "the cities of America" flourishing in the region, and, with keen interest, he sent a sketch of the proposed town for Harrison's perusal since he could not "decide from the drawing you sent me, whether you have laid off streets round the squares thus or only the diagonal streets therein marked. The former was my idea, and is, I imagine, more convenient."[11] While such a scheme had, indeed, found receptive ears in urban locales, population growth rendered such plans untenable in the long term. Not surprisingly, Jeffersonville's original design was abandoned by 1810 due to the impracticalities of so many open lots in a state that saw massive population growth—a staggering 413 percent—during the first decade of the nineteenth century.[12]

While the federal government struggled to determine the best means of reaping revenues from settlement in the region, land speculators such as John

Armstrong and William Wells (the latter was a speculator in the 1790s and an Indian agent for the U.S. in the 1800s) endeavored to turn a profit by buying extensive tracts and offering loans to individuals with signed contracts. Like federal policies, Wells's correspondence reveals not a lack of settlers but rather a frustrating lack of *legal* Euro-American settlers in the region. Wells informed Armstrong that he encountered "numbers of people" wanting "to purchase lands but they are mostly poor, destitute of money, and wish to purchase on long credits." As a result, "the sales of lands at Cincinnati were very small, when we consider the number of settlers, and the immense quantity of superior lands there offered for sale."[13] With legal Euro-American settlement and land purchases, speculators and the government alike hoped to reap revenues and manage squatters.

Federally directed economic investment promised to support the changes of the regional economy already underway and generate revenues for the government and speculators alike. Agricultural missions complemented the federal and speculator quest for settlement in both the long and short term. And not simply because farming would free Native nations to sell much of their increasingly commodified lands to the United States—though that was, of course, part of the story. The Northwest Indian War was a still-fresh memory to many Americans—particularly in the Ohio and Indiana territories and Friends' and other missionaries' work offered a means by which the federal government could deal peacefully with Native peoples. Friends' own reputation for diplomacy, further entrenched in the 1790s, contributed to such efforts. Their work targeted Native nations' young men, in particular, and those men were often in fact and certainly in Euro-Americans' imaginations the warriors who wrought bloody havoc among squatters. Native men, according to Euro-Americans' logic, should learn useful pursuits such as agriculture rather than hunt and make war. Many government officials, Friends, and settlers therefore hoped that Natives' "transition" to farm life would secure peace. With peace—or with the illusion of peace—secured by educators who enjoyed a positive reputation among the region's Native nations (as opposed to the more suspect reputation of government officials) would come, in the minds of many, regional stability; with that would come increased land sales, settlement, and state and federal tax revenues. Because peace was a protracted process, however, agricultural civilizing mission efforts were also crucial to the United States' short-term economic policies: they aimed to convert to the ways of civilized economy those who many

Americans deemed uncivilized. In turn, they created and expanded U.S. markets and consumerism.[14]

In many ways the *aim* to convert—economically, socially, culturally, and politically—was, for economic and political purposes, most important. Both the nation's finances and its humanitarian reputation were at the forefront of officials' thinking. Governor William Henry Harrison wondered in 1801, for example, "whether some thing ought not to be done to prevent the reproach which will attach to the American Character by the extirpation of so many human beings."[15] Though he ultimately concluded that such matters were better left to the president to decide, his concerns echoed those of the first secretary of war, Henry Knox, who in 1789 contended, "How different would be the sensation of a philosophic mind to reflect that instead of exterminating a part of the human race . . . [we] had imparted our Knowledge of cultivation, and the arts, to the Aboriginals of the Country."[16] Paternalistic rhetoric bolstered U.S. claims to benevolent power fit for a republic even as it facilitated the development of an imperial market system. Such rhetoric mattered not only on the continent, but it traversed oceans as well: capitalist philanthropists coveted moral capital and, as Chapter 7 will show, so, too, did Euro-American nations. The veneer of benevolence was central to U.S. imperial economic transformation, and the mission complex wedded both U.S. officials' and speculative philanthropists' ideas for Indigenous peoples.

Baltimore Quakers' brand of mission work borrowed from their urban reform impulse, and it intersected with Euro-Americans' ideas regarding Native peoples' supposed "extinction," the republic's benevolence, and a desire and need to build an economy that could support the republic and its growing empire. Baltimore Friends' mission work, focused on "useful" agricultural education, encouraged a commodification of Native land and labor that erased the individual and their need for numeracy as part of an agricultural education, even as it mobilized Friends' own work on behalf of their religious society and the federal state. For their work, Friends received pay from the federal government in ways similar to the tax benefits, grant money, and funds granted to other voluntary organizations in the nineteenth century and beyond. Though Friends' compensation was piecemeal at first, the Civilization Fund Act of 1819 institutionalized such pay and guaranteed that missionaries of all sorts received $10,000 annually. Federal power and funds combined with Friends' own private funds and goals to mobilize Friends and, later, other missionaries in the effort to solve an ongoing "Indian problem."[17]

Similar to ideas of disciplining in other contexts, the U.S. state worked with missionaries to define and class its labor force using categories of civilization and savagery.[18] Quakers' efforts helped shape nineteenth-century rhetoric that proclaimed Indigenous populations to be working *toward* civilization—they were never all quite "civilized" despite the rhetorical exceptions of the "five civilized tribes." The civilization project was, then, a constant work in progress, a never-to-be-completed work, and it set precedents for the federal management of labor on the continent and abroad, even as it contributed to economic transformation. The complex was a supposedly benevolent, free-labor answer to the problems presented by federal desires for land, revenue, economic development, and remaining Indigenous communities: agricultural uplift produced agricultural production, markets for American manufacturers, and, in turn, increasingly valuable land.

* * *

When Baltimore Quaker Phillip Dennis arrived in Indiana Territory alongside Gerard T. Hopkins in 1804, he embarked upon the first of Baltimore Friends' agricultural efforts by forming "Dennis's Station" near Miami, Eel River, and Delaware Indians on the Wabash River southwest of Fort Wayne. Friends later established at least two other mission sites in the region at Captain Lewis Town (Lewistown) and Wapakoneta both among the Shawnees in western Ohio. The Miami chief Little Turtle was thoughtful in his selection of a spot for the mission, and he placed the farm several miles away from the Miamis' village. Such placement was likely an effort both to manage the Quakers' work and keep the Euro-American men at a distance. The mission was nonetheless just south of the Forks of the Wabash—a valuable location where the Little River joined the Wabash in Indiana. Though it took over twenty years for the United States to claim ownership of the spot, Dennis's work of clearing and fencing fields, producing crops, and constructing a cabin for his residence not only showcased for the local Miamis and some Delawares the intricacies of becoming a "proper" agriculturalist, but also offered an opportunity to expand an agricultural market at a lucrative location.[19]

By the end of 1804, however, only one Delaware family relocated to the farm school lands. Dennis offered his colleagues in Baltimore some hope for the future, however, by noting that "55 Eal river Indians had been at his station."[20] Just as Jesuit missionaries wrote of their successes in an effort to raise sums of money from their literary audiences in France, Dennis's hope that

Eel River or Delaware peoples would join his enterprise encouraged both Friends and federal officials to continue their support of the mission project.

And, indeed, that support came. In 1807 Wapakoneta, Quaker William Kirk agreed to offer agricultural education to the Shawnees there for "one thousand dollars, as pay" along with a federal budget of $6,000 "on condition" that he would "undertake the Superintendency and . . . procure the necessary Assistants and labourers, together with such implements of husbandry and horses as [his] proposed system embraces." The Quaker kept secretary of war Henry Dearborn informed of his progress and, in doing so, revealed the vast amount of physical work that he, his fellow Quaker employees, and the Shawnees performed. After several months in Ohio, he had "placed all the young men among the Shawnees (except while three of them were imployed in making a small improvement for a few Dellawares)" and had high hopes that he was "likely to succeed as fast as the most Sanguine could have expected as they work constantly with my young men." Together, Shawnees and Friends "built several Cabins," "made Rails & fenced in about one Hundred Acres of Ground," "cleared about thirty" more "& planted in Corn better then two Hundred Acres." By 1816, moreover, Baltimore Friends' mission among the Shawnees at Wapakoneta yielded "between 7000 & 8000 Bushels" of corn, and they "found many of [the inhabitants] at work, in their fields" with "a considerable portion of them . . . becoming industrious" and raising poultry.[21]

With missionary and Indigenous labor, the federal government produced and managed workers but also contributed to both the transformation of landscapes and the expansion of present and future markets. The missions were labor-intensive ventures that fostered U.S. economic development, and the federal government viewed them as worthwhile investments. Kirk's mission at Wapakoneta, located just north of the Greenville line that separated Indian Country from the United States in Ohio, offered an opportunity for the U.S. to reap economic benefits from lands that remained unceded by Native peoples. Though Kirk departed the region in 1808, Friends agreed to sustain the mission site in 1810 after secretary of war William Eustis wrote that "the Government has consented to relinquish . . . the public property at that place to [Friends'] discretion and management" and that "the Government is to be at no expense hereafter in conducting this establishment."[22] The deal saved Friends the cost of buying land for their missions, minimized federal costs, and allowed the government to pay for services with a currency that was, at the moment, much more readily available than government cash—land. It also pleased regional Indian agent John Johnston, who, prior to the agreement, argued that abandonment of the settlement at Wapakoneta would "give a stroke to the buisness in this country from which it will not soon recover." He explained that "all the Tools necessary for the purpose of Farming on a large scale is on the spot," that "a waggon road from the Settlements in ohio to the Town is cut out," and that he knew "of no place in the Indian country where money could be so usefully expended as with the Shawanoes [*sic*] at Kirks Settlement."[23]

Johnston's words, coupled with the actions of Friends and government officials, reveals that civilizing missions in the Ohio Country could promote not just subsistence farming among "poor Indians" but "Farming on a large scale." Friends noted in 1813, for example, that three thousand bushels of corn were sold that season but also explained that "when Peace is restored in that Country, these People will be more than Ever disposed to pursue the farming business."[24] Native lands, both Friends and officials thought, could contribute to the development of U.S. territory, Indigenous communities, and agricultural markets, but it was no easy task. Missions required roads to connect the farms with nearby towns, and the work of civilization required textiles, agricultural implements, and stores for Native peoples' future consumerism.[25]

The early republic's factory system offered a key means of bolstering consumerism in the region and securing the necessary goods for agricultural production. It connected eastern manufacturers and developing regional centers such as Cincinnati with the rural interior, and the factory stores, along with the civilization plan, were key components of the mission complex in the Ohio Country. The factories offered for sale the manufactured agricultural implements, textiles, and other goods requisite for what Euro-Americans claimed was a "civilized" lifestyle—the Fort Wayne factory store, for example, had nearly five hundred hoes on hand in 1806. More broadly, however, the factories aimed to wrest control of the fur trade from private traders and establish stores as well as an administrative hierarchy of Indian factors and agents in Indian Country. The stores, along with the Trade and Intercourse Acts that established the federal government as the overseer of the Indian trade, meant that the federal government controlled both trade and market expansion in Indian Country. Because Miamis, Shawnees, and their neighbors' lands were so near the official boundaries of the United States in the upper Ohio Country, federal expansion of markets there expanded both Euro-Americans' access to markets and in turn the regional and national market economy.[26]

The work performed by the purveyor of public supplies and later the Superintendents of Indian Trade offered federal backing to the creation of an economy built upon the shared interests of agriculture and manufacturing. Tench Coxe, in particular, as one of the first to procure goods for the federal Indian trade and factory system, set the model for the later superintendents. Coxe was a strong supporter of manufacturing and industry, and he supported government regulation of "revenue and commerce." He argued that manufactures should aim at "accommodating the interests of agriculture, manufactures and commerce in such a manner, as to render them reciprocally a support to each other, and mutually beneficial to the interest of the nation." For Coxe, agriculture and manufacturing went hand in hand, and together they contributed to national political independence and power.[27]

The purveyors and later the Superintendents of Indian Trade procured goods from merchants and manufacturers in cities such as Philadelphia and Baltimore, or in western towns like Cincinnati; they utilized the republic's rivers and fields to ship the wares to factory stores for both purchase and distribution as Indian annuities. In 1810, for example, Coxe paid one man \$837.42 for "ironmongery," another \$111.90 for "50 axes & 40 grubbing hoes," and still another \$1,426.35 for "axes, ploughs, etc." "Blacksmiths tools" from Philadelphian Nicodemus Lloyd and 120 medals from the silversmith Liberty Brown were also paid for with federal funds.[28] In 1814, moreover, the Superintendent of Indian Trade John Mason informed then secretary of war John Armstrong that "a considerable portion of Woolens can be bought at Cincinnatti on pretty good terms."[29] As Mason's statement suggests, federal officials sought the best prices for their business. Once officials were satisfied with the specifics of procurement and shipment, the items traveled to the factory stores at Fort Wayne and Piqua in the Ohio Country and elsewhere throughout the heart of the continent, and the trade thereby supported U.S. manufacturers but also those engaged in occupations such as shipbuilding, roadbuilding, and transport. The expansion of markets in Indian Country had far-reaching economic consequences.

Once procured, Native nations and individuals purchased and received trade goods with their annuity funds. In 1802, the Wyandot, Delaware, Shawnee, Odawa, Ojibwe, and Potawatomi nations obtained \$1,000 each in the form of "Thirty Rifles, Thirty pounds of Powder, sixty pounds of Lead, one hundred small corn Hoes, and sixty small axes."[30] Eel River Indians, Wyandots, Weas, Kickapoos, Piankashaws, and Kaskaskias received similar items but in proportion to their number such that each nation received \$500 worth of goods.[31]

Offering such goods as Indian annuities translated rhetorical support of urban manufacturing into real federal financial backing: the purchase of goods aided manufacturers in the short term, while the potential to expand markets in Indian Country offered hopes for a new consumer base that included both Native peoples and, with regional peace, migrating Euro-American settlers. The United States thus compensated Native peoples for their lands with annuities, but then used those annuities to invest in its own economy.

Because the wares possessed the power to transform U.S. officials' economic aspirations into reality, their quality mattered. When John Johnston complained that some wares were defective, Superintendent Mason therefore informed him, "The Rifles you complain of were made in Philad. . . . I request you will continue to make your observations on the goods sent, to forward samples, to describe the articles best suiting Indian Trade out of this much good will grow & every attention shall be paid in the soliciting."[32] The stores' accounts thus reveal the simultaneously diffuse and centralized power necessary for the maintenance of the mission complex as well as the extent to which Native nations' consumerism influenced the development of the U.S. economy. A combination of federal and local power made the mission complex work.

Between 1807 and 1811, the factory store at Fort Wayne made a profit of $10,502.77—a pittance in terms of the national GDP but a significant sum in Indian Country nonetheless. The decreased military activity in Indian Country—in part the result of U.S. imperial policies, along with Friends', Indian agents', and Natives' diplomacy in the region—combined with these profits and the expanding reach of U.S. markets to render the factory system and missionaries' efforts worthwhile, co-constitutive investments. In 1806, moreover, the factory's accounts reveal that more than one-third of the debts owed to the store—$1,203—belonged to Native American individuals.[33] The stores therefore not only encouraged Native people to participate in the U.S. economy but also welcomed them—along with the Euro-Americans who owed the remaining two-thirds of the debt—into a cycle of credit and debt. Though the factory system's success was inconsistent, and "factory" stores ceased to exist after 1822, government-run stores and Indian agencies remained central to Indian policy throughout the nineteenth century, and their connection with officials' desire both to expand the U.S. economy and undermine private and foreign traders aligned with broader U.S. policy.[34]

Just as popular notions of the national defense supported both the development of the U.S. standing army and tariffs on domestic military manufactures, similar concerns about the virtue and industry of the nation's republican citizenry rendered any state-directed commerce required to "civilize" Native Americans commensurate with notions of the nation's benevolence.[35] In many Americans' political imaginations, Indian factories and annuities likely were connected with the "Indian problem" and notions of U.S. benevolence—not to federal economic policy. Because of this, neither Federalists nor Democratic-Republicans bemoaned—or explicitly recognized—the expansion of the mission complex in the Ohio Country, and U.S. Indian policy changed little as a result of the "Revolution of 1800."[36] Such ideas of benevolence proved to be pivotal to the republic's identity as an exceptional polity: they grounded the United States' imperial project in Indian Country throughout the nineteenth century, and they would undergird the empire's Pacific and Caribbean projects into the twentieth century.[37]

* * *

None of this would have been possible without individuals' efforts on the ground. The federal government held much sway over the civilizing project, but U.S. officials such as Johnston, along with Friends and Native people, ultimately made the work happen and in turn shaped the growth of the mission complex and U.S. imperial power. The combining of disparate ideas, actions, relationships, and goals meant that the growth of the federal state was a negotiated process. Federal directives were interpreted by agents on the ground, and they drew upon the labor of Euro-Americans and Native Americans alike. Native peoples, meanwhile, debated the merits of accepting federal labor and funds, and they worked to make federal policies work to their own ends.

Indian agents such as Johnston sold and distributed farm implements—rails needed for fences and the supplies necessary for the construction of mills—and they also constructed political alliances with settlers, Native leaders, Quakers, and government officials. Such activities ensured that federal goals were, at least in part, realized on the ground. Indian agents William Wells and John Johnston, for example, worked with Baltimore Friends and kept them abreast of developments in the region. Wells informed Quakers in 1805 that "there would be 100 acres of Land under good fence at the Little Turtles Town (15 miles north of Dennis' Station) by the 1st of the 6 mo" and that "they had obtained a large number of Hogs and some Cows."[38] When Philip Dennis returned to his family in Maryland, Friends asked Wells to place one of his men at Dennis's Station, at Friends' expense, until they could find another Quaker to carry out the work. Friends likewise informed Johnston that "we request thee to do us the favour to hire two suitable men . . . and draw on our Treasurer Elias Ellicott at sight for the amount of expence incured; we also request thee to write to us about the middle of the 7th mo (July) and let us know what aid is rendered."[39] Wells, Johnston, and other Indian agents thus oversaw U.S.-Indian relations at Fort Wayne, Piqua, and elsewhere in the region, but they also maintained connections with the religious society that provided diplomatic and educational support to the federal government's plans. They served as the crucial links between Friends, the federal government, and Native peoples.

Sometimes, Friends benefited from these connections through tangible markers of legitimacy. Friends often arrived at western posts, for example, carrying letters signed by the secretary of war mandating that post officials welcome them and treat them with hospitality. Secretary Dearborn wrote to territorial governor William Hull and John Johnston in 1808, for example, in order to ensure that they offered Elisha Tyson and James Gillingham a warm reception. The secretary informed his men that "any civilities you may afford them in the execution of their benevolent intentions will be grateful to them and their Society & pleasing to the Pres^{t}. of the U.S."[40] When Friends and other missionaries carried such letters, they not only showcased federal officials' approval of their work; they also supported both federal and local claims to control citizens' movement. Such letters would not have been necessary if movement had been entirely free in Indian Country. The federal government enhanced its authority over both citizens and non-citizens by managing its laboring and administrative bureaucracy, yet local officials such as Hull and Johnston also exercised the power to recognize and grant that authority. Indigenous peoples, too, had a say, and their connections with individuals likewise facilitated movement. Friends' agricultural mission work thus contributed to and intersected with a state-building project that took place in many forms and was built upon a combination of local, federal, and Native actions.

Baltimore Friends relied upon men like Johnston for assistance, yet they also influenced agents' hiring. After Johnston replaced Wells as an Indian agent in Ohio, the War Department recruited Quaker John Shaw to serve as Johnston's paid assistant.[41] Shaw continued the work at Dennis's Station after Philip Dennis and then William Kirk returned to Maryland. Baltimore Friends' influence, however, extended further. They encouraged federal officials to hire Hendrick Aupaumut as another of Johnston's assistants in 1809.

Friends deemed the experienced Mohican go-between "to be a judicious intelligent, worthy man, and well qualified for extensive usefulness" among the Miamis at Dennis's Station. Friends explained that "we so far interested ourselves in his behalf with the Government as to solicit some assistance for him, which has been granted and placed under thy superintendence, and we take the liberty to request thy friendly aid and attention to him, which will very much oblige us, and promote the benevolent view of Government."[42] In part because of Friends' influence, Aupaumut found employment with the War Department and maintained a vital presence in the Ohio Country during the War of 1812.[43]

While Friends and U.S. officials formed relationships with one another and ensured that their own ideas shaped federal policies on the ground, Native peoples, too, played a role in the maintenance and trajectory of the mission complex. Most contemporaries—and many historians—saw the 1795 Treaty of Greenville as the death knell for Native sovereign power in the region, yet such was not the case. Together civilizing missions, market expansion, and federal investment in Indian Country transformed Ohio Country inhabitants' ways of life, but they also enabled Indigenous peoples to continue to shape the state's policies, the U.S. economy, and American imperialism.

The mission complex worked to accelerate the incorporation of Native peoples into the U.S. market economy and offered them additional power as consumers in the early republic—even as it encouraged Native peoples' disengagement with other Atlantic markets. Shawnees, Miamis, and their neighbors, however, continued to make daily decisions based upon their needs and desires as well as upon the opportunities at their disposal. U.S. policies constrained these opportunities, but they did not eliminate them. The labor relations that accompanied the mission complex further centered Shawnees and their neighbors as key creators, links in, and manipulators of the U.S. economy, and this continued even during the volatile years of the War of 1812. The presence of individuals like Johnston, Wells, and Shaw, moreover, meant that Native people could continue forming relationships with outsiders, as they had for so long, to achieve their own ends. Because the War Department partially funded the civilization project by allocating annuity funds toward agricultural tools and missionary labor, in essence Native nations paid Friends and government officials to clear their fields, build mills, plant corn, fence lands, and build the roads that connected their crops with Euro-American markets. Shawnees, Wyandots, and their neighbors therefore found ways to take advantage of the United States' commodification of their lands: they adopted the practices undertaken by missionaries and the federal state, blended those with their own ideas of economy, and used Euro-American labor and resources, purchased with their annuities, to invest in their lands. They ultimately, then, helped shape the expansion of the U.S. market economy in the nineteenth-century Ohio Country before, during, and after the United States' war with Great Britain. Even more broadly, they continued to act as active participants, affected by the same squabbles, opportunities, and obstacles as their Euro-American counterparts, in the politics and economy of North America.

The Miamis, Shawnees, and their neighbors had already built economies upon a foundation of agricultural production, hunting, and international trading networks. In addition to trading with other Indigenous polities, the Miamis, for example, cultivated especially close relationships with French traders, while the Shawnees historically traded with both the British and French. From the seventeenth through nineteenth centuries, fur-trading partnerships, in particular, often blossomed as a result of intermarriage and the subsequent establishment of kinship ties by Euro-American men and Indigenous women. For some Ohio Country Natives, relationships with Quaker missionaries and other civilizing agents became simply an additional means by which their networks produced economic advantage. The mission complex in Indian Country thus enabled Native peoples to continue to employ Euro-Americans and their policies for their own purposes, albeit in new ways, even as it fostered economic change.[44]

For some Shawnees and Miamis, Friends' primary value was not in their instruction but in their ability to produce crops. In 1808, for example, when the Miami chief White Loon complained to Friend Elisha Tyson that some Quakers and government officials were being dishonest, he contended that they worked their own fields for profit and that the corn "was all gone" when his "people went down to receive it." Upon Tyson's inspection of the mission, White Loon proclaimed, "You expected to find your young men working in our fields; instead of which you found them working in a field by themselves, we would like it much better if they would work in our fields."[45] Here it seems that Euro-American laborers could use their employment to clear other fields—perhaps cultivate fields of their own—yet Native leaders protested and refused to let such practices stand. If Friends' efforts "taught" Native Americans anything, it was how to hire, deploy, and manage Euro-American workers with both cash and their federal annuities.

With missionaries and Euro-Americans providing them with the agricultural infrastructure, labor, and goods that produced crops and further connected their lands with diverse markets, some individuals and communities sought to reap the benefits of an evolving economy while remaining on their lands. As a result, a myriad of competing political opinions developed regarding the extent to which individuals should engage with the Euro-American economy. Just as one scholar deems the War of 1812 a "civil war" among Americans and British, so, too, were there divisions among the inhabitants of Indian Country.[46] In a report concerning Tecumseh's visit to the Shawnees at Wapakoneta in 1810, for example, Indian agent John Johnston informed Governor Harrison that the Shawnee leader "made no impression on the [Wapakoneta] Shawanese [*sic*], and went away much dissatisfied at their not coming into his views." Johnston went on to say that he "indirectly encouraged their emigration westward, and told them that their annuity should follow them. They appear determined to remain, and are much attached to the town and the improvements, which are considerable."[47] One should analyze such statements with care, but given that the Shawnees' appreciation of the town's "improvements" opposed Johnston's stated desire to push them west, and that they also refused to join Tecumseh's war against the United States in 1812, it appears that the Shawnees at Wapakoneta not only wished to remain on their lands but valued the results of Friends' labor and their own. In part, then, political divides between so-called "accommodationists" and "nativists" during this period were, just as among U.S. citizens, complex, political debates produced by a changing economic world.[48]

These tensions among regional Indigenous leaders were on full display at the Treaty of Fort Wayne in 1809. The negotiating parties included Indiana Territory governor William Henry Harrison and the region's Miamis, Delawares, Eel River Indians, and Potawatomis—though viewpoints were varied from nation to nation and individual to individual. The United States endeavored to buy a tract of land inhabited by the Weas on the Wabash, and Harrison promised the Potawatomis a share of the proceeds if the Miamis agreed to sell. The Potawatomis consequently pressured the Miamis to give up the lands in exchange for annuity payments, and, though Little Turtle expressed interest in selling, the Miamis near the Mississinewa refused. By this time, the Miami chief Little Turtle's influence was on the wane while that of Jean Baptiste Richardville, chief at the Mississinewa villages, was ascendant. Richardville did not attend the treaty, but rather sent words of support for a treaty agreement, a move that suggests that he anticipated complications would arise that would potentially harm his own trading business relations with the British, Americans, or both. Both Richardville and Little Turtle supported a

Miami political future based upon private property and wealth acquisition and also one situated in Indiana along the Wabash. Little Turtle, however, supported selling the Weas' lands in return for increased annuity payments, but the Mississinewa chiefs told Harrison that "you know when things are scarce they are dear, you know the price of lands. We are willing to sell you some for the price that it sells for amongst yourselves." The Mississinewa Miamis ultimately suggested that they would "sell their lands by the acre & that they should receive two Dollars for it."[49] Though Harrison refused the latter offer and Miamis ultimately agreed to accept annuities, the alternate proposal nonetheless shows that some Native peoples wished to negotiate as participants who could take advantage of Euro-Americans' commodification of their lands, while others, like Little Turtle, were more willing to accept annuities at the outset.

Such political debates also centered around the question of how closely to ally with the United States. The Shawnee brothers Tecumseh and Tenskwatawa, for example, endeavored to rally together a pan-Indian coalition of forces in an effort to halt U.S. territorial encroachments in the region through force. The Shawnees at Wapakoneta, however, chose not to participate in the attacks—as did others, particularly some Delawares in the region. Some did, however, join the effort, and the Shawnee Prophet Tenskwatawa established Prophetstown as a base from which allied Native people launched attacks between 1809 and 1812. After that town suffered a major attack during the Battle of Tippecanoe in 1811, regional Native leaders who had advocated for an alliance with Americans gained the political edge.[50]

With Tecumseh's death at the 1813 Battle of the Thames, and ultimately with conclusion of warfare in 1814, most regional Native nations treated for peace with the Americans. Though Native peoples' politics shifted after the war in order to adapt to the new realities of U.S. power in the region, they were not left powerless. Even during the years of conflict, individuals as well as nations found ways to benefit from the situation as best they could. During the war, for example, the U.S. Army Quartermaster paid Ohio Wyandots forty-eight dollars for beaver pelts, it offered the Seneca Tommy Smith forty-eight dollars for "one grindstone, one drawing knife and one Chissel for helving & repairing axes," and it paid the Shawnee chief Captain Lewis sixty dollars for "One Horse pressed into the public service."[51] Some individuals combined their existing economies with the emerging trend toward work-for-hire labor, while others provided a good or service for individual profit. Emerging economic practices traveled from the urban coast to the Ohio Country, and there combined with older ones to create an economic system that was marked, increasingly, by developing ideas of investment and production. Individuals like Tommy Smith, Captain Lewis, and others who provided goods or services for the U.S. government participated in the wartime economy in much the same way as did their Euro-American neighbors.

The War of 1812 could create economic opportunities, but it also disrupted life in the region in profound ways. Though the Miamis were of many minds when it came to the war, the U.S. army tended to overlook such differences and attacked numerous Miami villages near the Wabash, while William Henry Harrison's army attacked Little Turtle's Village as well as three others near the Forks of the Wabash. In December, moreover, Lieutenant Colonel John B. Campbell attacked the Mississinewa villages, though he received orders to avoid harming prominent leaders such as Richardville, White Loon, and Pacanne who were more open to working with the Americans on behalf of their people.[52]

Baltimore Friends' mission work, meanwhile, stalled during the years of the war, but John Johnston remained in the region. He retired from his post at Fort Wayne at the start of the war, but after removing to Piqua, Ohio, he nonetheless continued to serve the United States. The War Department, hoping to keep a man who maintained good relations with the region's Indian nations in its employ, opened an agency at his home. Delawares who desired to remain neutral in the conflict sought the assistance of agent John Johnston to do so, and the Indian agent hosted many of them—to the chagrin of his Euro-American Piqua neighbors—at his farmstead at Piqua during the height of the war. Acting on instructions from General William Henry Harrison, Johnston sold clothing, among other goods, and he reported in 1813 that such offerings would "take all that remains on hand."[53] In this way he ensured that those goods continued to find consumer markets, even during wartime. Nonetheless, when wartime rendered Delawares wanting, their relationship with Johnston enabled them to maintain their politics either in support of the war or of neutrality. Delawares' stay at Johnston's Piqua farm reveals not that they were "accommodationists" who sought either to support the United States or remain neutral, but rather that they supported a policy of alliance with the United States and its representatives—whether missionary or Indian agent. Such an alliance, they determined, offered the best prospects for the future but also for their endurance during the war.

In a number of ways, then, members of the Ohio Country Native polities continued to create, adapt to, and manipulate a dynamic economic world.

The later history of the Friends' mission at Dennis's Station, however, illuminates the contentious trajectory of Natives' and federal power as well as U.S. economic development. Neighboring settlers destroyed most of the original mission infrastructure at the start of the War of 1812, and such actions suggest that they viewed the site as an economic and political threat—a symbol of economic prosperity and enduring presence. Native nations possessed the power to take advantage of the mission complex, but that power could also make them visible targets of neighboring white settlers.

* * *

Though Native peoples' ongoing presence and manipulation of the mission complex threatened white Americans' dreams of an empire whose economic heart lay in Ohio Country fields, it also bolstered U.S. claims to Indians' economic dependence. By attempting to monopolize the sale of agricultural manufactures, linens, and other goods, moreover, factory stores and the broader mission complex contributed to federal overtures of Native dependence on U.S. manufactures during the early nineteenth century. Though this dependence was mainly rhetorical, U.S. officials nonetheless used the notion to promote fictional ideas of Native nations' *political* dependence. Much of Indiana Territory governor William Henry Harrison's correspondence dealt with the problems of Indian affairs, and it reveals the extent to which Native nations continued to wield power in the Ohio Country. Despite this reality, the governor informed his territorial legislature in 1805 that the region's benevolent Indian policies had secured Native nations' "entire dependence." Recognizing his territory's incredible potential and emphasizing peace, he continued to remark that "the mighty river which separates us from the Louisianians will never be stained with the blood of contending nations; but will prove the bond of our nation, and will convey upon its bosom, in a course of many thousand miles, the produce of our great and united empire."[54] Indian affairs, statehood, and economic production were linked in Harrison's mind, and the mission complex offered evidence of "dependence"; it offered a veneer of legitimacy to U.S. political claims in Indian Country.

For Harrison, Natives' "entire dependence" led to increased land sales, "settlement and improvement," "produce," tax revenues, and economic stability. The mission complex was thus crucial because it aided in the distribution of farm implements, gave the federal government hope that those tools would, in fact, find use among Native populations, and offered officials like Governor Harrison evidence of Native economic and, in turn, political "dependence." Such "evidence" would, officials hoped, encourage the settlement of the "right sort" of people and in turn boost land sales and increase revenues. These points were crucial in the maintenance of the civilization project in the Ohio Country, and they explain why, despite the limited success of the *explicit* goal of complete assimilation, it endured and shaped U.S. imperial policy throughout the nineteenth century and beyond.

Despite the far-ranging effects of the mission complex, it added to the transformation of the region's political and economic order with little public fanfare. What many Euro-Americans *did* notice, however, were the long-term consequences that were made possible by both civilizing missions and Indigenous dispossession. A "transportation revolution" as well as a "communications revolution" knit the territories of the United States together in rapid fashion after 1815, and they were phenomena that fostered awe and debate among American citizens and politicians. Canals, steamboats, railroads, and the telegraph—the proliferation of these technologies were obvious; yet Euro-Americans only acknowledged the fact that they were made possible by Indigenous dispossession when it suited. As Chapter 6 will show, when citizens petitioned the U.S. federal government to remove Miamis from Indiana Territory to make way for the Wabash and Erie Canal in 1830, for example, they recognized that dispossession needed to precede any transportation revolution.[55]

When one travels through Wapakoneta, Upper Sandusky, and Lewistown, Ohio, as well as Fort Wayne and Huntington, Indiana—all central locations of missions and Indian trading posts—the remnants of old railroads and canals still remain, many of which were built not long after Quakers and Native peoples helped build the mission complex and the U.S. imperial market economy. These remains reveal that the layered development of the U.S. economy—but also American imperialism—was both a top-down and bottom-up affair. As such, tracing the federal state's power in building a mission complex reveals that Friends' missions and the civilization plan were not simply tools for "assimilating the Indians," but rather were crucial means by which the U.S. state consolidated its power and spread its economic influence in the early nineteenth century. At the same time, Friends' mission work and the relationships that grew between Miamis, Shawnees, Delawares, and officials as a result of federal Indian policies likewise offered ways by which Native peoples could make a living during the War of 1812, and they enabled Native people to use missionary labor to their advantage.

Such trends continued even after the war, and they reveal the importance of understanding the growth of the federal state as a negotiated phenomenon that drew upon a blending of top-down and bottom-up power. Though the mission complex ultimately bolstered federal power in the Ohio Country, Indigenous peoples employed and manipulated Euro-Americans' ideas of "civilization" and economy for their own purposes beyond the War of 1812 in ways that had lasting consequences.

PART III

Negotiations

CHAPTER 5

"A Damnd Rebelious Race"

Native Authority in the Aftermath of War

> These Miamies Genl are a damnd rebelious race and I believe it true what Lafountain tells me that Richardville caries the Key and nothing can be done without his assent.
>
> —Hugh B. McKeen, 1826

When peace returned to the towns and fields of Ohio and Indiana after the War of 1812, the economic and political changes underway in the region continued apace. For some, 1816, in particular, ushered in cause for celebration: The Euro-American inhabitants of Indiana Territory found themselves citizens of the United States endowed with all the political rights and privileges (if they were white males) that accompanied statehood. Many of Indiana's Native peoples, meanwhile, continued to cultivate and dwell upon their lands much as they had prior to the state's incorporation into the official limits of the metropole. Statehood meant, however, that Indiana—and Ohio as well—boasted a growing population. Surges in population continued after statehood, and it encouraged the ongoing development of interstate infrastructure that facilitated settlers' movement and employment. In the ongoing struggle to give order to Euro-Americans' migration to the region, myriad agencies materialized to address the problems of labor and economy that accompanied U.S. colonialism on the continent.

In 1817, for example, Nathan Guilford, Ethan Stone, and Daniel Roe organized the Western Emigration Society in order to facilitate American movement into this "Western Country," newly free from British occupation. They declared Cincinnati "the most proper place for such a Society" because of its size, "local situation," and the fact that it operated as "a thorough-fare through which much of the migrating population passes."[1] By the time of the Society's founding, Cincinnati contained a much larger population than either the more northern expanses of the state or its neighbor to the west, Indiana. One inhabitant estimated that the city boasted "about 9,000 inhabitants, 15 lawyers, not the most eminent, 20 physicians" and that "the number of emigrants that are daily arriving are imense."[2] The emigration society eased the "great uncertainty and embarrassment" in "not knowing where to seek employment, where to apply for information," or knowing "where they can find a situation best suited to their circumstances."[3] The society thus functioned as a matchmaker in the business of employment, receiving applications from "persons wanting to employ Mechanics, Tradesmen, Labourers, &cs.," as well as from "persons wishing for employment of any kind," and it connected them with employers seeking to bolster their fortunes through hired labor.[4] These connections proved essential to the practical functioning of everyday life in the nineteenth-century Ohio Country, and by the 1820s the challenges of making ends meet shaped the lives of Euro-Americans and Native peoples alike.

Native nations and individuals used their market and government connections to earn a wage and assert authority during the War of 1812, and they continued to do so through the 1820s and 1830s. The mission complex, the U.S. civilization plan more broadly—and, crucially, the rhetoric of civilization that accompanied these—offered them tools, labor, and a language that was intelligible to Native peoples, settlers, and U.S. officials alike. It offered Native peoples further means to engage the changing regional economy, demand goods and labor, and complain when such things failed to materialize. Miamis, Shawnees, and their neighbors, accustomed to dealing with U.S. officials and their missionary partners, manipulated the tools and language of civilization and Euro-Americans' speculative philanthropy, and they employed a variety of strategies that ensured that they continued to possess and wield authority in the region despite the increasing pressures of U.S. settler colonialism.

Many Indigenous peoples who remained in the Ohio Country after the war became neighbors, employees, and employers in a region that boasted a growing Euro-American population, and they employed a variety of strategies to do so. Some used their connections with Euro-Americans to invest in their lands and engage the growing regional economy; others employed the discourse of civilization to secure both material goods and bolster their political agendas through petitioning, while others wielded a language of rights to do so and contemplated the advantages of participating in nation-building projects in places such as Missouri and beyond. Such strategies illuminate the ways in which Shawnees, Miamis, and their neighbors found ways to remain on their lands and, when that appeared impossible, remain connected to their people.

* * *

After the War of 1812 concluded, some Shawnees and their neighbors in the Ohio Country endeavored to continue to take advantage of missionary and federal labors. Leaders like Captain Lewis at Lewis Town and Black Hoof (Catecahassa) at Wapakoneta maintained relationships with Friends in order to secure material advantages, organize their own labor force, and cultivate closer political relationships with U.S. officials; they requested and accepted Friends' assistance and instruction in cultivating their crops. The Shawnees explained that "the war swept away every thing from us," and that, despite the fact that "the United States have been very charitable to us," they required renewed assistance.[5] When Friends visited Wapakoneta in 1816, they noted that several hundred acres of corn and other infrastructure remained intact, yet Black Hoof and his people nonetheless had endeavored to take advantage of the benefits Friends offered, writing before Friends' visit that they were hopeful of the "prospect of the same help that we received from our friends the Quakers before the war."[6] As political allies who had historically advocated for Shawnees, Friends offered the means to facilitate Shawnees' own economic projects. In maintaining and cultivating their connections with missionaries as well as federal and local officials, Shawnees, Miamis, and their neighbors engaged a strategy that drew upon older paradigms of interaction and offered additional opportunities for Indigenous peoples' success in a region undergoing increasingly rapid change.

For their part, the Baltimore Friends wasted no time in traveling to Ohio to assess the condition of the region's Native communities.[7] Their report to the secretary of war William H. Crawford stressed that the Shawnees required further instruction from Friends to complete their transformation into so-called civilized peoples. Writing to the secretary from Baltimore in August 1816, James Ellicott and Philip E. Thomas informed him that they had recently traveled among the Shawnees at Lewis Town and Wapakoneta and found both Shawnees and Wyandots in Ohio "anxiously disposed to obtain instructions relative to the cultivation of their lands."[8] In a population of

Figure 5. The Shawnee chief Black Hoof, also known as Catahecassa. National Portrait Gallery, Smithsonian Institution; gift of Betty A. and Lloyd G. Schermer.

eight hundred at Wapakoneta, for example, the Shawnees had "400 acres of ground enclosed by tolerable good fences, 250 acres being planted in Indian corn."[9] They cultivated that land "principally with hoes," however, because they had only two plows. That lack encouraged Ellicott and Thomas to reiterate that the Shawnees and Wyandots yet required instruction; to Friends, the use of hoes indicated Shawnees' continued ignorance of agricultural techniques. The Friends remarked that they had successfully overcome the Shawnees' "general indisposition" to work, "which prevailed . . . when the Society of Friends first embarked in this concern," and they were pleased that "the principal obstacles which retarded our successes are in a great measure removed."[10] If they obtained their projected budget for work among the Shawnees and their neighbors ($4,720), Ellicott and Thomas concluded, the Friends could alleviate "the situation of these Indians," which was "peculiarly calculated to awaken the commiseration and excite the benevolence of all who feel for the sufferings of their fellow men."[11] The Friends' report to the War Department reflected an ongoing blindness to Shawnees' economic ingenuity and success as agriculturalists: they either could not see the Shawnees as proficient or they weighted their record to reflect their own agenda and desire to engage in acts of philanthropy.

Despite Friends' assessments, Native peoples had continued to take up roles as consumers, employers, and participants in the regional economy during the war, and they continued to do so after. Shawnees at Wapakoneta, for example, embraced and manipulated commercial market relations, but they also combined the concepts of debt and market exchange with those of older, trade-based forms of exchange with which they were familiar. According to George Johnston's 1829 promissory notebook (a collection of receipts that record Wapakoneta Shawnees' names, debts, and the items they purchased), approximately two hundred Wapakoneta debtors failed to pay off their loans, and a roughly equal number of receipts were torn out of the notebook, signifying debts canceled.[12] Johnston's notebook provides evidence of the Shawnees' participation in a cycle of credit and debit and in the larger U.S. economy, just like the large number of Euro-American debtors of the republic.[13] What is more, the book charts Shawnees' proximity and ongoing participation in the regional and continental economic networks: every needle and yard of cloth marked as sold signified the connections to and profits of merchants and entrepreneurs elsewhere. Given that the Shawnees possessed a robust gift-exchange tradition, they may have viewed the goods as gifts—though it is equally plausible that they simply understood this as a means to acquire the goods they needed and desired. What is certain, however, is that they borrowed Johnston's money to secure items such as cloth, knives, bridles, and teakettles, and they did so to the detriment of Johnston's finances. The ambiguities of the evidence reveal the consequences of the intertwining of a variety of economic understandings. While President Jefferson and William Henry Harrison conspired to drive up debts in an effort to facilitate land sales in the early nineteenth century, some Native peoples nonetheless found ways to take advantage of those who would have them accrue debts.[14]

While most Shawnees obtained these goods in cash or future cash payments, some secured the wares or canceled their debts through barter. Such transactions included Native women, and they offer a clear sense of Indigenous women's roles in the development of early American markets. "Turkey Feathers wife," for example, obtained goods at Johnston's store, as did Mary DeShane who paid off part of her debt with "winter Deer Skins" in the "amount of fifty cents."[15] The latter transaction offers a glimpse of the ways in which multiple economies collided with and became intelligible to one another in Wapakoneta. In this instance, DeShane exchanged skins, a crucial part of the region's historical and contemporary economy, for both wares and for a cancellation of standing debts. As with white women in places like New

England and urban markets, it is clear that Native women in Wapakoneta likewise undertook some of the shopping for their families.[16]

Wapakoneta Shawnees partnered with Quakers at their town and accepted the agricultural infrastructure they offered, but their willingness to use Friends and other Americans like George Johnston for economic investment purposes suggests that their engagement was selective, purposeful, and grounded in their own sense of economy and exchange. They adapted to regional shifts and envisioned a future for themselves on their lands that was grounded in their own practices. When Friend Isaac Harvey, then a missionary at Wapakoneta, attended the funerary services of the aged Shawnee chief Black Hoof in 1831, he observed that the Shawnees intensely grieved the man's death and that they marked their loss with food and ritual. He noted that "twenty deer were killed, beside a large number of turkeys and what smaller wild animals they considered fit to eat—no tame animal or fowl was suffered to be eaten on that occasion, though there was a large quantity of bread prepared."[17] Here is revealed Shawnees' selective appropriation of Euro-American goods and practices: "tame" or domesticated animals had no place in this ritual of death. In 1810, Wapakoneta Shawnees had turned Tecumseh away from their midst and refused to buy into Tenskwatawa's spiritual message of difference. In 1831, they maintained their acceptance of Euro-American labor and infrastructure but also revealed that they valued their own cultural practices. Such episodes further demonstrate that cooperation with the U.S. government and its imperial agents was selective and politically and economically purposeful rather than accommodation of U.S. imperialism. At Wapakoneta, Shawnees held a vision for their future that was grounded in their own practices, in a market economy, in selective partnerships with outsiders, and in their land.

Native people participated in local exchanges, and they also invested in their lands in part by taking advantage of Euro-American labor, government money, and annuity payments. At the same time, however, the War Department bolstered the local economy and facilitated settler colonialism by hiring men in need of work. Though the number of men hired to labor on Indian lands was relatively small, the government hired them to perform the same tasks that Friends once handled. John Johnston wrote to William H. Crawford in 1816 that "labouring men is much wanted to instruct them [the Indians] in farming and to enable them to live on their own industry."[18] He went on to request a budget of $2,000 that included payment for the labor, sustenance, and tools of six men—two for Shawnees, two for Wyandots, and two for Delawares and Senecas living near Johnston's Piqua agency.[19] By 1829, moreover, the Miamis were due to receive the services of "10 Labourers" as part of the fulfillment of their annuity payment for that year.[20] Those ten hired hands each received forty-five dollars and worked at either the "Miamie Villages" or they received their compensation for "labour performed for [the] Thorntown party [of Miamis]."[21] These workers may have thus supplemented their household subsistence economy with wages earned for work performed on behalf of the Miamis.[22] U.S. settler colonialism in the Ohio Country thus increased tensions between Euro-Americans and their Native neighbors, but it also offered Native peoples and the War Department a growing labor force.

While the federal War Department arranged for Euro-Americans to labor on Ohio Indians' lands, Miami and Shawnee leaders such as the prominent Richardville family among the Mississinewa Miamis contracted settler-laborers on their nations' lands to perform the same tasks as Quaker missionaries like William Kirk once had. While histories of the region view Shawnees and their neighbors' cooperation with both Quaker missionaries and the civilization plan more broadly as evidence of their desire to appear as a peaceful people capable of living among the Euro-American population of Ohio, we must add to this Native peoples' desire to manipulate U.S. policies for their own purposes.[23]

The Richardvilles, like Little Turtle among the Miamis during the first decade of the nineteenth century, cultivated connections with Euro-Americans that facilitated Miamis' ability to hire and manage labor on their lands. These relationships similarly served to bolster Jean Baptiste Richardville's political position in Miami Country, even as it offered opportunities for the region's settlers to find work. Though Miamis' relations with Friends were more distant and infrequent after both the War of 1812 and the destruction of Dennis's Station, the mission complex dovetailed with and complemented the ways in which Miamis took advantage of expanding Euro-American markets and the presence of U.S. officials, and Miamis would nonetheless interact with other missionaries such as the Baptist Isaac McCoy after the war. Friend Philip Dennis's labor at Dennis's Station, moreover, remained a not too distant memory, and Miamis took advantage of the shared language of economy and improvement that was in part a consequence of the U.S. civilization plan and its rhetoric.

Richardville, in particular, used his presence in both the regional fur trade and as an employer in Indiana to cultivate connections with the U.S. federal government. Richardville's father was a Frenchman and his mother was a prominent Miami. He received a Euro-American education and was well-versed in the ways of European politics, economy, and diplomacy. Richardville profited from both the fur trade and Euro-American immigration to the region, and his accumulation of wealth—he was rumored to be the wealthiest man in Indiana by 1840—suggests that his economic aims were personal. He nonetheless worked to secure a prosperous future for the Miamis in Indiana by ensuring that his economic interests intertwined with Miami political interests.[24]

To that end, Richardville and his son John secured laborers for work on Miami lands. They hired out tasks that reflected both what U.S. officials understood to be civilized ideals and that strengthened their own economic positions. They invested in their lands in order to become formidable economic players. In 1824, for example, the Richardvilles arranged for William Ewing to make "a Contract with the Miami's to Make rails and fence their ground" and, the following year, William Caswell earned three dollars in return for making a plow frame.[25] In the case of Ewing, the elder Richardville, in particular, used the resources at his disposal to hire out work that promised future returns. Ideas of investment lurked behind such labor contracts. Hiring Ewing to fence ground with a contract, moreover, suggests the adoption of evolving ideas of free labor and private property. U.S. market practices combined with the existing exchange economy in the Ohio Country to create a market system characterized, increasingly, by dynamic ideas of investment and production and that included Native and non-Native workers and employers. The emerging Ohio Country economy was one wherein all inhabitants struggled to assert themselves at the top of an economic hierarchy. The fact that Euro-Americans were willing to perform such tasks reveals both their desire and need to work as well as their willingness to labor for Miami or Shawnee employers.

Richardville was largely responsible for cultivating a connection with the Ewing brothers, and while he used them to invest in Miamis' lands by contracting them to fence, clear, and plow lands, he also used the relationship in other productive ways. The Ewing brothers and their father were experienced traders who sought profit, and they demonstrate the extent of economic change underway in the nineteenth-century Ohio Country. Whereas regional traders once offered goods in exchange for valuable furs, these men made their profits by offering goods on credit, and they often succeeded in racking up Natives' debts that could then translate into profit during treaties with the U.S. government since debts were often deducted and paid out of treaty annuities and payments. Richardville was himself a shrewd businessman, however, and he knew the power of consumerism. As historian Stewart Rafert makes clear, "the Ewing firm could not survive without Miami annuities, and the Miami could not have resisted demands for removal as long as they did without the influence of the Ewings."[26] Thus, as Miamis secured annuities from various land deals, they offered business to the profit-minded Ewings who supplied them various goods; this in turn ensured Richardville and his countrymen Euro-American allies who shared an interest in Miami persistence in Indiana. The regional economy thus offered Miamis opportunities to thwart both U.S. imperial ambitions and U.S. colonists' efforts to remove them until 1846. Even then, many Miamis remained in the state after Richardville and another chief, Francis Godfroy, purchased lands and allowed their countrymen to remain on those lands after removal.

In addition to forming connections with regional economic players such as the Ewing brothers, Richardville maintained a public role as a chief among the Miamis, and he attended many treaties and councils prior to and after the War of 1812. As a consequence, he cultivated and maintained connections with both Miamis and federal officials, and such a strategy served him well as a political and economic leader in Indiana. When in 1824 Indian agent John Tipton declared that traders in the region were "not to employ directly or indirectly any other than natural born american citizens of the united States" whether "as clerk or otherwise," Richardville made sure to apply for a trading license regardless.[27] Upon hearing of the application, and the subsequent political problems that Richardville's application created due to his position of power, then territorial governor of Michigan Lewis Cass urged Tipton to approve the application since "it is impossible to mark the difference between whites and Indians, so as to determine where the political rights of the one cease and of the others begin. It is a mixed question, depending for its solution, not so much on the relative quantity of Indian or white blood in the veins of the person, as upon his education, habits or pursuits."[28]

Richardville frustrated U.S. desires to render Indigenous peoples culturally dead or vanished as a result of civilization policies. As Cass's statement to Tipton suggests, the civilization plan and the economic and social relations that resulted from the mission complex meant that race alone would not serve to "other" all Native peoples. Cass seemed to suggest that Richardville was of mixed heritage, but "education, habits or pursuits" mattered as well. Men like Richardville were important politically but also economically: it was in U.S. officials' interests to keep such individuals satisfied. Richardville possessed the power to contribute to both U.S. economic growth and the maintenance of U.S. imperial dreams of uncontested rule in the region while also claiming power for himself and the Miamis in Indiana. Richardville's application for a trading license ultimately reveals, then, that in the early nineteenth-century Ohio Country, practical concerns of politics and economy could trump other considerations, and economic success and Euro-American ideals regarding education could provide a gateway to political power.

Richardville's economic and political power in Indian Country, moreover, intersected with U.S. state and national politics in crucial ways. When John Tipton became Indian agent for the Miamis in Indiana, he made the mistake of complaining about the ways in which Richardville conducted himself as leader of the Miamis. Interpreter John Boure informed Tipton in 1829 that he should be acquainted "with the feelings of Cheef Richardville to wards you."[29] Boure continued to explain that the powerful Miami "was very much dissatisfied with you sow far as to say should thay Bee a treaty hee wood treet with Govr Cass But not you."[30] By 1830, the Miamis wrote a memorial to Lewis Cass, the Superintendent of Indian Affairs, complaining of Tipton. They informed Cass that "it seems as if our Agent wished & has usurped a power which we do not believe properly belongs to his office."[31] They went on to say that Tipton "selected a place for the payment of our annuities contrary to our wishes. Our Principal Chief T B Richardville remonstrated & positively objected going to the place selected by our Agent & requested him to pay the annuities at or near the same place they were paid last year./ on a reserve made at the Wabash Treaty expressly for that purpose/. to which he objected."[32]

What began as a dispute between Richardville and Tipton escalated to involve key federal officials like Lewis Cass and the secretary of war. After the Miamis' memorial, Tipton wrote to secretary of war John Eaton and informed him that "in 1828 I paid these people at a place selected by their chiefs where there was no good *water*, in a *river bottom covered with nettles*. I told the chiefs I would not pay at that place again. in 1829 I proposed to pay on their *reservation* near the Treaty ground *20 miles* nigher to the residence of the principle chief. but this was ten miles from a point where *two chiefs have stores*. I then appointed a place 8 miles below on the wabash to which the chiefs would not come."[33] The Miamis' grumblings forced Tipton to explain himself to his superior. Such politicking demonstrates the authority that Ohio Indian leaders possessed. In that same letter to Eaton, Tipton warned that "the chiefs of this Tribe will controul the operations of the Government unless the Department sustain the ground I have taken."[34] Miamis' persistence and chastisement of Tipton reveals the necessity of blended state power as well as the power of individuals on the ground; federal and local officials remained at the mercy of Indigenous leaders into the nineteenth century. The completion of federal objectives would require negotiation and diplomacy.

The dispute between Tipton and the Miamis would have been problematic for any U.S. Indian agent interested in removing Indian peoples, but it was particularly troublesome for Tipton, a Democrat, in 1830. That year William Ewing, a pro-internal improvement Whig, wrote to Tipton supporting the state legislature's recent passage of a Canal Bill. Ewing's connections with Richardville, the Miamis, and U.S. officials like Tipton positioned him as a nineteenth-century go-between who, in an effort to best satisfy his own financial interests, encouraged Tipton to facilitate a policy that was amenable to the Miamis. Though Indiana citizens sent a memorial to the U.S. Senate and House of Representatives demanding Miamis' removal westward in order to make room for the proposed Wabash and Erie Canal, Ewing told Tipton that "their Removail from the State now I believe to be impracticable—would it not be well to suffer them to occupy back & unimportent situations for a while, as their increased annuity will be of material benefit in the first settleing of our county and there is yet room for all."[35] Ewing, then, in an effort to ensure continued profit from Miamis' annuity, encouraged Tipton to "restore . . . influence over old Richardvill" in order to "[gratify] the Malicious Minority, and false faced, formerly your hypocritical friends, who hope to throw obsticles in your road, when serving your country & its best interest."[36] Gratifying Richardville and allowing the Miamis to remain in the state not only benefited the Miamis but also enabled Tipton, a Democrat, to indulge his Whig political opponents.[37] What was more, Ewing openly stated that Miamis' annuities stimulated Indiana's economy. Indian affairs were bound up in individual profit schemes as well as state and federal economic policies

When, in the early 1830s, the United States endeavored to buy the remaining Miami lands in Indiana, Tipton and others knew that Richardville was savvy, and they knew that he stood in the way of completely swindling the Miamis. George B. Porter, a U.S. commissioner, wrote to Cass in 1833 that he "cannot . . . believe that these Indians will dispose of the whole of their Lands:—nor are they willing now to move West of the Mississippi:—nor is fifty cents per acre a sufficient price. Chief Richardville knows, as well as anyone else their value. They are worth at least two dollars per acre."[38] Playing the property game according to Americans' own rules of market economy and value increased Miamis' ability to remain on their lands, and it explains in part why they were able to maintain much of their territorial holdings into the 1840s and beyond the time when most other regional nations sold their holdings to the United States. Though it is possible that Tipton was truthful when he informed Eaton in 1830 that many Miamis "have many times requested me to pay the heads of *families*, or *individuls*, alledgeing that the *village chiefs cheate them*," cheating their fellow countrymen or no, Miami leaders such as Richardville cultivated connections with Euro-Americans and their economy in an effort to ensure the best possible political and economic future for his people even as he turned a profit for himself.[39]

While the Miamis engaged a variety of Euro-American connections, the Shawnees at Wapakoneta maintained close connections with the Society of Friends after the War of 1812, and they thus continued to directly utilize the connections established by the mission complex to invest in their futures. Black Hoof and other Wapakoneta Shawnees invited Friends to visit their town and resume mission work there in 1815, and, in response, Friends arranged for Joseph and Martha Rhodes to offer instruction in the agricultural arts, domestic production, and literacy. When Martha died in Ohio, Black Hoof and his countrymen grieved her passing alongside Joseph, and they lamented Rhodes's departure from the mission.[40] The relationship between Friends and the Shawnees continued to be simultaneously personal and practical, with the lines blurred between the two. Friends were political allies and useful sources of economic assistance, and their personal relationships with Native peoples, built upon a century and a half of cooperation, facilitated Natives' efforts to remain in their homes and ancestral lands.

Securing labor and maintaining connections with government officials and missionaries proved crucial for Native leaders, but those Shawnees, Miamis, and their neighbors who did not occupy positions of leadership also found ways both to participate in the expanding market economy and manipulate U.S. policies to their advantage. Shawnees at Wapakoneta adapted to the changing economy bolstered by Friends' mission work in their town, and they invested in their future. By the 1820s, Baltimore Friends partnered with Ohio and Indiana Friends to run the mission schools at Wapakoneta, Lewis Town, and Upper Sandusky.[41] With the new influence of these latter Friends, the schools began to offer not only agricultural instruction but lessons in reading and writing as well. In 1823, however, Baltimore Friends reported that many Shawnees in Wapakoneta "expressed a wish that their children might be taught to work as well as read and write. . . . They had also wholly abandoned all intention of removing, and appeared very desirous that Friends should continue the school."[42] Friends may have included the statement in order to justify their own efforts, yet sources suggest that the Shawnee parents at Wapakoneta valued the "improvements" made by Friends there, and they in turn likely encouraged their children to learn to labor in order to continue to invest in Shawnees' future in Ohio. For some, the key to maintaining a foothold in their home hinged upon the next generation acquiring trade skills and learning to take advantage of and maintain agricultural infrastructure.

Ohio Native leaders and their peoples in the early nineteenth century often possessed, wielded, and supported economic and political power in ways that harkened back to the ideals of reciprocity and leadership common among many of the region's peoples. Generous gift-giving once cemented hereditary chiefs' authority among their people, and chiefs' oversight of the distribution of annuities or land operated similarly in the nineteenth century. When Richardville or Godfroy offered their people the opportunity to remain in Indiana by offering a place for them on their recently purchased lands, they not only bolstered their own power; they served their people in much the same way as their forefathers had for centuries. These leaders took advantage of the connections and rhetoric established by the civilization plan and mission complex, used them to serve their people as best they could, and, while they were at it, continued to mold, as employers, traders, and farmers, the creation and expansion of the U.S. market economy in the Ohio Country.

* * *

Mission work and the civilization plan linked Ohio Native Americans ever closer to the U.S. market economy, and they opened new avenues of economic manipulation and strategic persistence for Native leaders and their peoples—avenues that simultaneously borrowed and diverged from earlier imperial precedents. As was the case prior to the War of 1812, such economic engagement continued to influence Indigenous peoples' politics. As the Miamis' 1830 complaint regarding Tipton's reported abuse of power suggests, Native strategies for combating U.S. power increasingly involved claims making, petition writing, and a general willingness to issue complaints to state officials. Such appeals often involved matters of investment, labor, debt, or claims for economic redress, and they often borrowed from the language of civilization. Sometimes these requests were successful, and sometimes they were not. Regardless, they strengthened the bonds between Ohio Country Indian leaders and government officials and Native nations and the U.S. state, just as economic strategies linked Native peoples closer to the U.S. market economy that they helped to create. And they were deliberate and purposeful; the petitions and requests showcase a variety of Native individuals and nations choosing to engage the federal state and use it to their own ends. As Native leaders like Richardville employed petitions, along with a variety of strategies, to secure a future for their people amid a rapidly growing Ohio Country population, they participated in the creation of the U.S. economy, and they continued to contribute to the development of the U.S. state by investing that state with authority.

The ability to make claims upon the U.S. federal government offered Ohio Country nations an opportunity to engage with the federal state, but it also reveals that, while there was power in making such appeals, Indigenous peoples' opportunities were increasingly defined by that growing state.[43] Native peoples in the Ohio Country used their connections with John Johnston, missionaries, and others to navigate the evolving U.S. bureaucracy and legal system in order to claim what was rightfully theirs, and they could do so in large part because of the authority of Indigenous leaders, the desires of U.S. officials, and the pressures of land-hungry United States settlers. On-the-ground individuals such as Johnston and Richardville reveal the ways in which both local and national power combined to produce and define federal authority on the edges of empire as well as the relationship between Native polities and the republic. As Richardville's successful application for a trading license suggests, Native leaders' power and relationships with traders and officials meant that regional peace and U.S. hopes for eventual removal often hinged upon these leaders' happiness; as a result, these relationships became crucial for Americans' own economic and political gains, just as they had during the heyday of the fur trade in the *pays d'en haut*.

Though some Native peoples used their connections with U.S. officials or missionaries to make claims against their Native neighbors, they also made claims upon the U.S. state for redress whenever they perceived a failure to fulfill a political or economic obligation. Such claims were often linked to promises made by the U.S. during treaties—promises intended to dovetail with the U.S. civilization plan and that included economic infrastructure and laborers. In 1826, for example, Meehcikilita (Le Gros), Richardville's Miami compatriot, issued a lengthy complaint on behalf of his nation that weaved together economic concerns with an assertion of political authority. He informed the secretary of war, James Barbour, that while the United States had fulfilled most of the provisions of the 1818 Treaty at St. Mary's, it had promised the Miamis a blacksmith and a gunsmith, two laborers whom had yet to be provided to his countrymen. Weaving ideas of economics, reciprocity, and sovereignty into his appeal, Meehcikilita asked, "Now father, who is to pay the damage which has accrued to my nation in consequence of this failure?" and he followed this query with a remedy for the United States' misstep.[44] He declared, "I wish to make a proposition to you, which is, that you will authorise our Agent, to employ a good blacksmith, who can repair our guns likewise, and a good trusty Miller in lieu of the gun smith as promised by the Treaty, to be placed at the mills, as that position will be central to the nation."[45] Though the treaty stipulations were eight years old, less than one week after the Miamis' complaint, the Superintendent of Indian Affairs, Thomas L. McKenney, agreed to find, employ, and send Meehcikilita his miller; by the summer of that same year, the miller was in Miami Country.[46]

Sometimes, language of rights could add to Native peoples' strategies of engaging the United States. In 1826, for example, Meehcikilita confidently informed governor Lewis Cass, "You have made a request of us for our land, which we have already refused. I told you our situation. We have a right to trade or exchange our property."[47] Discourses of right swirled throughout the Atlantic world, and Indigenous and African-descended peoples alike contributed to rights discourses, as Meehcikilita did in the 1820s.[48] Meehcikilita's insistence upon his and the Miamis' right "to trade or exchange our property" was not only an insistence upon Miami sovereignty; it was also an insistence that their rights were grounded in part in the land.

Just as they had during the earlier years of the nineteenth century, some Ohio Country Native peoples endeavored to work with the investment opportunities and language that accompanied the government civilization plan, and they made sure to do so even as settler movement pressured them to move. Indeed, the strategies that Native people developed to combat U.S. colonialism often drew upon ideas of civilization, and these strategies traveled with Native peoples as they moved throughout the continent. In 1820, for example, a group of Shawnees and Delawares who migrated from Ohio informed President James Monroe that since "our Tools will need frequent repair, and our Horses Shod, we ask if you are willing to give us a Black-Smith for five years only, to mend our ploughs &c. during that time, some of our Young Men, will learn with him to do it for us."[49] These Shawnees and Delawares kept plows and smiths at the center of their requests in order to showcase their engagement with Euro-Americans' civilization plan, yet they were equally careful to craft their request in a manner that drew upon their own understanding of political relationships. The stipulation that the blacksmith should stay for "five years only" suggested that the Shawnees and Delawares desired to extract knowledge and labor from the hired man but did not wish to tolerate an open-ended engagement with the American. Instead, they maintained a preference for reciprocal, gift-based relationships that strengthened political ties between nations, even as they asserted themselves as employers with the power to rehire or dismiss contracted labor at the end of a specified period of work. The Shawnees and Delawares integrated Euro-American ideas of apprenticeship, hired labor, and contract, but, as they built their own economic infrastructure, they asserted their relative autonomy, creating and reinforcing their political connections to the United States as contracting nations.

Political efforts to seek redress were not new, but by the 1820s, Native peoples' methods of seeking and exacting compensation for losses or grievances revealed the extent to which market considerations were at the forefront of their thinking. They reveal, too, the extent to which Native peoples' practical concerns had shifted by the nineteenth century, as well as the ways in which they used and grew the U.S. federal apparatus. Rather than seek gifts or adopt kin to remedy their losses during war with Osages, for example, Shawnees, Delawares, and others bargained for land in 1822. They "set up a claim against the Osages, of one thousand Dollars, for damages Sustained," and they rejected $500 worth of material goods in favor of a tract adjacent to their own in Missouri.[50] Employing U.S. officials in these claims-making endeavors became a key strategy for some Native peoples in the early republic, and the allied Natives' claim, in particular, demonstrates that the desire to remain united drove these Shawnees' and Delawares' politics. The aftermath of war with Osages thus offered some an opportunity to use U.S. policy to their advantage: the commodification of lands meant that Delawares, Shawnees, and their neighbors could bargain for Osage land in an effort to expand a territory in the west intended for the use of their people.

As these methods of combating and negotiating American empire traveled along with migrating Native Americans to places like Missouri, white settlers were not naive to such claims to power. Just as settlers destroyed Dennis's Station at the start of the War of 1812, they continued to attack Shawnees and their neighbors' agricultural infrastructure. The promises made by the civilization plan, meanwhile, meant that Shawnees, Delawares, and others could appeal to officials' own ideas and assumptions—while also insisting upon treaty obligations—and ask for compensation. "Six ploughs, and other Tools, were Stolen from us by the Whites," Shawnees and Delawares complained in

1820, and "our Houses have been broken open and our property robed [*sic*] by the Whites. Father! The Whites do not Steal these things merely for their value, but more to make us abandon our Land and Take it themselves."[51] Just as these violent settlers were savvy to Native peoples' ability to translate economic "improvements" or successes into political power and entrenchment in a coveted land, so, too, did Ohio Natives recognize Americans' greed: the thefts did not occur simply because the Shawnees and Delawares owned items of value, but rather because Euro-Americans wanted their lands. Framing their call for redress using "Father," moreover, underscored the obligations that these Shawnees and Delawares expected the United States to uphold.

Importantly, these Shawnee and Delaware victims of the thefts recognized their power to seek redress through petitions. They did not employ violence to remedy the situation, but rather they chose to implore the president of the United States to act. They actively sought compensation for their losses, and such efforts further cemented a political relationship with the United States that simultaneously undermined and solidified Native nations' independent power. From the U.S. perspective, these claimants depended upon the state for assistance; from the petitioners' perspectives, the familiar rules of political alliance and reciprocity demanded that the U.S. government make amends for the acts of its citizens. The politics of fictive kinship meant that the Shawnees and Delawares seeking redress possessed the right, from their perspective, to exact compensation from their "father." U.S. paternalism offered a means to erode Indigenous sovereignty, but it also provided opportunities for Shawnees, Delawares, and their neighbors to navigate and make claims upon the federal state bureaucracy in ways that reflected their own understandings of political reciprocity and association.

While the politics of petitioning involved the meeting of distinct political cultures, the claims nonetheless reveal how Native peoples endeavored to adapt their own economy in order to remain. In the same 1820 petition to the president, Shawnees and Delawares claimed that "Two White Men have Stolen Two Hundred Dollars in Species, One Rifle estimated at thirty Doll.s and one Bridle at Two Dollars."[52] Not only did these men demand redress in the form of monetary compensation, but they also demonstrated the extent to which ideas of private property were at the center of their demands. Like the locks placed upon Creeks' valuables by the nineteenth century, some likewise took stock of their possessions and quantified them in terms of monetary value.[53]

Though Native petitioners did not shy from addressing the U.S. president directly, more familiar relationships also, of course, offered numerous benefits to Native peoples, even if they were formed as a direct consequence of U.S. imperial ambitions. After years of hearing Euro-Americans' pronouncements regarding the benefits of civilization—and after receiving the material benefits that accompanied partnerships with civilizing agents such as the Baltimore Friends—Native peoples combined ideas of petition-making with ideas of either civilization or savagery, depending on their aims. Hendrick Aupaumut and his fellow Mohicans, for example, masterfully used the discourse of civilization both in an attempt to secure Indiana lands before and after the War of 1812 and, when that ultimately failed, to secure a place for the Stockbridge Mohicans in Wisconsin Territory during the 1820s and 1830s. Aupaumut himself cultivated relationships with government officials and Baltimore Friends during the 1790s warfare in the Ohio Country, and he also benefited from Friends' recommendation that he receive employment with the War Department as a civilizing agent. Aupaumut's initial petition, penned in 1819, suggests both that he saw himself as possessing a viable claim as well as a political relationship with the state. In 1818, White River Delawares in Indiana sold their lands to the United States, but members of the Stockbridge nation lived upon those lands with the Delawares since an 1808 treaty, and they were not consulted during the 1818 negotiations.[54] When the Christian Mohican petitioned the president of the United States and Congress for redress in 1819, he wove together discourses of religion, poverty, and missionary zeal in order to make his appeal. He claimed that his people were lately "few and weak," but that they and Americans were "all decended from one father and . . . acknowledge and worship one GOD."[55] He continued to explain that his "nation have long ago cast away their dumb idols which could not speak, and we now worship the only true GOD and Savior Jesus Christ. Our Children are taught to read and write, to Cultivate the Earth, and to worship, love obey and serve the Lord."[56] Not only did Aupaumut claim that his people held up their end of the bargain—they cultivated the earth according to the plans set forth by U.S. civilizing policies—but he also asserted that they could be instrumental in encouraging others to live in a "civilized" manner. A portion of the Stockbridge, Aupaumut explained, traveled to the White River in the hopes of civilizing the Delawares: "We saw them lying in darkness and paganism, and believed that our GOD called upon us to send among them a colony of our nation in which was built up a Church of our Lord and Savior, that we might be the means o [*sic*] Civilizing and Christianizing them and doeing to them great good."[57] The Stockbridge thus internalized the discourse of civilization and appealed to U.S. missionary ambitions: they offered government officials hope that "civilized" Natives could become civilizers.

Aupaumut laced the language of Christianity together with that of civilization and duty, and he used that rhetoric to assert Mohicans' rights. Complaining of the Stockbridges' loss of the lands sold in 1818, Aupaumut contended that the Stockbridges were "directed to leave them in a short time," and that their "right to them is denied."[58] Weaving ideas of property and investment into his claim, he continued to explain that "a part of our nation, as we have told you, removed to these lands and possessed them with the Delawares and Munsees and made large improvements on them, at great expense to our nation, to prepare them for us."[59] Aupaumut then closed his appeal with another consideration of the Stockbridges' rights: "we pray that you will consider our just rights, and set off to our Nation such a location of these lands as we are justly entitled to—that we may not suffer under this wrong and that we may thus be aided in our designs, and our nation again be . . . in peace and our hearts quieted."[60] Just as U.S. settlers claimed a right to the lands they developed, so, too, did these petitions. Though the Stockbridge eventually moved to Wisconsin Territory, civilizing mission work, its accompanying rhetoric and that of U.S. settler colonialism nonetheless offered Indigenous peoples additional means to use U.S. economic and political ideas in order to confront growing U.S. state power.[61]

Just eight years after making the 1819 appeal, couched as it was in language of Christianity and civilization, Aupaumut's signature graced a piece of paper that made yet another appeal, this time, to the ABCFM and for missionary aid. Rather than emphasize their civilized state or their belief in Christianity, however, the appeal began, "We thank the Great Spirit that he has favored your Society with compassionate feelings for our Nation. We rejoice greatly that you have sent the Rev Jesse Miner to pay us a visit for the purpose of ascertaining our true state & condition to enable you to know what you could do for us as also for those of our Brethren around us."[62] Here, the Stockbridge Indians appealed to their supposed "heathen" state by calling upon the power of the Great Spirit. They downplayed their "civilization" (which was, apparently, lost in the eight years between appeals) by thanking the ABCFM for being willing to witness their "true state." What was more, the Stockbridges, Aupaumut among them, were eager to discern what the missionary society "could do for us." The Stockbridges, armed with their long history of missionary encounters, knew that missionaries held many keys: to "civilization" and

Christianity, but also to powerful political alliances, economic infrastructure, Euro-American labor, and the U.S. government's ear.

Just as Aupaumut cultivated relationships with Euro-Americans and used discourse of civilization to political advantage, in the Ohio Country, Shawnees' close relationship with John Johnston offered a potential means to secure payment for crimes committed by Euro-Americans in ways similar to Shawnees and Delawares' petition to the U.S. president. Johnston complained to the commissioner of Indian Affairs, Thomas L. McKenney, in 1825 that he was "often compelled to grant renumeration to the Whites out of the Annuities of the Indians, and when an Indian suffers loss, which is now frequently the case . . . no redress can be afforded for want of funds at the disposal of the Agent. It is beleived [*sic*] $1000 would not satisfy the claims of this nature now pending, and which are just and equitable."[63] Johnston went on to submit a detailed list of "depredations committed on their property by our Citizens" on behalf of the Indians near his Piqua agency in 1827.[64] The Seneca Captain Smith claimed $35 for a horse stolen; John Sky, $65 for one horse shot and another stolen; Blue Jacket's daughter demanded $35 for a horse stolen; others listed saddles taken by Euro-Americans as well as horses and cows stolen, shot, or killed by the same, and money, furs, blankets, and a kettle stolen.[65] The goods ultimately totaled just over $1,000—a debt Johnston forwarded onto the U.S. federal government on behalf of the mostly Senecas and Shawnees near Piqua.[66] The agent performed this duty out of a concern for "the loss of their confidence in the justice of the United States," and such work served both his own interests and those of the Native Americans near his agency.[67] Indeed, it appears that the act of claiming damages against Euro-Americans became so common that, by 1828, Johnston needed to make clear to McKenney that a "list of Claims of Shawanoese [*sic*] who have emigrated from Ohio west of the Mississippi" were "unfounded and ought not to be paid."[68] The requests reveal Piqua-area Natives' recognition that cultivating a close relationship with Johnston offered a means to make claims upon the U.S. state.

As the next chapter will show, such claims could, however, prove to be a double-edged sword. Johnston fought for Senecas' and Shawnees' property rights, but he also advocated for their removal as a direct result of the damages suffered upon the peoples near his agency. Immediately following his recommendation that Piqua-area Indians receive compensation, he wrote, "These evils and a multitude of others which readily occur to your mind are rapidly encreasing upon us, and after a considerable part of my life spent managing this description of persons I am free to declare, that in my judgment there is no adequate remedy but removal to a Country of their own, where a suitable Government could be established over them."[69] While Euro-Americans would have called for removals regardless, Native peoples' authority, successes, and presence likely hastened Euro-Americans' calls for their removal from eastern lands.

Though claims-making produced mixed consequences, it nonetheless reveals the extent to which Native peoples engaged with the politics and strategies embraced by U.S. citizens more broadly. Petitioning formed a political bond between petitioner and the state, and oftentimes, Native peoples living in the Ohio Country or who migrated from that region not only employed the tools of petition writing and claims making, but they also employed the discourse of civilization to their own ends; they thus turned U.S. imperial rhetoric and policies on their head. Even when material conditions were harsh, they found ways to appeal to government officials' ideas regarding Native Americans, poverty, and civilization.

* * *

The mission complex in the Ohio Country could offer material benefits to the region's Indigenous peoples, but it also offered additional means by which Shawnees, Miamis, Stockbridges, and their neighbors could make claims upon the federal state after the War of 1812. A discourse of civilization increasingly intersected with discourses of rights and nation to create a complicated nexus of ideas that both rendered Native peoples further intertwined with emerging U.S. intellectual currents and offered them opportunities to manipulate policies to their advantage. Such strategies reveal the ways in which Native peoples adjusted to life in the increasingly populated Ohio Country: as Euro-American settlers endeavored to make a living, Native peoples confronted their own problems of money, work, and survival in a rapidly changing economy.

The various strategies adopted by Shawnees, Delawares, Miamis, and their neighbors—whether petition writing, cultivating connections with area traders, or asserting economic independence—reveal that economic and political change accelerated by the mission complex in the Ohio Country offered the means by which Indigenous peoples simultaneously continued to assert their cultural, political, and economic independence and consciously borrowed from and adapted to Euro-American ideals. Some Ohio Country Natives understood that they could carve a place with the emerging political and economic order in the region, and as they made steps toward doing just that, they increasingly frustrated Euro-Americans. By using the mission complex, civilizing policies, and broader economic changes to their advantage, Native peoples forced the United States and its inhabitants to recognize that Indigenous power was enduring.

Such efforts did not come, however, without a price. Natives' claims-making bolstered the U.S. federal state apparatus, and it linked them ever closer with the legal and bureaucratic policies of the United States. What was more, when Native peoples dared deviate from U.S. officials' ideas of "proper" Indigenous behavior—when they actually succeeded in adapting and adopting the ways of the American empire—they fueled calls for their removal. As Chapter 7 demonstrates, by appropriating U.S. Indian policies for their own purposes, some Indigenous peoples forced Americans to grapple with the contradictions that lay at the heart of their civilization schemes. Ideas of race, class, and difference increasingly rose to the fore of discourse as, ironically, the differences between Euro-Americans and some Native peoples eroded. Native power and authority endured, yet Americans increasingly supported removal policies in a quest to acquire lands but also to render the United States a homogenous, inclusive nation—a nation built on the policies and politics of exclusion.

When Hugh McKeen declared the Miamis to be a "damnd rebelious race," he expressed frustration at their unwillingness to disappear from the Ohio Country on Americans' terms. That he wrote the statement with Richardville in mind is not surprising. The Miami leader was, in many ways, the exemplar of what many considered to be Indigenous rebellion in the early years of American empire. Richardville, along with Shawnees at Wapakoneta, Delawares and Senecas near Piqua, and others who dared remain in the region, turned U.S. imperial rhetoric and policies on their head and adopted and adapted to civilizing policies and the economic, political, and social relations established by the mission complex and a changing economy. They took part in an imperial struggle on Americans' terms, but they eked out victories that frustrated U.S. attempts to take the region by force or for no financial compensation or simply entirely on the state's own terms. When Wapakoneta debtors ruined George Johnston's finances, they secured items that made their own lives a bit better, and they did so on their own terms by partially paying off debts through barter of furs and by becoming economically savvy neighbors in the midst of a population that sought their physical and cultural removal. When Delawares and Shawnees petitioned for economic redress, they invested the federal state with authority, but they also forced government officials to fulfill economic and political obligations that drew upon Indigenous peoples' understandings of reciprocity and political alliance. They secured, in some cases, funds and goods that frustrated, at least in the short term, Ohio Country Euro-Americans' attempts to drive them off their lands. Ohio Country Native leaders and peoples, then, ultimately used the tools available to them. They ensured that they continued to exercise their power to shape their own lives and also to mold the contours of American imperial policy and the U.S. market economy and state. Such tools would prove useful as they confronted Euro-Americans' growing calls for their removal.

CHAPTER 6

"The Best and Cheapest Way to Get Rid of Them"

Speculative Philanthropy and Indigenous Dispossession

In 1828, Indian agent John Johnston faced a series of conundrums. Euro-Americans living near his Piqua, Ohio, home and Indian agency pushed for the removal of the state's Indigenous peoples. At the same time, Shawnees and their Native neighbors pressured the cash-strapped U.S. federal government for financial compensation for their lands. Certain that the Shawnees "cannot go upon their own means," however, Johnston implored the superintendent of Indian Affairs, Thomas L. McKenney, for additional funds to facilitate their removal. He explained that "the best and cheapest way to get rid of them—would be to—afford aid to individuals, families, and small parties." Such assistance, he suggested, "would releive [*sic*] us from all within my agency," and "it would be much the cheapest plan and by far the most agreeable to the Indians." Such a scheme would then enable them to "purchase of each family when ready to go their right to the soil" as well as to "compensate them for their improvements, and this would nearly cover all expence of emigration." Failure to offer adequate funds, he argued, would ensure that "the whole business will be knocked in the head, and we shall be put back for many years." Johnston concluded his letter to McKenney by estimating that "$5.000 would be sufficient for a year."[1]

Johnston penned his letter soon after he returned from Columbus, Ohio, where he attended to his business as one of the state's canal commissioners.[2] One of the state's major canal projects, the Miami and Erie Canal, ultimately passed through his Indian agency seat at Piqua, Ohio. As canal commissioner, he had a personal and political stake in the success of the canal; as owner of a farm at Piqua, he had a financial stake in the canal's progress; as Indian agent at Piqua, he had the power to negotiate Natives' removal from the waterway's path. As the Miami Tribe of Oklahoma would eventually note, that canal, and, more particularly, the lock located near Johnston's farm, controlled the water that carried Miamis southward and away from their homes during their forced removal in 1846.[3]

Johnston's letter to McKenney, his cost-conscious request for aid, as well as his own interest in canal politics demonstrate the extent to which individuals' speculative philanthropy facilitated both what scholars term the "transportation revolution" and Indigenous dispossession in the Ohio Country. Johnston shows, too, that speculative philanthropy was not merely the realm of missionaries and reformers: government rhetoric and personnel—from high- to low-level officials—also wed ideas of benevolence and interest in profit together. The 1820s and onward saw Euro-American population growth in the region, and it also ushered in a period of rapid transformation in economic infrastructure—canals and railroads in particular—that rendered, from settlers' perspectives, the presence of Native Americans increasingly intolerable.[4] Euro-Americans' quest for economic and moral capital, as well as their belief in their ideals of civilization and their own enlightened exceptionalism—and, as Chapter 7 will show, their desire to convince others of that same exceptionalism—however, meant that they increasingly cloaked the intertwined work of Indigenous dispossession, economic transformation, and profit in the garb of humanitarianism.

Missionaries' work was part of this effort, and they increasingly and explicitly wove ideas of economy into their civilizing projects, ensuring that the mission complex continued to facilitate those changes and contribute to Euro-Americans' desire to claim the mantle of benevolence. In some cases, mission work took on the characteristics of a business enterprise: cost-efficiency and systematic organization came to the fore. What was more, the very same missionaries who spearheaded the U.S. government's civilization—those whose work U.S. officials could point to in making a case for U.S. benevolence—were, in some cases, among those who stood to reap—and did reap—financial and political benefits from Indian removals. As the United States pushed Native peoples from their homes, missionaries followed, and they facilitated the endurance of the mission complex that made some new lands even more valuable from the perspective of land-hungry settlers as they simultaneously worked to empty the lands Native peoples left behind to make way for economic innovations.

As the balance of power tipped ever more in favor of Euro-Americans in the region, and as settlers endeavored to portray themselves as benevolent participants in a grand republican experiment that was, in actuality, premised upon the profitability of seizing Indigenous lands, Native peoples continued to work to maintain their homes and their authority. Some did so in part by engaging in and shaping settlers' own politics and policies of philanthropy and speculation and by continuing their engagement with the regional economy. Indeed, Johnston's letter made it clear that the United States government should "compensate [Shawnees] for their improvements." Those improvements and Johnston's call for compensation were the tangible results of both Shawnees' own labors and Euro-Americans' labors as part of the federal government's civilization plan, and they were a direct consequence of enduring Indigenous authority and presence. As Chapter 5 demonstrated, some Native peoples utilized connections with nearby missionaries, laborers, and markets to invest in their lands as part of an effort to realize their own visions of a future in their Ohio Country homes, and they continued to do so even as settlers' calls for their removal escalated. Shawnees, Miamis, and their neighbors thus navigated the political landscape of the early republic, often manipulating settlers' own ideas regarding Americans' philanthropic sensibilities to their benefit when they could, even when they saw their hopes for the future shattered by imperial policies and settler greed. They continued to use to their advantage—sometimes successfully and other times less so—both the politics of speculative philanthropy as well as the very philanthropists who contributed to the American imperial project. While speculative philanthropy, Indigenous dispossession, and in turn the growth of American capitalism were each key to the development of American empire, Native peoples' own negotiation of U.S. policies and politics likewise ensured that Miamis, Shawnees, and their Indigenous neighbors not only survived but left their mark on North America's newest imperial power.

* * *

The years following the War of 1812 saw dramatic changes in communications and transportation technologies such as canals, railroads, and the telegraph, and the Ohio Country was the locus of much of this activity.[5] While the mission complex further integrated Indigenous lands into the U.S. market economy, the transportation revolution promised to better connect those and other "improved lands"—along with their agricultural surpluses—to continental and global markets, particularly as the waning of the British and French Empires in the Atlantic facilitated Euro-Americans' own access to the seas.[6] Investment in the Ohio Country's transportation and agriculture fed the cotton-producing markets in the south, New Orleans, and beyond, and it translated into opportunities to reap vast profits. Agricultural production and transportation innovations, then, each bolstered the slavery-based economies of the south—economies that were likewise integral to the rise of American capitalism in the United States. Indigenous dispossession in the Ohio Country thus possessed both regional and continental consequences—for peoples throughout the continent as well as for the U.S. economy. Economic growth went hand in hand with imperial development as the U.S. metropole endeavored to incorporate more and more agriculturally rich and increasingly well-connected lands. With profits on the horizon, Indigenous dispossession and displacement became, from the perspectives of Euro-American settlers and investors, all the more imperative. Transportation technologies promised additional markets for agricultural goods that were increasing in demand, and settlers clamored to build canals, turnpikes, and eventually railroads in the Ohio Country's agriculturally rich and increasingly population-rich areas.

While many missions of the 1820s were in Choctaw and Cherokee Country, both federally and privately funded missions coupled with the rhetoric of the civilization plan in the Ohio Country to complement the region's transportation and economic changes more broadly, and they continued to support the government's desire to accumulate land. In addition to the Society of Friends' ongoing work among the Shawnees, missions at Fort Wayne and Upper Sandusky received federal funding in the 1820s. Such funding was a direct result of Congress's passage of the Civilization Fund Act of 1819.[7] That act offered $10,000 annually to support missionary projects, and it codified twenty years of partnership between Friends and the federal government. Drawing upon the example of Friends' cooperation with the state, the War Department incorporated other societies into its cadre of philanthropic partnerships—most especially the American Board of Commissioners for Foreign Missions (ABCFM), established in 1810, as well as Methodists and the Baptist Board of Foreign Missions in America—by offering funds with the act.[8]

Individuals and societies received the civilization funds for building schools—not for theological purposes—and the monies were contingent upon those institutions' success and number of pupils. The institutions that received funding during the middle decades of the nineteenth century included literacy education in their curriculum, yet mechanical and agricultural education and labor remained central.[9] Not only were the funds' recipients charged with basic construction of educational infrastructure such as schoolhouses and mills, but the government also expected them to "impress on the minds of the Indians, the friendly and benevolent views of the government towards them."[10] In addition to bureaucratizing missionaries' relations to the state, then, the act institutionalized both the United States' desire to become a benevolent empire and the role of speculative philanthropy in building economic infrastructure.[11]

Funding such projects with federal funds reveals that missions and civilizing work continued to have long-term investment implications for both the federal government and private individuals alike, just as they had during the earliest development of the mission complex. Such investments also, however, offered an effective means of circumventing political debates that grew increasingly pressing after the War of 1812. While secretary of the treasury Albert Gallatin pushed for federal support of infrastructure development during the earliest years of the nineteenth century, the war with Britain and Native peoples encouraged U.S. government officials to realize anew that roads and canals were vital to the republic for both economic and political reasons. Individuals such as Henry Clay worked to find solutions to the republic's infrastructure problem in response.[12] Politicians and policymakers, however, disagreed on whether the federal government should spearhead such efforts or whether the states should do so along with private investors. Speculative philanthropy—in the form of civilization funds and general funding of civilizing efforts in Indian Country—offered a means to contribute to those economic projects in the Ohio Country, what is now western New York State, and in the south (all of which had federally funded missions) through a combination of federal, state, and private funds. The Civilization Fund Act's offer to federally subsidize infrastructure and the so-called "improvement" of Indigenous lands complemented both the burgeoning economic changes already underway in the Ohio Country along with those hoped for by settlers and settler-investors. The civilization scheme's intersections with economic projects reveal once again that a combination of local, federal, and individual power, investment, and interests were key to nation- and empire-building.[13]

Any settler-conceived revolution in transportation or economy, however, first required the presence of what Euro-Americans declared to be evidence of economic progression, including marketable agricultural commodities and Indigenous dispossession.[14] Civilizing work contributed to both simultaneously. With civilizing efforts and funds, the federal government, along with private individuals, contributed to the presence of U.S. authority in the region and to the increase in what Euro-American settlers understood to be "improved land"—land upon which economic infrastructure existed. That "improved land" was precisely what canal-builders and, later, railroad investors prized. As one team of researchers shows, investors in transportation infrastructure such as railroads did not plan lines randomly. Rather, factors such as agricultural output and (Euro-American settler) population density aided in the selection of railroad routes: increased agricultural outputs mitigated risk for investors as those places tended to possess the population numbers and markets that would ensure a railroad's success.[15] So, too, did the removal of the region's Native peoples. A program that increased agricultural production in an area thus contributed to the likelihood that those lands would be targets for infrastructure investment, particularly in the years following the War of 1812.

Both the developing U.S. economy and the Civilization Fund Act encouraged missionaries to conceive of and brand their mission endeavors in a manner tailored to ideas of economy, "improvement," and profit. Such framing captured on paper how the worlds of business and mission work collided. It also, however, suggests the lucrative nature of Native peoples' lands, as well as their potential to become even more so with additional infrastructure. In preceding centuries, missionaries in the field, such as the Moravians and Jesuits, usually wrote to their home congregations with news of their feats of conversion among the "heathens" in efforts to solicit funds for future work. By the 1820s, however, Baptists, Friends, and Methodists often wrote not merely of religious or moral triumph over savagery but of economic change, and their audience now included the U.S. government officials from whom they solicited funding to support civilizing missionary endeavors. In 1816, for example, Friends Philip E. Thomas and James Ellicott penned a letter to the secretary of war describing several Shawnee and Wyandot towns. They noted the number of fenced acres, planted crops, and at one town they also "ascertained that there is a good mill seat convenient to their village which may be improved at a moderate expence." They went on to note "that there is a good mill seat on the Sandusky river near this [Wyandot] village and that these Indians are extremely anxious to receive instruction in their farming business."[16] Such information bolstered missionary appeals for support, and it offered a means to envision the possibilities for infrastructure and "improvement."

In the early 1820s, moreover, Baptist missionary Isaac McCoy traveled to Miami Country, and he opened a school near Fort Wayne, Indiana, that offered reading and writing instruction. That school also ensured, however, that males were "instructed in agriculture, and Mechanic Arts," and "the Females in Spinning, Weaving, Knitting, Sewing &c."[17] In an effort to obtain federal support for his mission near Fort Wayne, McCoy informed secretary of war John C. Calhoun in 1821 that "our prospects in relation to those several tribes . . . are truly inviting. And we trust that the patronage of the Government, And the liberality of the public, will render our funds adequate to the undertaking: I therefore humbly solicit a share of the 10,000 Dollars appropriated by Government for Indian reform."[18]

To bolster his argument for funding, McCoy detailed both the immense labor required for his mission work as well as ample evidence of his mission's economic contributions. He explained that "beside the Superintendent & the Directress, there are belonging to the Establishment. A School Teacher, An Agent to procure Supplies of provision &c- And four labouring men. two assistent females. and a labouring woman." McCoy then wrote, "We have cultivated this season 35 Acres of Land, 100 have 8 spinning wheels and a Loom—The property belonging to the Mission consists of Land improvements, Horses, Cattle, Hogs, farming utensils, Houshold furniture. &c—and estimated at 1,800 Dollars."[19] Thus, McCoy recognized that a successful appeal for federal monies depended upon the extent to which he could make a case for his essential role in what Euro-Americans understood to be economic progress. The prospect of receiving U.S. federal funds encouraged him and other missionaries to offer a particular type of missionary work and reporting.

McCoy's letter points to a shift in how missionaries publicized and reported their work in the early republic, and his example also illustrates the extent to which both individuals and philanthropic societies participated in and intertwined their work with the developing economy and ideas of profit. McCoy's own Baptist Board increasingly wed mission work with ideas of business. Writing to a missionary in Cherokee Country, Lucien Bolles, executive secretary of the board, wrote, "The missionary must want to know his own limits exactly, what he may do under the sanctions of his employers and what he may not do; what money he may call for and what he may not." Bolles went on to say that the board was "forming a plan of systematic operations" and that the missionary should take note of "whether the number of persons employed as teachers, or otherwise, cannot be immediately reduced; whether the lands under improvement cannot be made more fully to furnish the support of the station."[20] Here, the board considered the bottom line as paramount—in part due to the fact that civilizing mission work was expensive. A changing economy and rising costs encouraged missionary societies to both appeal for more money from the federal government and their congregations, as well as work to improve the efficiency of their sites.

Isaac McCoy's voluminous writings demonstrate that the mission complex continued to operate in Indiana into the 1820s and beyond and that he supported it wholeheartedly. After working in Fort Wayne, McCoy opened the Carey Mission on Potawatomi lands in what was then Michigan Territory, and he ultimately traveled to Kansas to continue his work when U.S. policymakers and settlers forced the region's Native peoples from their Ohio Country homes. Throughout his journeys, issues of economy and profit were at the heart of his operations, and he connected his religious and economic work explicitly with a broader American imperial project. Individuals like McCoy thus demonstrate the extent to which economic change combined with speculative philanthropy and rhetoric of humanitarianism to facilitate a process of Indigenous removals and dispossession that unfolded over time. In 1827, McCoy published his *Remarks on the Practicability of Indian Reform, Embracing Their Colonization*. McCoy framed Indian removal explicitly as a colonization scheme—drawing direct parallels with African colonization in Liberia—even going so far as to title one chapter "The only hopeful Plan for reforming the Indians is that of colonizing them."[21] The Baptist's vision was grounded in his belief that Native peoples would flourish best if removed from Euro-American society. He was, quite simply, a pro-removal missionary imperialist, and, like other missionaries of the time, his work facilitated U.S. policies of Indigenous dispossession, albeit in a more explicit manner than others.[22] Superintendent of Indian Affairs Thomas L. McKenney took McCoy's plan seriously and offered the missionary his encouragement.[23] McCoy wrote that other missionaries did too little to better Native peoples' conditions, that their efforts worked merely to "soften, as it were, the pillows of the dying."[24] Though this was his estimation of missionaries in 1827, the perpetuation of the mission complex across space and time revealed that missionaries were complicit in much more than he gave them credit for.

Colonization of Native peoples, McCoy argued while drawing upon the Bible, could save those "scattered, pealed [*sic*], and perishing people" from "their total extermination."[25] He also made it clear that it could prove a financial boon for the federal government. Rather than allow Native peoples to remain on their lands until treaties extinguished their claims, McCoy proposed that they receive continued compensation for their lands in the form of interest payments over a period of thirty years. To this plan, McCoy devoted several pages of his work, writing, "I suppose there is yet within the States of Illinois and Indiana, and the Territory of Michigan, 10,000,000 of acres of Indian land, not ceded to the United States, which, added to the 45,000,000 mentioned above, make 55,000,000 acres. This, at the rate of sixty-two and a half cents an acre, would be worth to us, free of all cost, $34,375,000. The interest on which, at six per cent per annum, would be $2,062,500."[26] He continued to argue that

> If our Government should choose to positively invest the stock under consideration, then there would be at the end of these years, belonging to the United States, not only the country itself, but also a disposable fund of $34,375,000. This, we recollect, is only one verse in the chapter. The calculations which have led us to this fund, include only the Indians south of the 46th degree of northern latitude, east of the Mississippi river, skirting for its southern limits, the northern parts of Illinois and Indiana, and extending a little distance into Michigan Territory, east of Lake Michigan. All others, with their millions of territory, have been left out of our calculations.[27]

U.S. financial interests were similarly at the heart of McCoy's argument regarding "the most eligible Situation for the Colony."[28] Ultimately claiming that west of Missouri was most ideal for the colony, he wrote that "obviously no part of our sea coast ever could have been, nor ever can be, spared for such a purpose. In point of commercial advantages the shores of our Lakes on the north, are second only to our sea-coasts on the east and south, and do, therefore, for the same reasons, forbid them a home on their borders."[29] He ultimately concluded that "a good grazing country must be, of all others, the best adapted to the condition of a people in their transition from the hunter to the civilized state."[30] McCoy made clear that commercial connections and considerations undergirded his plans for Native peoples' futures.

In the midst of his planning and calculations, McCoy was clear to argue that the proposed removal plan also ensured a steady stream of funds for the government's civilization work. McCoy's plan thus left room for the United States to achieve both an economic boon and a benevolent reputation. He wrote that "without doubt, the revenue would commence and would increase on a scale sufficiently large to meet the necessities of any civilizing operations that our Government would choose to adopt."[31] Though he argued that the government's current combination of treaties and annuity funds were "a lamentable waste of publick treasure," both the $10,000 annual Civilization Fund and treaty stipulations pertaining to education were "two items of annual expenditure of Government on the Indians which have not been wasted or lost."[32] McCoy here made it clear that the civilization plan should continue undisturbed. "Civilizing operations," he argued, could continue and would be paid for out of the interest payments made to removed Native peoples as well as the Civilization Fund. In other words, the money *McCoy* received from the federal government—and from Natives' own annuities—should, in his estimation, continue to flow undisturbed. This was a plan that appealed to government officials, settlers, and people like McCoy alike.

McCoy usually lamented his own financial limitations and endeavored to pull upon potential philanthropist-donor's heartstrings, and his work in places like Fort Wayne and at the Carey Mission ultimately alerted some who viewed his efforts with a critical gaze. One writer, Timothy S. Smith, suspected that McCoy strove for personal profit and ran his mission to fulfill that quest. While we should treat such indictments with care, Smith's claims do resonate with the broader trends that marked missions in the early republic. Smith claimed that McCoy's Carey Mission "was a mercantile trading post, rather than a sanctuary. It was a place of resort for the purchase of cattle, grain, potatoes, bacon, etc. The Blacksmith that was deployed by Government to work for the Indians was a great part of his time working for the whites, and the iron and steel that was annually sent to the Indians, by stipulation of the treaty, more or less, made use of by those superintendents, which caused the poor Indians to complain. . . . Such were the speculations for the good of the poor Indians (as Mr. McCoy termed it)."[33] Smith went on to claim that McCoy would travel to solicit funds for his work, writing that McCoy "could perform his tours to the East and the South, setting forth the mighty works which he had wrought in the West, and soliciting charity with a gracious face, which no doubt caused, in many instances, the poor and oppressed to contribute, through godly motives, only to enrich the pockets of a sinister and artful speculator."[34] McCoy's record-keeping, as well as the Baptist Board of Foreign Missions in America's notion "that our expenditures for a living were too great," lent credence to this charge.[35] In 1840, McCoy endeavored to defend himself and wrote that the board "desired me to accept a specific salary for the support of myself and family, and that these accounts should embrace only what they termed extra expenses. But the Indian pupils of our school, and all whom we employed to aid us, either in the school or elsewhere, fed at the same table, and the Indian youths were also clothed and lodged at the mission; so that it was impossible for us to keep accounts of expenditures for others, distinct from those of myself and family."[36] Such may have been the case, yet McCoy's history of skimming from federal funds—the executive secretary of the Baptist Board noted in 1827 that McCoy used $700 from the Civilization Fund monies to send his son to Columbian College—suggest that Smith's accusations had merit.[37]

Smith's indictment explicitly laid bare the economic considerations behind mission work. Since the earliest years of the nineteenth century, missions had operated as part of a broader economic network. The Indian factory system ensured that Native people as well as neighboring Euro-Americans could purchase goods that were usually shipped to places like Fort Wayne, Indiana, from urban manufacturing and shipping centers like Philadelphia and Baltimore.[38] McCoy operated the Carey Mission toward the end of the factory system and after, and it is therefore likely that the mission was, in many respects, "a mercantile trading post" that borrowed from the earlier pattern of consumerism in the name of "civilization" established by missions' connections with the factory system. McCoy's own reporting in 1820, when he requested federal funds to bolster his mission work, reveals that his missions employed laborers from nearby towns and agents to procure supplies. And indeed the Baptist Board, too, was concerned with the uncertainty surrounding how much money went to employed laborers at mission sites. Smith, whether he had a personal grievance against McCoy or no, rightly noted the business that was agricultural mission work in the early republic. The mission complex was alive and well in the Ohio Country and beyond—into 1820s Michigan Territory.

Perhaps even more illuminating is that Smith repeatedly—and accurately—refers to McCoy's work as a form of speculation. Individuals and the U.S. government alike could profit from mission expenditures—both in the short and long term. According to Lucien Bolles of the Baptist Board, McCoy funneled the society's federal funding to send his son to college, and he was not alone. Bolles also noted that another missionary, Luther Rice, used $1,300 of the Civilization Fund money to pay off his own debts.[39] Yet it was not just individuals who benefited financially from civilizing mission work. Missions were premised on the hopes that investment in Indigenous peoples' education and civilization would eventually solve what was, to many, an "Indian problem" of immense proportions. They used federal funds, and they harnessed the labor of missionaries and Euro-American settlers in efforts to build buildings, fences, and infrastructure. To some, missions were investments in a peaceful future full of agrarian Native Americans who required fewer lands; to others, they were a means to transform landscapes—free of Native peoples—in ways that would contribute to the linking of the region's agricultural bounties with global markets. In myriad ways, then, missions could be both profit-minded and investment opportunities.

While the examples of McCoy and Rice suggest that some settlers found ways to profit from civilizing work individually, Indian agent John Johnston's own position as an Ohio canal commissioner, a federal Indian agent, and the owner of land through which a canal ultimately passed at Piqua illustrates the combination of federal and local power that contributed to the growth of the republic. What is more, it illuminates the ways in which speculative philanthropy, the transportation revolution, and dispossession went hand in hand after 1815. Johnston, who worked to supply goods to Delawares during the War of 1812 and who frequently wove rhetoric of charity and philanthropy into his official letters, understood that civilizing work was but a preamble to a broader story. Writing from his agency and home in Piqua in 1816, Johnston wrote to secretary of war William Crawford to ask that he be allowed to hire men to labor on area Delaware, Wyandot, and Shawnee lands, explaining that "labouring men is much wanted to instruct them in farming and to enable them to live on their own industry." Yet such labor, Johnston noted, would be needed only temporarily. He concluded his letter by proposing that "the expence be deducted from the first purchase of land made from these Indians it would be but a few years and the Government would be amply reimbursed."[40] While Johnston refrains from explicitly saying that civilizing efforts would add to the government's ability to be "amply" reimbursed, the implication is clear: philanthropic efforts could be and were an investment in a future where Native people lived on smaller plots of land or lived somewhere else entirely.

Johnston was not alone. The efforts of Baltimore Friends such as Philip E. Thomas and other members of the Ellicott family also illustrate the ways in which individuals and speculative philanthropy rendered civilizing work and civilizers central to the political and economic growth of the imperial state. Philip E. Thomas, a prominent Quaker and clerk of the Indian Concerns Committee for the Baltimore Yearly Meeting, looked to the Ohio Country and saw profit. As clerk for the Indian Concerns committee, he was directly involved with the missions' project in Ohio and Indiana, and he worked with the Ohio and Indiana Yearly Meetings to facilitate their operation. Thomas also, however, served as president of the Baltimore and Ohio Railroad during his tenure as clerk. He was not alone: other individuals used their positions of power to dispossess the Haudenosaunee in what is now western New York State and line their own pockets.[41]

The efforts of men like Thomas actively engaged the politics of risk and profit, and they reveal the extent to which policies in Indian Country were both a product and producer of the emerging U.S. economy. In 1827, Thomas, clerk of the Indian Concerns committee, penned, along with a committee of like-minded citizens, the *Proceedings of Sundry Citizens of Baltimore, Convened for the Purpose of Devising the Most Efficient Means of Improving the Intercourse Between That City and the Western States*. The publication sought to convince fellow citizens and entrepreneurs that the Baltimore and Ohio Railroad was a lucrative investment. Thomas served as the chairman of the committee, and for Baltimore land owners he estimated a "50 pr. ct. appreciation upon the value of this real estate in consideration of the increase of the Trade of that city from the opining of this new and cheap means of communication between it and the west."[42] He further estimated that the "appreciation of real estate in the counties adjacent to the line of the road, as above estimated by the United States Board of Engineers. $12,000,000," while for "the Western States directly benefitted by the road, $17,280,000."[43] To "convince any one that there is no probability that the Trade here estimated will be likely hereafter to decline," Thomas insisted that "it will only be necessary to observe, that the population, upon which the calculations are founded, is rapidly increasing every year, and that it must for several succeeding generations, still continue to increase."[44] He continued to write:

> There is now a dense population extending as far west as the junction of the Osage River with the Missouri: which is about nine hundred miles west of the Ohio River at Wheeling; of course the white population has, within the last thirty years, travelled that distance, or more than thirty miles each year, and is at this time advancing with as great, if not greater impetus, than at any former period: and according to all probability, if not checked by some unforeseen circumstances, it will, within the next thirty years reach the Rocky Mountains, or even to the Pacific Ocean. We have therefore, no reason to look for any falling off in this Trade, but on the contrary, for an increase of it, to an extent of which no estimate could now be formed.[45]

Missing from this argument was an obvious issue—*especially* given Thomas's role as clerk of the Indian Concerns committee in Baltimore. The obvious issue was, of course, the continuing presence of Indigenous peoples in areas both proposed as future sites of railroads and canals, as well as in the locations where he prophesized that the Euro-American population would grow. Railroads were about commerce, and Thomas made it clear that commerce and population—Euro-American population—went hand in hand. Thus, the clerk of the Indian Concerns committee himself imagined profits, and he premised those profits on the disappearance of Native peoples, even as his work on Indian affairs perpetuated the mission project in Ohio. The civilization plan and its emphasis on agricultural education and labor supported his vision: Native peoples would either continue to move further from Euro-American settlers or they would disappear within the ranks of agrarian laborers who would produce the crops that would ultimately enrich urban investors.

While Thomas represents one of the more obvious instances of the intersection between profit and acquisition of Indian lands, leading Baltimore Quakers' own business ventures in Baltimore shed some light on just how closely U.S. Indian policies—particularly removal—were caught up in an emerging economy that revolved around profit and speculation. Prominent Baltimore Friends engaged in speculation just as many non-Quakers did. The Ellicotts, in particular, but also the Thomas and Tyson families, worked together to secure contiguous land holdings in rural Baltimore as well as key locations along the city's waterfront. In 1804, for example, Jonathan, Elias, George, John, Benjamin, and James Ellicott, along with Isaac and Elisha Tyson—most of whom sat on the Baltimore Yearly Meeting's Indian Concerns committee—bought a piece of property in Baltimore City for $700, and they received all buildings and infrastructure that the previous owner, Matthew Pawson, had built.[46] That same year, the same group of Friends purchased another piece of the city's wharf for $500.[47] The Ellicotts, meanwhile, purchased a number of rural plots. Such purchases were not new, but had been a key piece of the Ellicott business model since the eighteenth century.[48] The family built a major flour business and, with their lands, was able to largely control the management of grain and thus the industry in the area. Each purchase—plots named "Newtown," "Parish's Range," "Georgia," and, perhaps most creatively, "Cuckold-Maker's-Palace-Enlarged"—came with all the "Land, Houses Mills Buildings Improvements and Premises."[49] They also received access to all "Roads Paths Passages Waters Watercourses Woods

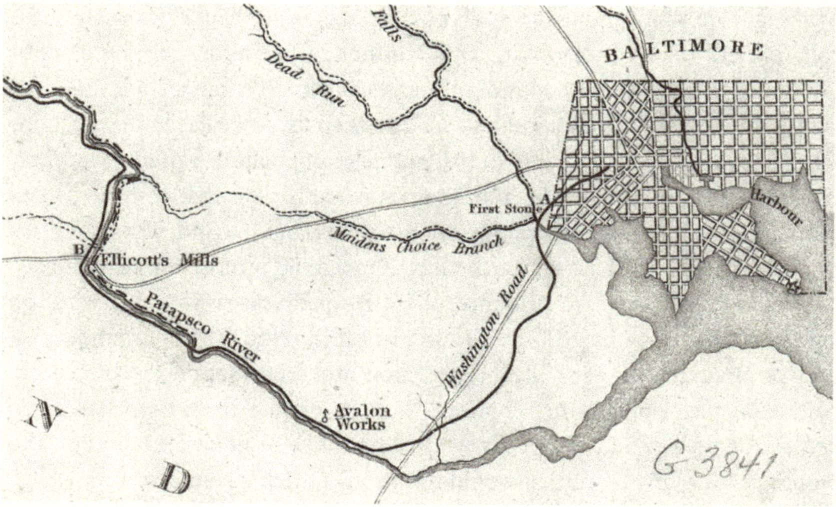

Figure 6. Map of the routes surveyed for the B&O Railroad. One such surveyed route passed through the Ellicotts' land holdings near Baltimore. Library of Congress, Geography and Map Division.

Underwoods Mines Quarries Minerals Liberties Easments Privileges Advantages . . . and Appurtenances whatsoever, unto the said hereby described and granted."[50] Not coincidentally, the early plans for the Baltimore and Ohio Railroad, spearheaded by Quaker and friend Philip E. Thomas, would pass through the seat of the Ellicott family's land holdings at Ellicott City. Thomas Ellicott—president of the Union Bank of Maryland, a bank intimately involved with both the B&O Railroad's financing *and* the financing of Baltimore Friends' civilizing missions—sat alongside his fellow Quaker Philip Thomas on the committee that advertised the railroad to investors.[51] Baltimore Friends' web of connections was robust and family-based, and it linked their civilizing mission work with their own personal investment projects.

Friends' land purchases and economic entanglements demonstrate both that civilizing work shared connections with their other investment projects and that prominent Baltimore Friends were willing to engage the economic paradigms of the world around them to turn a profit—just as missionaries like McCoy and Rice had. They also, however, showcase a pattern of speculation that marked Indian removal as well. Baltimore Friends' own histories of business and land deals were, of course, shared by other policymakers and officials in the early republic, and that history and experience ultimately shaped Indian policies. Just as Friends did when they acquired lands upon which "improvements" were located, the federal government acquired Native peoples' "improvements"—their homes and fields and infrastructure—when it purchased lands and carried out forced removals in the Ohio Country. Those improvements, along with their position on lands desired by settlers and transportation boosters, increased the value of lands—value added in part, but certainly not always, thanks to U.S. investment in civilization projects that were often spearheaded by the very Quakers who engaged in similar acquisitions in the Baltimore region.

In performing an analysis of Indian removal, federal officials and their correspondents made it clear that improved land was more valuable—such land could produce abundant agricultural goods, and, with further growth in transportation networks, those products could then feed continental and world markets. In 1820, John Scott wrote to John C. Calhoun regarding the sale of Shawnees and Delawares' lands. "The Bargain to the U States," he determined, was "a good one." The Indians' land had "Houses, Towns, and farms thereon," "Their Animals are domesticated to the place," and they had "all their property there." The proposed land west of the Mississippi, on the other hand, was "not of equal quality by a great difference" and would not be as valuable as the lands they were leaving for a long time. Regarding the U.S. government's initial investment of $20,000 for the removal scheme, Scott speculated that "the Very first sales will more than remunerate this disbursement—and the Land [the Indians] will receive would not do it in many years."[52] Improved lands translated into profits. Native peoples' participation in the U.S. market economy, and their investments in their lands, ultimately incentivized, from the perspective of the United States, Indian removal.

* * *

When the ABCFM, Baptists, Methodists, and others accepted a portion of the civilization funds after 1819, they not only ensured that the mission complex endured, but they also ensured that Native peoples could continue to maintain relationships with missionaries and to call upon those relationships when needed. Since the earliest years of the nineteenth century, Shawnees, Miamis, Potawatomis, and their neighbors endeavored to employ missionaries and federal agents in an effort to reap the advantages that the civilization plan might offer. When Native peoples admitted civilizing missionaries to labor on their lands, they built upon their own modes of diplomacy and economy and formed new diplomatic connections with the United States, and they also invested in their lands and their future. Though speculative philanthropy worked to facilitate Indian removal, grow individuals' profits, and bolster the image of the United States as a benevolent power, it also offered an additional means by which Native leaders could negotiate, manipulate, and combat U.S. policies. Individuals like John Johnston, John Shaw, Isaac McCoy, and Philip E. Thomas each played a role in propagating and employing ideas of benevolence for their own economic and political purposes, yet so, too, did Indigenous peoples.

The Miamis' experiences in Indiana demonstrate the extent to which some individuals could negotiate dispossession and the politics of exclusion. While leaders such as Jean Baptiste Richardville and Frances Godfroy built and cemented connections with missionaries and U.S. officials beginning in the early nineteenth century, as well as with American, British, and French traders, they also sought economic advantage that was built upon the premise that forming connections and strategically engaging with Euro-Americans could pay off in both the long and short term. Miamis like Richardville seized upon missionaries and the politics of philanthropy in order to engage in their own speculation on behalf of themselves and their people. The risk was great: most Euro-Americans had proven themselves to be wily partners who readily altered or ignored treaty obligations when the situation suited their interests. Yet missionaries like members of the Society of Friends had offered economic and diplomatic advantages in the past, and they made the risky proposition somewhat more palatable.

When the Baptist McCoy began his school at Fort Wayne, Richardville's son and grandson were among the pupils.[53] McCoy noted that "Pishewa appeared to interest himself much in favour of our school; being related to the French, he professed to be a Roman Catholic, in matters of religion."[54] Here it is clear that Richardville engaged the missionary and the school, likely endeavoring to use both strategically to serve his own and his family's ends. In this, Richardville was not unique: other leaders in eastern North America likewise used missionaries and mission schools to advantage. In the Southwest, for example, elite Choctaws, too, sent their own children to Great Crossings, the site of the first official Federal Indian School. Elites among Native nations presumed that their children would eventually lead their nations, and that they would benefit from the connections made and education received at such places—both could equip them to deal more effectively with Euro-Americans and the United States.[55]

While Richardville engaged the mission in ways that were shared by other leaders, he also likely drew upon Miamis' past experiences. As with Little Turtle's positioning of Philip Dennis's farm school several miles from Miami villages in the early years of the nineteenth century, the location of McCoy's school is telling: the mission school was located at Fort Wayne, not on the Mississinewa River where many Miamis' homes were located. McCoy blamed the school's ultimate location on the efforts of an intervening U.S. Indian agent, but it is possible that, like Little Turtle before him, Richardville hoped to maintain connections with missionaries at a distance.[56]

Miami leaders' abilities to cultivate business and diplomatic connections meant that, by the 1820s, their visions for the future remained firmly rooted in Indiana. During treaty negotiations with the U.S. government in 1826, Meehcikilita (Le Gros), for example, another leader among the Miamis, stated, "We want to live like neighbors, and barter and trade with each other, if we can agree, if not, to part peaceably and each keep his own."[57] Meehcikilita envisioned Miamis remaining on their lands as neighbors, and showing support for federally funded mission work such as that offered by McCoy was one way to visibly demonstrate Miamis' willingness to partake in Euro-American modes of living even as some Miamis managed to reap advantages from the connections and labor that accompanied mission projects. What was more, some Miamis, like Richardville, recognized that Euro-American–style education could prove useful to future generations. Not only could such education make Miamis appear, to Euro-American eyes, as neighbors, but it could offer additional means to ensure that Miamis thrived. Euro-Americans' own speculative philanthropy in the form of civilizing work thus continued to offer a possibility for negotiating U.S. settler encroachment and imperial policies.

To an extent, men like Richardville and Meehcikilita succeeded in their efforts, though by no means completely. By the 1820s, transportation innovations were, for the Miamis as with settlers, one key piece of their considerations when retaining lands. While Chapter 5 revealed that Richardville used his connections with the Ewing brothers to secure a presence for Miamis in Indiana during the 1826 treaty proceedings, that same treaty nonetheless resulted in the creation of reservations in Indiana and a good deal of land cessions. Yet, again, the locations of the reservations were key: Richardville and his compatriots ensured that the Miamis maintained the most lucrative lands—those in the proposed pathway of the Wabash-Erie Canal. Miamis understood the value of lands and the potential of transportation innovations, and their continued hold on the potential canal lands did not please

Indiana residents; it became a political headache for both state and federal officials over the next several years.

In 1829, a group of settlers sent a memorial to the federal government in an effort to eliminate, once and for all, the Miamis from their midst. Their petition amply demonstrates the ways in which speculative philanthropy converged with transportation investments and profit to amplify settlers' calls for Indigenous dispossession: the settlers combined their pleas for Indigenous dispossession and the construction of the canal with potent humanitarian rhetoric. The memorialists opened their letter stating, "the interest of the United States and of the State of Indiana, require, at this time, a course of appropriate measures to be pursued, calculated to extinguish the claim of the Indians, (more particularly the Miamies [*sic*]) to their reserved territory, lying upon the borders of the contemplated Wabash Canal, and within the boundaries of this State."[58] The writers were careful to say that they would "not fatigue your honorable body with detailing the evils which will necessarily follow the longer continuance of the Indians in the possession of their reserved territory." Instead they simply explained that "humanity dictates their immediate removal from a place where they are exposed to many evils."[59] Though these memorialists were the very people who possessed the power to ensure Miamis' protection from "evils," they nonetheless chose to ignore that point by obscuring it with language of philanthropy in an effort to conceal less-than-humanitarian motives. The petition demonstrates that settler colonialism was a powerful force that was made stronger with government assistance as well as with ideas of humanity. The Indiana petitioners added that the presence "of these few savages within our limits, who claim so large a space of the best soil . . . circumscribes in its practical effects, the usefulness of the privileges we enjoy as a free and independent State."[60] The petitioners showed their hand most clearly when they wrote of Miamis' prosperity and their possession of "so large a space of the best soil," yet they couched their appeal in political and philanthropic terms. By allowing Indigenous peoples to remain, they argued, the federal government threatened Indiana's sovereignty as a state and flirted with a human disaster.

The canal lands remained an issue into the 1840s, and many—though not all—Miamis ultimately lost their lands and their homes. Miamis sold more lands in 1834, yet they still retained holdings, in the form of grants to individuals, near the Forks of the Wabash. Those individual grants proved to be crucial to the maintenance of Miamis' foothold in Indiana. By the 1840 Treaty of the Forks of the Wabash, Richardville and other families were exempted from removal and they retained their allotments, while the U.S. federal government, now with Lewis Cass's support, informed other Miamis that they must leave their lands within five years. Here it may be seen that those elite Miamis who were able to engage the emerging economic paradigms most directly, who made the most money, and who cultivated relationships with outsiders were able to combat U.S. policies most successfully. Richardville, now nearing the end of his life, as well as Francis LaFontaine both ultimately relinquished the Miamis' lands in exchange for lands west of the Mississippi—though the allotments remained in Indiana—no doubt in part in the hopes that some Miamis would be able to remain together as a people. Roughly one hundred fifty Miamis avoided removal, yet the U.S. government forced others onto steamships headed southward, on the waters controlled by John Johnston's canal lock, toward present-day Missouri and Kansas and then, by 1867, to present-day Oklahoma.[61] Despite this, today, a number of citizens of the Miami Tribe of Oklahoma remain in the area near Fort Wayne and the Richardville and LaFontaine land holdings, many of whom are descended from those who thwarted removal.[62]

* * *

Like those of the Miamis, Shawnees' experiences, particularly those who dwelled at Wapakoneta and who worked with Friends since the first decade of the nineteenth century, reveal starkly the ways in which all these impulses—profits, speculative philanthropy, Indigenous dispossession, and Native peoples' negotiation of each—combined to transform the continent, build Americans' territorial empire, and provide space for some Native peoples to ensure their survival. Wapakoneta Shawnees engaged missionaries and the civilization plan even more directly after the War of 1812, and they, like Miamis, maintained visions of the future that were grounded in their Ohio Country homes. Black Hoof, chief at Wapakoneta, maintained a close relationship with Friends, and through them he sought to secure material advantages, mobilize labor, and cultivate closer political and diplomatic relationships with U.S. officials. During the Treaty of the Maumee Rapids in 1817, Wapakoneta Shawnees' relationships with the Friends, as well as their refusal to join Tecumseh in the war against the United States just several years prior, encouraged the U.S. government to allow Shawnees at Wapakoneta to maintain "a tract of land, ten miles square, the center of which shall be the council-house at Wapaghkonnetta."[63] Shawnees at Wapakoneta were thus were able to stay in their homes, though others of the Shawnees were not so fortunate.[64] Quaker Henry Harvey, who would lead Friends' mission efforts at Wapakoneta and then beyond the Mississippi in the 1820s and 1830s, noted that "in these tracts of land there were allowed for each male person of the Wapaughkonnetta band, about five hundred and nine acres each, and those of Hog Creek, about, or nearly, one thousand acres each."[65] The civilization plan had long aimed to shift gender relations within Native communities, and such a distribution of land to "each male person" continued that work.

Such gendered divisions of property was but one element of the civilization plan's quest to spread patriarchic ideals. By the era of the civilization fund, white women increasingly participated in the work of civilization by both traveling to mission sites and by supporting mission societies near their homes. By the 1820s, white Americans increasingly associated the work of reform with the feminine: Women took on increasingly robust roles in reform societies and took on a number of different issues—temperance, anti-slavery, poverty, and Indian affairs.[66] The inclusion of white women in the work of civilization was part of this larger shift. By 1815, for example, the Indian Concerns Committee of the Baltimore Yearly Meeting included women among their ranks. Quaker Henry Harvey's wife joined him in his work among the Shawnees, as did the Baptist Isaac McCoy's—indeed, in general, missionaries increasingly performed work as families as time wore on. The work of settler colonialism and empire increasingly hinged on the presence of white women—both on the ground and in the imaginary. White women performed crucial domestic labor that allowed their missionary husbands (and the men of settler families more generally) to attend to other tasks. Whereas men like Philip Dennis had modeled farming in the earliest of Friends' missions in the Ohio, by the 1820s, white families could model the gendered division of labor as well. White women, such as those included among the ranks of the Indian Concerns committee—as well as those who accompanied other missionaries of the ABCFM, Baptists, and other societies—contributed much to the work of empire on the continent.[67]

Isaac Harvey (not to be confused with Henry Harvey) spearheaded Friends' efforts at Shawnees' town in 1819 when he became "superintendent of the mills, etc. erected for the benefit of the Shawnees."[68] Harvey had been "sent there by the committee having charge of the Indians, to take these mills off the hands of the contractors, so that he had become well known to a number of the chiefs, and others of the Shawnee nation, as well as to become acquainted with his valued friend, John Johnston, then agent for the Indians in the north."[69] Here it is clear that economy took center stage: Isaac Harvey was to be "superintendent of the mills," a crucial component task of the civilization project.

Isaac and then Henry Harvey led the civilizing project among Shawnees in the 1820s and beyond after tensions caused a rift between the Baltimore Friends on the one hand and members of the Ohio and Indiana Meetings on the other. Baltimore Friends—who had worked so closely with the government and had accepted public support and a parcel of land for their work—lamented Ohio and Indiana Friends' desire to accept a portion of the civilization fund. Baltimore Friends wrote that "a difference of opinion . . . has arisen between us, upon so essential and important a point as we have believed the receiving of the public Money by us, as a Society and the rendering ourselves responsible to the Government for the manner & terms of its disbursement to be." They went on to say that historically they have performed their work out of "a sense of religious duty" and that "there is no instance of the Society of Friends, having in the prosecution of any of those religious concerns and duties to which they have apprehended themselves called, ever uniting themselves to the policy or principles of the Governments of this world or in any manner voluntarily made themselves amenable to, or controulable by them."[70] Of course, such language did not adequately capture the truth—Baltimore Friends had worked closely with the government and received support in several different ways. By the time Baltimore Friends sent this letter, the committee's membership had changed somewhat since the earliest years of their work in the Ohio Country. Yet there were still some members who participated in and recalled those efforts. Nonetheless, clearly, Baltimore Friends were articulating a different vision for their work in the Ohio Country by 1820. The committee's insistence that "religious duty" formed a core of why they conducted their civilizing efforts is a reminder of the difficulties inherent in ascribing motivations to actions. A desire to fulfill religious duty could coexist with a desire to make profit, to alter lands, to garner moral capital—and these could vary widely from individual to individual—even if the consequences of such efforts could be quite disastrous for Native people.

Beyond the funds, it was the issue of a school that also divided the Friends. Baltimore Friends did not want to open a school, while Ohio and Indiana Friends did. Indeed, it was for a school that these latter Friends wanted the civilization funds. They proposed that "the boys might be instructed in agricultural pursuits & the girls in such branches of industry, as belonged to them." Friends proposed a gendered division of labor that, as civilizing efforts long had, adhered to Euro-American ideals. What was more, these Friends suggested that the school adhere to a boarding school model: "we are united in believing that it would be best to remove from the Indian reservation & purchase a tract of land adjoining, on which to make such an establishment as may suit our purpose. . . . The children seperated from the immediate company of their idle associates, will be more under the controul, and attached to the company of their preceptors."[71] Removing children from their families—from "idle associates," as Ohio and Indiana Friends phrased it—was, to these Friends, the best course of action. Referring to parents as "idle" recalled the rhetoric of poor relief—white reformers often assumed the "undeserving poor" to be idle—and their efforts shed light on the many ways in which missionaries viewed and hoped to conduct their work.

Ultimately, Baltimore Friends agreed to hand the day-to-day operations over to their counterparts in the Ohio Country, yet they would maintain a role in handling the finances. The funds for Baltimore Friends' civilizing work were held with the Union Bank of Maryland—a pet bank during the bank wars, the bank for which Thomas Ellicott served as president, and a bank that had financial ties to the Baltimore Indian Concerns Committee clerk Philip E. Thomas's B&O Railroad. Friends in the Ohio Country agreed to this proposition and both societies maintained access to the funds. Baltimore Friends noted in their minutes that their funds—$10,000 to $11,000—are "principally invested in Bank Stock & may be expected to yield about $600 per annum in half yearly dividends."[72]

While Friends worked out how they would handle the finances and management of their civilizing work, Shawnees and neighboring Euro-Americans openly acknowledged the economic payoffs that accompanied such efforts. In 1825, Isaac Harvey did help establish a school, located five miles south of the Shawnees' town.[73] The location, however, was not the Quaker's first choice. Henry Harvey noted that "some bad white men persuaded the young men to believe that, if the Quakers continued to make improvements on their lands, the white people would take it from them."[74] As a consequence, "buildings were erected, a farm opened, and a school established about five miles south of Wapaughkonnetta, until the Shawnees left their homes for the country west of the Missouri."[75] Here, then, in the 1820s—and certainly by 1854 when Henry Harvey wrote his history of the mission work—was a recognition that mission work offered "improvements" or additional infrastructure to lands that "white people" found enticing. Those "improvements" appealed to Shawnees at Wapakoneta. They understood them as investments, and those investments were appealing to Euro-American settlers if they could acquire them for themselves.

Employing missionaries to secure infrastructure and labor could sometimes offer advantage to Shawnees and their neighbors. As Isaac Harvey's statement suggests, however, such employment was part of a longer-term economic investment project that was riddled with risk. Buying into—and taking advantage of—Euro-Americans' civilization plan for their own purposes meant that leaders like Black Hoof formed political ties with the United States government via its agents on the ground and its intermediaries—in this case, both Indian agent John Johnston and members of the Society of Friends—and it meant that they participated in a broader economic development scheme that would increase the value of their lands. Mills, roads, and fences added to the value of Shawnees' already fertile—and thus valuable—lands, yet they also made those lands even more desirable to land-hungry settlers. Indeed, John Johnston's suggestion that the U.S. government compensate Shawnees near Piqua for their lands as well as for their improvements illustrated the financial payoffs that could come with participation in the civilization plan. By engaging with the United States' philanthropists, Native leaders like Black Hoof became implicated in the web woven by speculative philanthropy. Black Hoof and others like him would also discover, however, that that web could offer both payoffs and devastation.

For Shawnees at Wapakoneta, Black Hoof's gamble did not pay the dividends for which he had hoped. Shawnees at Wapakoneta ultimately removed westward, and they lost their homes and infrastructure as well as their lands. Yet their removal reveals that while speculation in philanthropists' labor and infrastructure did not save them from the violence of settler colonialism and U.S. policies of exclusion, philanthropy played a role in their survival and in the negotiation of the terms of their removal. After Isaac Harvey's death, Henry Harvey led Friends' efforts at the Shawnee town, and he continued the work of schooling and farming there until removal.

In 1831, U.S. commissioner James Gardiner visited the Shawnees at Wapakoneta to convince them to sell their lands and remove to lands in Missouri. The commissioner, employing the rhetoric of poverty and charity as well as profit, informed the Shawnees of their "deplorable condition" and promised that if "they would now sell their land and go west . . . their great father, General Jackson, would make them rich."[76] Harvey noted that the commissioner's proposition divided the Shawnees, but that, nonetheless, the Shawnees agreed to the commissioner's terms. It soon became clear, however, that the commissioner had done his best to confuse Shawnees about what, exactly, those terms were. Shawnees understood that, as part of the sale, the federal government would cover their debts, survey and value their Wapakoneta lands, pay them according to the value of both the lands and the infrastructure on those lands, and then offer lands in the west.[77] Upon hearing, however, that in actuality the United States would deduct the price of the new lands from the sale price of their current lands—making Shawnees pay for their own removal—several Shawnee leaders actively sought out assistance from the Quaker Harvey as well as from the Ohio and Indiana Yearly Meeting of Friends.[78]

The Shawnees at Wapakoneta maintained a relationship with the Society of Friends since the first decade of the nineteenth century, and here, nearly thirty years later, that relationship endured, and they called upon it for aid. Harvey noted that Shawnees lamented,

> We are sorry to find that it is to be the price of our farms that is to take us to our new homes. We expected no such thing—we understood plainly that the government was to be at all that expense, and that what our improvements here were worth, after being valued by good men, was to be paid us in money, to assist us in making farms at our new homes. We have good homes here, and had abundance of labor and pains to make them. We wanted good men to value our improvements, for we are not ashamed of our homes. We are surprised to hear that the treaty is not as we understood it was, in that matter. . . . My friends, we are in a difficult situation. We cannot let our property go in this way; if we do, we are a ruined people.[79]

Here, Shawnees knew that Friends' labor on their lands should have been an investment that paid off even in the face of removal. In an effort to combat the terms of the treaty, they reached out to Harvey and the Society of Friends in hopes that they might still recoup some of their losses. Shawnees' outreach paid off. Friends worked with Shawnees and pieced together a delegation to travel to Washington, a delegation that included Shawnee leaders John Perry and three others, as well as members of the Society of Friends. Their goal was to secure greater compensation for the Shawnees.

In Washington, the delegation met with both Lewis Cass and representative Joseph Vance of Ohio. Not only did Shawnees employ their relationship with the Society of Friends in order to spur that society to action, but with the Friends' assistance, they pursued a political course that reflected a sophisticated understanding of the U.S. political process and the politics surrounding U.S. Indian policy. According to Harvey, the delegation brought the recent land treaty to the attention of Lewis Cass, and he expressed sympathy. Cass then informed them that he would bring the issue before President Jackson. Jackson, however, reportedly refused to aid the Shawnees.[80] Undeterred, the delegation shifted their attention to Congress, effectively circumventing the executive branch. They approached Joseph Vance, a Whig with political ambitions who championed congressional power, and he successfully brought the Shawnees' claim before the congressional Ways and Means committee. The delegation made a claim for $100,000 in additional compensation, but, according to Harvey, recognizing that Jackson could veto the bill, they asked for only part of the sum up front. Congress approved a bill for $30,000 to be distributed to the Shawnees in fifteen annual installments—a partial success, yet one that would not overburden the federal government by any means.[81]

The Shawnees' efforts to combat the unacceptable terms of their removal treaty—though by no means completely satisfying—reveals that when confronted with removal, employing philanthropic networks (in this case, the Society of Friends) and manipulating politics offered some room to negotiate and shape the terms of the government's actions. Here, however, caution is required: Shawnees did not avoid removal nor did they avoid the economic, physical, and emotional violence that accompanied it. Soon after the delegation returned from Washington, the Shawnees at Wapakoneta prepared to remove beyond the Mississippi. The Shawnees "sold two hundred head of cattle, about twelve hundred hogs, and many other things" ahead of a government-planned spring departure, but that date was pushed back to fall.[82] Though the Shawnees secured additional funds for their lands, they soon faced starvation due to that delay. Once again, however, they contacted Harvey and the Society of Friends for aid.[83] Harvey secured assistance, but he also went one step further and utilized his connections with the secretary of war Lewis Cass and Indian agent John Johnston, successfully requesting provisions from the federal government. Though their investments in their lands may not have paid off, their investment in constructing a political partnership with Friends did. Shawnees used their networks and secured the items necessary for survival.

And endure they did, and Harvey followed. Soon after removal, Harvey and two other Friends visited the Shawnees in their new lands. He noted that the "purpose of our visit to them was to offer to erect buildings and establish a school among them."[84] Harvey informed the Shawnees that "we had taught their children, and wished to apply the proceeds to a like purpose at their present homes, if they desired it, and that we wanted none of their money, but would do it all at our own expense, as we had ever done, only we wanted to have a farm as large as we might need and timber to keep it up." He added, "To these propositions they at once consented."[85] The mission complex endured.

By the 1840s in what is now Kansas, Shawnees, including those removed from Wapakoneta, continued to receive instruction from the Society of Friends. The school, known by government officials, settlers, missionaries, and pupils alike as Friends' Manual Labor School, had roughly forty students. In 1844, the superintendent of Indian Affairs Thomas Harvey noted that "the boys are taught to farm, the girls the domestic arts suitable to their sex."[86] Henry Harvey and then other Friends continued to work among Shawnees, offering their labor and money for infrastructure, until, together with Shawnees' own labor, they once again rebuilt their community. The Shawnees and Friends were joined by Methodists who also opened a manual labor school on Shawnee lands in Kansas.[87] One writer indicated that the Methodist mission's "financial support came principally from the Methodist church, supplemented by government grants and Indian education funds. An important part was derived from the school farm which produced in 1840, the first year of operation, 2,000 bushels of wheat, 4,000 of oats, 3,500 of corn, and 500 of potatoes. There were then 130 head of cattle, 100 hogs, and 5 horses. Indian boys, as part of their education, supplied farm labor, aided by hired help at planting and harvesting seasons."[88] Missions, along with missionary and Native labor, continued to feed local economies as the century wore on.

Much of Henry Harvey's work was written as a forceful indictment of U.S. Indian policy, and therefore we must approach his rhetoric—as with any rhetoric—with care. His writing offers compelling narrative arcs, for example, that neatly detail crests and troughs of Shawnees' progress toward civilization. Those crests usually aligned with Friends' presence; troughs with removals. Yet, despite this, we should not dismiss his descriptions of Shawnees' experiences nor those of their efforts when rebuilding their lives again and again. Indeed, Harvey's description of Shawnees' community in 1854 Kansas is an important one: "many of them have good dwelling-houses, well provided with useful and respectable furniture, which is kept in good order by the females, and they live in the same manner as the whites do, and live well too. They have smoke-houses, stables, corn-cribs, and other out-buildings. They have a good supply of horses, cattle, hogs, and some sheep. They have many farm wagons, and work oxen—some carriages and buggies, and are generally well supplied with farming implements, and know how to use them."[89] Here it is clear that Harvey brought his own Euro-American judgments to this description—"kept in good order by the females," "useful and respectable furniture"—but the passage does point to a recurring pattern that characterized speculative philanthropy's intersection with Indian removal: Euro-American settlers profited from philanthropists' efforts, Shawnees' labors, and Shawnees' employment of missionaries' labor. Harvey noted, "the avaricious grasp of the white man has fixed its eye on these rich acres, and the fine Indian farms."[90] Shawnees' investments in their daily lives and in their economic futures—their success in meeting the Euro-American standards of "civilization"—encouraged more settler greed and, ultimately, additional removals. Shawnee wealth—and Native wealth more broadly—simply did not align with settler expectations. The federal government removed these Shawnees to Indian Territory not long after.

And this pattern endured in other places and among other peoples. Missions continued to be intimately involved with economic development as they stretched deeper into the heart of North America. Baptists, Methodists, the ABCFM—all continued their work into the midcentury, a period when mission schools were often explicitly manual labor schools. Ideas of labor and economic development remained central to the institutions' mission, even as they continued to transform landscapes and further embed economic networks. While "useful knowledge" had been the euphemism for the kind of agricultural education and labor deemed fit for Native peoples by missionaries and officials, by midcentury, missionary philanthropists abandoned that language in favor of more explicit language: to them, Indigenous peoples, and Native children especially, needed to learn to be manual laborers.

Despite this (and, more likely, because of this), ideas of philanthropy, too, remained at the heart of this project. By the early 1860s, the local Indian agent indicated that twenty-two Shawnees attended a manual labor school run by Friends, and that Friends maintained the institution "from motives of pure benevolence" at the discretion of the federal government.[91] This paradigm, established during the earliest years of the nineteenth century, continued throughout the nineteenth century as Friends took the lead on President Grant's "Peace Policy" and spearheaded the United States' boarding school efforts that removed children from their homes in favor of labor-intensive and—as children's burials at places like the Carlisle Indian Industrial School in what is now Pennsylvania reveal—often deadly education.[92]

Ultimately, Harvey captured the multifaceted story of speculative philanthropy and removal in his book *The History of the Shawnee Indians.* He wrote in 1854, "tell [Native peoples] they are too near the whites, and they will say that that is to their advantage, for there is where their market is. Tell them of what you will, and they will believe just as much of it as this: they believe the whites want their country because it is rich."[93] Shawnees, Miamis, and their neighbors built their own homes, and they produced their own crops. Yet in lands near mission sites—which increasingly included more lands as reservations grew more circumscribed and missions grew more plentiful—missionary labor and resources facilitated their efforts, and they further encouraged the growth of markets in lands where many U.S. officials and policymakers believed that market participation needed to be taught. Of course, North American Indigenous peoples did not need to be taught how to participate in wide-ranging commercial networks; they had done that for millennia and with various foreign partners over time. But it was both the boost to infrastructure and the promise of peace and U.S. authority that mission sites and labor offered that did, in fact, make Indian lands appear to be even more prosperous and valuable than they already were to Euro-American eyes. Shawnees in 1830 Wapakoneta knew as much when the government expressed a desire to buy their lands in Ohio. Harvey wrote that Shawnees worried that "if they did improve their land the whites would want it, and persuade government to drive them off."[94] Harvey wrote that he had told the Shawnees that they worried too much, that never would "the United States . . . be so intolerably hard . . . that if they would improve their lands and be at peace, that they never should be asked for their land." Perhaps recognizing his own complicity in the growth of Americans' empire, Harvey then lamented, "But alas! What a mistake!"[95]

* * *

In his recent work on "northern Indian removal," historian John Bowes reminds us that Indian removal was a process rather than a singular event, and that it was a process that differed from place to place and from people to people.[96] Understanding the intersections between philanthropy and economy in the Ohio Country is crucial for understanding the process that was Indian removal as well as the ways in which Indigenous dispossession both created and was born out of the political economy of the early republic. Politics and policies in Indian Country facilitated both the creation and entrenchment of the ideas of poverty, charity, and morality that accompanied the development of American capitalism and empire, and Native peoples' lands and homes served as fuel for the growth of the same. At the same time, however, U.S. Indian policies were not simply asserted and implemented by Euro-American actors. Instead, Native peoples cultivated relationships that enabled them to secure additional funds, provisions, and aid when they required it, and they combined those relationships with their own desire to remain in their homes in order to shape the terms of both their removals and their survival. While the United States wove its empire and economy out of the threads of Indigenous dispossession, Native peoples seized upon Americans' efforts to assert benevolence at home and on the world stage, and they ultimately exposed the contradictions that lay at the heart of the American republic.

CHAPTER 7

"Of Mercy and of Sound Policy Too"

Cultivating American Empire on the Continent and Overseas

While mission work and speculative philanthropy intersected with and facilitated Indigenous dispossession, they also offered a means by which federal officials could shroud both that violent process and other of the republic's shortcomings with a veil of benevolence. By the 1820s, the republic grappled with a number of moral quandaries: the question of slavery loomed with no politically amicable solution apparent, people experienced poverty that seemed out of step with the republic's promise of prosperity, and Indian removal was increasingly at the forefront of debate. The discourse of philanthropy became both a means by which individuals grappled with these issues and a veil that shrouded the violence and pain that accompanied them. Against this backdrop, many Americans worked to reconcile U.S. Indian policies with both their own and others' ideas of philanthropy and morality. As settlers' and officials' calls for removal escalated by the 1820s and 1830s, representatives of the U.S. government endeavored to maintain ideas of morality and benevolence while also carrying out the desired policies yearned for by both emigrating settlers and local U.S. officials. They did so by employing a rhetoric similar to that used by those Indiana settler-petitioners who had called for the removal of Miamis during the quest to build the Wabash and Erie Canal in 1829—they cast removal as a benevolent answer to a moral problem.

While Americans engaged in a discourse of philanthropy internally, they also employed it in their international dealings. Great Britain, in particular, loomed as the imperial power to which officials most liked to declare the United States' status as a benevolent power. The two polities' history of war, along with their status as neighbors on the North American continent, meant that their competition took place on the ground and in print. Thus, at the same time that Euro-American settlers and government officials in the Ohio Country dispossessed Native people and invested in transportation technologies, policymakers and officials together worked to cultivate and maintain a benevolent reputation for the young republic on the world stage—and they did so while struggling to contend with the reality of enduring Native presence.

A single moment in 1820 captures the ways in which the rhetoric of philanthropy intersected with both international imperial rivalries and Native peoples' own politics and hopes for the future. In that year, Indian agent John Johnston's agency at Piqua, Ohio, was low on cash. Amid the agency's financial woes, Delawares living near Johnston's agency prepared to remove westward. Some had already departed, but others remained, waiting for promised provisions from the U.S. government. Johnston informed Lewis Cass that he had done his best but that additional goods were necessary. It was not only the agency's financial straits, however, that worried Johnson: so, too, did Delawares' solution to the agency's failures. Johnston informed Cass that "almost all the Indians of this Agency has been at Malden the present seaso[n] to receive goods from the English. Necessity has been the chief motive, as it is found their annuities is totally inadequate to cloth their population." Johnston continued to describe the problem, writing, "I humbly conceive the character and dignity of this Government will be somewhat affected by these visits[.] These Indians have parted with their Country and are now oblidged to solicit charity from a foreign nation, whose Agents will not fail to improve the occurrence in a way the most disadvantageous to us." He added, "As the residence of the Tribes here cannot continue over a few years, would it not be an act of Mercy and of sound policy too, for the Government to send on Annually Three thousand Dollars worth of cloathing for them?"[1]

Johnston's letter to Cass makes clear that in the midst of the United States' struggle to assert the moral virtue of its government, acts of speculative philanthropy could be conceived as simultaneously merciful, practical, and politically shrewd: in this case, offering clothing to Delawares could address a number of problems. By highlighting Native peoples' material needs, as Johnston did in his letter to Cass, U.S. officials drew upon ideas of poor relief and aid to assert the empire's benevolence. Johnston's emphasis upon Delawares' failure to adequately "cloth their population" aligned with a broader intellectual paradigm that imagined Indigenous peoples as "poor Indians" who required Americans' assistance.[2] A discourse of poor relief thus became an accompaniment to removal schemes. As settlers' calls for removal escalated in the Ohio Country, representatives of the U.S. government endeavored to weave ideas of Natives' poverty and their own philanthropy into their rhetoric while carrying out the desired policies championed by both Euro-American settlers and U.S. officials.

Johnston's letter reveals much about U.S. officials' strategies and insecurities, yet it also reveals that Delawares near Piqua were well informed regarding international politics: their act of approaching the British for assistance—borne out of need as well as savvy—left the U.S. federal government in an awkward political position. By seeking out aid from the British, Delawares exposed the international complexities that accompanied the United States' desire to position itself as an enlightened republic. Foreign policy intersected with ideas of benevolence, charity, and Indian removal in the Ohio Country, and both Delawares and Johnston knew it. Johnston's request for aid ultimately demonstrates that ideas of mercy, charity, and morality colored Indian policy politics, and that speculative philanthropy could have local and international ramifications.

By considering how Americans' policies and rhetoric contributed to an international dialogue, we can trace how speculative philanthropy in Indian Country offered a means by which the United States cultivated a mantle of benevolence on the world stage and justified its emergence as a world imperial power. Just as ideas of "usefulness" traveled with Friends between Baltimore and the Ohio Country in the early years of their civilizing efforts, rhetoric of poor relief similarly permeated U.S. officials' ideas regarding Native peoples and their own empire's benevolence in the world. U.S. officials' deployment of the rhetoric of poor relief and humanitarianism on the world stage emerged as one of the dividends of missionaries and U.S. officials' speculative philanthropy in Indian Country. Officials no doubt hoped that such rhetoric would secure a benevolent reputation, moral capital, and, in turn, power and authority.

If scholar Susan Ryan's work on "the grammar of good intentions" shows that a discourse of benevolence was ubiquitous in the antebellum United States, attention to the ways in which U.S. officials deployed that discourse in international relations offers a means to trace the consequences of such rhetoric and how it was part and parcel of the making of U.S. empire on the continent and overseas.[3] Poor relief—and its accompanying rhetoric of deserving and undeserving poor—offered a means by which reformers could make sense of and seemingly combat the disparities and inequalities associated with changing economic realities, and, like "useful knowledge," the language of poor relief intersected with racial and class hierarchies. Operationalized in world affairs, such rhetoric could mask the violence of Americans' empire, an empire that grew upon a foundation of the accumulation of Indigenous land and resources and enslaved labor. Such rhetorical efforts reveal the connections between U.S. empire on the continent and the world, and they also reveal much about the builders of empire themselves.

The individuals who wielded such rhetoric no doubt did so while experiencing a variety of emotions and holding a myriad of ideas. While some actors' intentions and motivations are difficult to pin down, the consequences of philanthropy and its accompanying rhetoric are somewhat easier to trace. Writing of Britons' pity for Indigenous peoples, one historian reminds us that "pity can be morally problematic even when authentically felt."[4] The ways in which acts and language borne of pity and philanthropy reified social hierarchies and bolstered the emergence of the U.S. imperial state in the early republic are no less problematic: a disavowal of violence was and is both powerful and a mainstay of settler-colonial polities.[5] While we must take such rhetoric seriously—refraining from dismissing its articulators as mere hypocrites—we must also understand that conversations regarding philanthropy—and of what counted as philanthropy—were both deeply embedded in the culture of the early republic and very much up for debate.[6] While many wove ideas of philanthropy into the work and discourse surrounding Indigenous removal, others pointed to the problems of doing so. Missionaries' work in the early nineteenth century helped lay a groundwork for U.S. officials to claim the mantle of benevolence in the world, yet they themselves—as the example of Henry Harvey in Chapter 6 shows—often saw the devastating consequences that such work wrought. Tracing the connections between Americans' speculative philanthropy on the ground, then, offers additional means to understand the ways in which peoples and policies in Indian Country helped cultivate a reputation of benevolence and a foundation for Americans' empire in the world during the nineteenth and twentieth centuries and beyond. It also highlights the contested nature of that process.

* * *

White reformed-minded Americans knew that poverty, Indian policies, and slavery posed moral dilemmas for the republic, and they created categories and policies that helped them grapple with those issues. By the 1820s, white Americans had increasingly hardened their attitudes toward those who experienced poverty. In urban spaces, they were more sympathetic to those who were "deserving" of public assistance—widows, children, and the "impotent poor"—and they moved to institutionalize these individuals by placing them in public almshouses, removing them from the public.[7] Boosters of African colonization, meanwhile, advocated removing free African-descended people to Liberia, claiming that in doing so those removed could better thrive and civilize their fellow Africans. Like Indian removal, both public almshouses and colonization offered a means to eliminate from the United States the specter of difference as well as those whom many white Americans deemed undesirable through a framework of philanthropy.[8] Together, these schemes represent quite clearly that a politics of exclusion held great purchase with white Americans—and that ideas and a discourse of philanthropy could bolster such politics. Doing so enabled Euro-Americans to envision the existence of an ideal nation that was premised on benevolence, virtue, and, ultimately, whiteness.

Some missionaries explicitly considered the problems presented by both Native American and free African-descended populations to be similar. Both posed challenges to ideas of citizenship, for example: both were free, but they were non-citizens. One missionary wrote to superintendent of Indian Affairs Thomas L. McKenney in 1818 in the hopes of convincing him to consider forming an American Civilization Society. This society, the missionary contended, would act "as a sister establishment to the Colonisation Society. The object of which should be to patronise the exertions of such Societies of different denominations as are actually engaged in civilising and educating the American Indians & otherwise to promote this verry important work." Such a society would "form a connecting chain to them, & harmonise their operations, & more effectually prevent any clashing between them than perhaps any other method."[9] It was a proposal that revealed that some considered the "Indian problem" to be akin to that posed by free Africans, slavery, and the problem of freedom.

In an era when Euro-Americans increasingly saw their claims to North American territories as boundless, geographic space became an obvious way to consolidate a nation both by claiming the right to a continent—and the right to carve up that territory as the republic saw fit—as well as by excluding certain people—free and enslaved African-descended peoples and Native peoples alike—from the nation-state geographically. In 1806, Quaker John Parrish, the diplomat who factored so heavily into the United States' efforts in the 1790s, argued that the United States should establish a territory beyond the Mississippi where free African and African-descended people might settle. He wrote, "Have not the General Legislature a right to instruct a committee to assign a tract within some part of the western wilderness (where there are millions of acres likely to continue many ages unoccupied) for colonization of those already free and disposed to remove thither?"[10] As early as 1806, then, removal offered a possible solution for confronting the problem of African-descended peoples' freedom. Parrish envisioned a "western wilderness" as a land unoccupied—perhaps a somewhat surprising observation for a Quaker so involved in Indian affairs—that would offer African-descended peoples refuge from the scourge of racism and the threat of re-enslavement.

Efforts to remove freed people gained popularity—among reformers but also among enslavers—after Gabriel's Rebellion in 1800 and 1802, and as the numbers of freed people grew after the American Revolution.[11] Gradual emancipation and wartime service meant that more and more African-descended people gained freedom—to the consternation, and sometimes fear, of white Americans. In 1816, Presbyterian minister Robert Finley established the American Colonization Society (ACS) for the purpose of removing free Blacks to Africa. Importantly, Great Britain, with the aid of the Committee for the Relief of the Black Poor, had already begun to send free Africans to Sierra Leone. The British committee's work was partially the consequence of the British government's increasing tendency "to think of black loyalists as wards of the state," and the removal of Black loyalists to Sierra Leone was similarly couched in terms of charitable aid.[12] After an exploratory mission to the continent, the ACS similarly decided that Liberia, just north of Sierra Leone, presented an ideal location for emigrating Africans. It supposedly offered a haven away from the poverty of the republic's urban spaces; it offered a means by which enslavers could hide the example of freed people from the enslaved; it offered freed people an opportunity to gain the kinds of political freedoms longed for after the American Revolution; and it offered white American reformers a chance to further claim benevolence.[13]

Removing impoverished laborers by placing them in almshouses, sending free African Americans to Liberia, and shuffling "poor Indians" onto lands beyond the Mississippi meant that poverty, difference, and supposed failure disappeared behind walls, oceans, and rivers in the early republic, and such exclusions fostered the ongoing development of ideas of race in the early republic. Ideas of poverty coupled with the notion that Natives' vices were the result of contact with unruly Euro-Americans and this meant that some white Americans framed Indian removal in terms of—and sometimes as a form of—morality-based public assistance.

* * *

By the 1820s and 1830s, U.S. officials spoke of benevolence, poor relief, and mercy in the context of Indian policy in large part thanks to missionaries and Indian agents' decades-long efforts to "civilize" Native peoples. The development of such rhetoric took place over time and was the product of both white settler and Indigenous influence. Civilizing missionary work followed an old script intelligible to the world's European empires—missionaries had been, after all, key players in the French, Spanish, and British Empires. The United States reimagined that old script to accommodate new economic and technological realities, yet it nonetheless held purchase in international relations during the nineteenth century. Rhetoric of pity and "poor Indians" had abounded in British missionary writing in the eighteenth century, and it worked to cultivate a culture of sensibility and community among the English and then British.[14] When U.S. missionaries traveled to agricultural missions in the Ohio Country during the earliest decades of the nineteenth century, they carried with them similar ideas as well as their own notions regarding poverty in the early republic. Native peoples, in turn, combined these notions with their own, appropriated them to secure wares, infrastructure, and labor, and used relationships with missionaries to their advantage.

Myriad Native peoples had long employed a discourse of impoverishment or lack, appealing to their own sense of community responsibilities and reciprocity, though the connotations of such appeals changed over time.[15] During the earliest years of the nineteenth century, for example, the Miami leader Little Turtle strategically employed a discourse of poverty in his dealings with both the Society of Friends and U.S. government officials. Such rhetoric related to an older mode of diplomatic condolence speechmaking, and the relationship between language of pity and lack continued to be linked with the establishment of social and political ties in the nineteenth century.[16] Individuals like Little Turtle heard the rhetoric of settlers' philanthropy and used it to achieve their own ends—they used it to establish or cement relationships, even if they may also have used it to secure material goods.

Little Turtle likely linked officials and missionaries' notions of poverty and "poor Indians" with his own. When he spoke of lack, Little Turtle did not seek sympathy for sympathy's sake; he sought both material goods and a relationship. Speaking of traders in 1802, for example, he told Baltimore Friends, "Our repeated entreaties to those who bring this evil [liquor] amongst us, we find, has not the desired effect. We tell them; brothers, fetch us useful things—bring goods that will clothe us, our women, our children."[17] Here, the Miami brought his own ideas regarding gift-giving, political alliance, and need, evoking pity in order to secure economic advantage and a political relationship. Yet he did not want just anything that traders or the U.S. government might feel like offering, but rather he wanted "useful things" like textiles. Little Turtle went on to say that the liquors that were often obtained in exchange for furs, "made us poor," and that it caused "our young women to go without clothes, our women & children to go without any thing to eat."[18] Such gendered appeals bolstered his appeal for his audience: white settlers often centered white women in their appeals for aid.[19] A savvy statesman, Little Turtle made these appeals to his political allies, the Baltimore Society of Friends—themselves an ally of the U.S. government and a society that aided Baltimore's own poor. When Friends received Little Turtle's pronouncements in 1802, they moved to send Friends Gerard T. Hopkins and Philip Dennis to Miami lands in order to begin an agricultural mission. Dennis began his mission work among the Miamis just two years later; Little Turtle's appeal worked. He succeeded in strengthening a relationship with Quakers, and he received goods and the work of laborers as well.

Such rhetoric enabled individuals like Little Turtle to secure missionary labor and connections and facilitated the cultivation of a relationship that he could then use to assert power and make claims upon the state and its recruited laborers. Such claims also, however, simultaneously bolstered Americans' assumptions regarding Native peoples' dependence upon the U.S. federal government in the early republic. Ideas of poverty, dependence, and charity became foundations for a fiction embraced by many Americans: by assisting poor Indians, the U.S. government—and its missionary partners—could cancel a "moral debt" while simultaneously revealing itself as a benevolent empire. In this way, the United States shared much in common with the British Empire, and it offered a means to dialogue—and compete—in the realm of international relations.

The idea of a moral debt that the United States could somehow repay to the continent's Native peoples through charity became a centerpiece of the young republic's claims to benevolent power in Indian Country by the 1820s and 1830s. In the 1820s Ohio Country, government assistance for removal became more frequent, and it coupled with missionaries' civilizing efforts to offer a crucial and, importantly, visible foundation for the United States' supposed benevolence. The government could offer provisions and aid to Natives beginning their removal trek, yet officials like superintendent of Indian Affairs Thomas L. McKenney proposed that that would not be the end of American aid. Rather, McKenney informed the ABCFM that "the Indians hold us in great arrears, and the Missionaries go to aid in cancelling them."[20] McKenney's hope was that missionaries would follow Shawnees and their neighbors as they traversed the heart of the continent from the Ohio Country to Missouri and Kansas, and, in doing so, that they would aid them as well as pave the way for virtuous settlement across the continent. As Henry Harvey's journey with the Shawnees demonstrated in Chapter 6, McKenney's hope was partially realized, and, indeed, missions would continue to stretch into the heart of the continent.

With McKenney—a Quaker—at the helm of Indian affairs in the 1820s, ideas of removal became concerned not only with the emptying of lands that, supposedly, could be better employed by Euro-American agrarians, but also with the expansion of American ideas of morality in North America. McKenney explained that in order for Native peoples to become "a portion of 'our great American family of freemen,'" Natives' condition should be "held up to the view of our citizens, that the trophies of reform be pointed to—I say, it needs only this to enlist in their favour the whole civilized population of our country; for could the extent of their wretchedness be comtemplated with indifference by our citizens, if it were known? And would not the charities of seven millions of men warm into animation their sad and dismal torpor?"[21] Here, discourse of civilization combined with that of poverty to appeal to Americans' own sense of and claims to civilization. Natives' "wretchedness" required Americans' charity, and such philanthropy possessed the power, ultimately, to translate into moral capital. The language of poor relief fostered reform in U.S. urban centers, and it offered powerful framing for Americans' supposed benevolence in Indian Country and in the world.

Of all Quakers employed in the service of the War Department, McKenney attained the most prominent position, and his rhetoric and policies reflect his spiritual beliefs. As superintendent of Indian Affairs, he institutionalized the paradigm of federally subsidizing mission work by aiding in the crafting of the Civilization Fund Act of 1819. His belief in the Inner Light, familiarity with Quaker reform efforts, and his business savvy gleaned as a result of merchant work in Maryland all shaped his policymaking and manner of business. He believed that Native peoples were the spiritual equals of

Euro-Americans, and he endeavored to maintain what he considered to be a generous and philanthropic attitude toward them. McKenney became an advocate for removal, however, supporting his position with ideas of humanitarianism and morality. He traveled through Anishinaabewaki in 1826–27, witnessed what he described as suffering and poverty (though his journals offer very little evidence of such helplessness), and endeavored to ameliorate the condition of Native people by removing them from the proximity of white people. McKenney's concern for Indian affairs continued even after he left office, and he went on to publish his multivolume *History of the Indian Tribes of North America* (1836–1844).[22]

Though President Jackson eventually removed him from office, McKenney's work as superintendent of Indian affairs was nonetheless critical to the development of Indian policy on the continent. The 1820s marked a crucial turning point: it was during this decade that removal as official policy began to coalesce in citizens' and policymakers' minds more firmly. What was more, McKenney's rhetoric of debt, charity, and poor relief reveals the extent to which both missionaries' partnership with the U.S. government and U.S. Indian policies more generally were connected with the republic's burgeoning economy. Just as civilizing efforts ensured that "poor Indians" received an education that was tailored for their assumed station—most often agricultural education and manual labor more generally—ideas of mercy, charity, and poverty, articulated by U.S. officials, continued to wed Native peoples to the republic's emerging socioeconomic hierarchy, just as it had during the earliest years of the nineteenth century.

Ideas of success and virtue, born out of the development of the republic's economy, ultimately gave U.S. Indian policies the benevolent sheen that officials hoped would translate into authority at home and abroad. Native peoples' supposedly sad state offered the United States a chance to offer aid that then demonstrated the republic's generous character. Central to this intellectual somersault was the tendency, evident in McKenney's rhetoric as well as that of others, to frame Native peoples as "poor Indians"—not merely in the eighteenth-century sense of "savage" or misguided but as poverty-stricken populations. As Michael Katz's work shows, ideas of the "deserving" and "undeserving" poor abounded during the era of the early republic, precisely when Americans worked to define ideas of race and class.[23] Such ideas applied to Native peoples as well. For some Americans and U.S. officials, those Miamis or Shawnees who attempted to become civilized—but who in actuality appropriated some of the ideas of the civilization plan in order to mold and combat U.S. imperial policies or to maintain their own lands—earned a place among the republic's "deserving poor."

These ideas of philanthropy and economy translated into on-the-ground transactions. John Johnston's concerns regarding Delawares' journey to receive "charity from a foreign nation" at Malden, for example, underscores the importance of speculative philanthropy, this time in the form of poor relief, to U.S. officials in Indian Country. And at times, U.S. government officials were happy to offer aid to those Native peoples they deemed "deserving," both in the Ohio Country and elsewhere. In 1821, for example, Indian agent John Shaw, a Quaker, wrote to Lewis Cass that Wyandots near Upper Sandusky were "intirely destitute of many usefull Tools, and their dispositions to use them are equal at least to any other Indians that I am acquainted with, they in my opinion deserve as much of the bounty of Government as any other Tribe."[24] Shaw continued to assure Cass that the Wyandots, who "may be considered poor," demonstrated appropriate "signs of thankfulness when they receive favours."[25] Wyandots' manners—no doubt, for Shaw, evidence of their propensity for civilization—also convinced Shaw that those near Upper Sandusky were worthy of government aid.

Shaw also offered evidence of Wyandots' destitution and virtue. He noted that "as a proof of the poverty, as also of the Acconomy of these Wyandots they dress very much in leather, and very seldom see them wear any costly clothing or ornaments of Silver as is customary with some other Tribes."[26] Shaw's argument makes clear that Americans' ideas regarding poor Indians were, by the early republic, grounded in observable notions of destitution. The Wyandots' dress demonstrated their "Acconomy" and, in turn, virtue: they refrained from wearing items that they could not afford. That virtue rendered these Wyandots among the "deserving poor." Shaw's assurances of Wyandots' worthiness contrasted their supposed poverty with government abundance and generosity. It was a discourse that positioned the United States as Indians' merciful benefactor even as the burgeoning empire reaped the financial rewards of dispossession and removal. What was more, it offered federal support to settler cries for Indigenous lands while also facilitating the acquisition of moral capital.

Other middling officials continued to appeal to humanity in order to secure federal assistance in removal as well. In 1828, for example, William Clark lamented that "as the wild game deminishes, the pressing calls of those unfortunate people upon the humanity of the Government for assistance increases."[27] Here, however, Clark exposed the continuing disconnect between ideas and reality from which so many Euro-Americans suffered. The "unfortunate people" to which Clark referred in this case were Delawares migrating from Ohio, Delawares who had undoubtedly sufficient knowledge of agriculture and who were by no means completely dependent on "the wild game." Nonetheless, even this intellectual blindness offered a means to construe the U.S. government as humane.

In December 1820, moreover, just two months after Johnston documented Delawares' trip to Malden, Johnston remarked that Delawares near his Piqua agency requested half of their annuity, $2,750, before attempting to remove. Johnston encouraged Cass to agree to the deal since "otherwise it will be impossible to get them off on account of their poverty." He continued to state that "some provision should be made for furnishing them with subsistence and amunition [*sic*] to prosecute their journey." Ultimately, he lamented that "it is a troublesome and expensive affair to get rid of about 1800 sou[ls] many of them the most miserable and wretched o[f] their race. The Government as an act of Mer[cy] and justice too should present them with $3000 worth of goods, to clothe and send them awa[y] confortable [*sic*]. . . . Their claims for depred[a]tions could be commuted in this way."[28] Johnston combined harsh language—"get them off" and "get rid of"—with ideas of paternalistic benevolence in a way that he believed would appeal to federal officials and in a manner reflective of the growing tendency to couple their ideas regarding Natives' poverty with poor relief.

* * *

While men like Shaw and Johnston mostly acted on a local and regional level, they interacted with men like McKenney and Lewis Cass in their letters, and they shared in a dialogue that wed U.S. Indian policies with a discourse of philanthropy on the local, national, and international levels. Such a dialogue contrasted with some evangelicals' and reformers' growing disdain for the U.S. approach to Indian affairs, yet some of these reformers' own efforts—their endeavors to civilize, in particular—figured into their political opponents' arguments. The growing number of civilizing missions helped create a sufficiently coherent portrait of Euro-Americans' efforts to "save" or aid Native peoples, and policymakers held up that portrait to cast Americans' U.S.-Indian policy as benevolent. Civilizing missions helped U.S. officials to craft a lineage of philanthropy—stretching from the earliest days of the republic—that possessed great value in international affairs.

By 1825, nearly forty mission sites, run by a variety of religious societies, received federal funding.[29] Others continued to operate with private funds. The bulk of these were among the Cherokees and Choctaws, yet the geographical reach stretched from Passamaquoddy Country in what is now Maine to Haudenosaunee Country in what is now western New York to the Ohio Country and Great Lakes to Osage Country in what is now Missouri and Arkansas. Each mission site adhered to the broader paradigms of the mission complex: missionaries partnered with the state to offer instruction—including agricultural education—and build infrastructure at the site. Each site also, however, differed according to politics, the Indigenous nations engaged, and the individuals involved. At Choctaw Academy, for example, instructors offered instruction in reading and writing, yet there enslaved people often bore the brunt of the day-to-day labor that maintained the school.[30]

U.S. officials and missionaries dialogued in letters, circulars, and regulations that governed civilizing work, yet there was an international conversation occurring as well. Reformers, including Quakers, corresponded and shared ideas and literature during the nineteenth century, and they kept each other abreast of their respective empires' policy initiatives. Indeed, the Philadelphia and Baltimore Yearly Meetings had, since the eighteenth century, regularly discussed the issue of Indian affairs, and London even offered some funds for North American Friends' initiatives to civilize Native peoples. Such trends continued into the nineteenth century. In 1817, for example, Baltimore Friends recorded that "by a letter received from Elizabeth [Pickessew] a friend residing in Cork, Ireland . . . we have received £100 Sterling, to be appropriated to the use of the Indians to assist in procuring tools or other conveniences for their advantage."[31]

In Australia, members of Britain's Aborigines Protection Society (APS) developed their ideas regarding Indigenous policies in light of and in tandem with those of the United States. Quaker Thomas Hodgkin, for example, encouraged the APS to adopt an assimilationist policy in South Australia as a result of his contempt for Jacksonian plans of removal.[32] One British reformer, Adam Hodgson, moreover, applauded Jedidiah Morse's 1822 plan to civilize Native peoples in communities near Euro-American settlements, and deemed the plan a humanitarian one in his 1824 *Letters from North America, Written During a Tour of the United States and Canada*.[33] A global discourse of benevolence drew upon not only the continental politics of benevolence and civilization, but it was also part of a larger paradigm of settler colonialism around the world.[34]

By the late 1820s and 1830s, British officials, reformers, and thinkers considered U.S. Indian policies to be decidedly less philanthropic, and those policies served as a means to highlight the crucial differences between the British and American empires. In 1837, for example, Saxe Bannister, an official in New South Wales and later a member of British Parliament, applauded the United States' civilizing efforts but decried Jackson's harsher policies of removal. He also made it clear that Britain and the United States were in close competition for the right to claim moral authority. He remarked that "no more honorable rivalry can be imagined than that of the British Parliament with the American Congress in the difficult task of elevating the ignorant and protecting the weak."[35] As both the British and American empires sought to expand their territorial claims, such a competition mattered. The discourse of morality and humanitarianism offered a common language that rendered each power intelligible and comparable to the other.

Cultivating the image of a benevolent empire was not easy for a republic tainted by its notoriety as a slaveholding power. In 1827, Lewis Cass, future secretary of war under Andrew Jackson, nonetheless made the attempt by penning an eighty-page document that compared the treatment of North America's Indigenous peoples during the eras of both the British and American empires. Cass, the architect of Jacksonian removal schemes, had served as the territorial governor of Michigan from 1813 until his appointment as secretary of war in 1831. He was renowned as an expert on Indian affairs and penned works relating to various Indian nations, perhaps most famously, the Delawares in 1821–22, and he continued to write in defense of removal into the 1830s. He was a Democrat, and central to his pro-removal arguments were ideas of benevolence and civilization.[36] His 1827 article was an attempt to position Indian policy as evidence of the United States' enlightened state in contrast to Great Britain. His essay was in response to an indictment, recently printed by the *London Quarterly Review*, of the U.S. government's handling of Indian affairs. Cass's response reveals the extent to which such criticism riled U.S. officials. He began his discussion of Indian affairs claiming that "the true character of this policy has not been well understood, even in this country, and abroad it has too often furnished the motive or the pretext for grave accusation and virulent invective."[37] The document, written for a British but also a global audience, references the United States' reputation numerous times, and, indeed, Cass insisted that "to the judgment of the world we may safely commit the conduct of the American government, in regard to the particulars here touched upon."[38]

Those particulars included extensive analysis of wars conducted by Great Britain and the United States alike and of the virtues of U.S. efforts to offer Native peoples annuity payments and civilization. Cass deemed annuities to be a particularly enlightened policy. He argued that "the plan of *permanent annuities* guaranties to the Indians a never failing resource against want, and its beneficial effects are apparent in the improved condition of the Wyandots, the Shawnese, and the Miamies."[39] As Chapter 5 demonstrates, of course, any "improvement" of Ohio Indians' condition, according to Euro-Americans' standards, was the result of Miamis, Shawnees, and Wyandots' own adaptability and ingenuity. Nonetheless Ohio Native Americans were Cass's rhetorical foil; Indigenous peoples of the southeast, he largely ignored. The situation of Shawnees and Miamis offered Cass his best talking points, largely thanks to mission work, land sales, and, importantly, the absence of slaveholding. "Civilization" in the Ohio Country was tied to ideas of market economy, not slavery, and thus Cass offered little mention of elite Cherokees or Creeks of the southeast, many of whom held enslaved Africans in bondage.[40] In this way, Cass diverted attention away from the issue of slavery in the United States, while simultaneously pointing to Indian policy as the realm in which the republic could stake its benevolent reputation.

Discussion of annuity payments and civilizing policies enabled Cass to draw explicit comparisons with the British Empire. Annuity payments, he argued, ensured Ohio Natives' well-being, and Cass placed the policy—and others—in direct contrast with that of Great Britain in both Canada and Australia. He wrote that "the inquiries, which we have instituted, have satisfied us, that no system of permanent annuities has heretofore been adopted in the Canadas, as a consideration for cessions obtained from the Indians."[41] Great Britain likewise offered no compensation to Indigenous peoples of Australia. "We hear of no treaties of cession," he contended, "no 'purchases compulsory,' or voluntary, no mutual discussions, no annuities for future relief." Instead "*the land is wanted, and it is taken*."[42] The comparison with Britain's colonies suggests not only the extent to which Cass endeavored to portray the United States as an enlightened power but also the degree to which U.S. officials understood the United States as an empire among empires. Employing a direct comparison with Britain in the world, Cass took issue with the *London Review*'s suggestion that the United States was among the most land-hungry of polities, "Has England furnished us with any example of such a system of self denial, or rather of canting weakness?" he asked. "We will not inquire in India, for there no barbarians, strictly speaking, are found. But the Australasian continent is now a British province, acquired and settled within the memory of the present generation. And where are its aboriginal inhabitants?"[43] The idea of "self denial" is particularly striking, and it recalls Johnston's refusal to consider settlers as the true problem on the ground.

Britain, Cass went on to contend, failed to ensure Indigenous peoples' well-being. He censured the British government for neglecting to pass "any prohibition against the introduction of spirituous liquors in any part of their Indian country," and for failing to "to provide a permanent residence for the Indians."[44] Indeed, he wrote, "there were no schools, and no efforts to introduce agriculture, or the mechanic arts. There were no annuities, no regulations to direct the conduct of the traders, and no law to prevent the sale of ardent spirits."[45] For Cass, then, government regulation took on the cast of benevolence. Trading laws, civilizing schemes—these were the tangible evidence of the United States' "benevolent empire," evidence that the British Empire did not have.

According to the *London Quarterly*, however, there was "'not to be found, on the face of the globe, a race of men, so utterly abandoned to vice and crime—so devoid of all fear of God and regard towards man, as the outsettlers of Kentucky, Ohio, and the other back states.'"[46] Cass defended the reputation of Ohio Valley settlers, but also raised the issue of removal in an effort to confront the issue of vice. "Revolting scenes" of Native peoples falling victim to traders' liquors, Cass argued, were limited to areas where Indians and settlers lived in proximity to one another.[47] "In the interior," on the other hand, he insisted that "we have seen many Indians, remote from the white settlements, who had never tasted of spirituous liquors, and we can testify, from personal knowledge, that the evil itself is almost unknown there."[48] Such an argument suggests that Cass viewed removal from the "white settlements" as a potential remedy to Indigenous peoples' problems.

Cass was clear to say, however, that the issue of removal was contested. He explained that "we have brought it before our readers merely as an evidence of the feelings of the American government, and of their earnest desire to discharge with fidelity a great moral debt, which is neither concealed nor denied."[49] By recognizing and attacking the republic's missteps head-on, the United States could remedy past faults. Cass pointed out that in British Canada, no "plan has been digested or proposed for removing the Indians from any part of the lands they now occupy, where they are peculiarly exposed to temptations and danger."[50] By framing the "Indian problem" as an ethical quandary with which the United States actively grappled, Cass offered evidence of American moral superiority, and he framed removal as evidence of Americans' enlightened approach to empire.

The civilization plan and missionaries' labor also figured prominently in Cass's evaluations of U.S. morality. Once again invoking an imperial comparison and quoting a British publication, he informed his readers that "we are told, that 'in Canada, there is but one regular protestant Indian mission!'"[51] As a result of Britain's failure to engage in mission work, Canada suffered "no want of physical wretchedness, or of moral depravity."[52] That "moral depravity" was the result of British indifference and vice. Ultimately, Cass was able to detect only minimal "interference of the British government in any plan to improve the moral condition of the Indians."[53] American missionaries, however, actively sought to spread knowledge of agriculture and the mechanic arts, and they did so at the behest of the U.S. government. Here it is clear, then, that missionary efforts became an important element of American imperial rhetoric. Missionary societies' work was crucial to U.S. claims to benevolence in the early republic.

Cass's article ultimately sought to restore and bolster the humanitarian reputation of the United States abroad, but it was also an attempt to rally his fellow citizens to his side. He insisted that Americans could not "sit still, with folded arms, while the civilized world are believing, and judging, and condemning, deceived, as they well may be, by such bold assumptions" of the United States' Indian policies.[54] He contended that "vainly shall we look back with pride, or forward with hope, or around us with congratulation, if we do not cherish a sacred regard for national character."[55] Connecting Indian policy to the nation's character raised the stakes at home, even as it established Indigenous affairs as a pivotal battlefield upon which U.S. officials endeavored to build and protect the republic's global reputation. The American empire, Cass suggested, was an enlightened one; Indian policies were a means by which Americans could claim moral and political authority.

Cass's frequent allusions to the virtuous nature of American intentions in Indian Country reveals the extent to which considerations of morality factored into claims to global authority. If domestic politics and divisions ensured that the United States could not compete in the race toward abolition, then a "merciful" Indian policy could perhaps offer a means to claim political durability and enlightened standing in the world. Speculative philanthropy in Indian Country was an investment in moral authority on the world stage, and it could serve to elevate the American empire in ways that echoed the imperial competition spurred forward by the discourse of a Black Legend in preceding centuries. Indeed, in a last biting remark, Cass drew upon a vast historical chronology of downfall and wrote that "sincerely do we hope that [Britain's] day of glory will not be shrouded in a night of gloom," and that "what has happened to other nations may happen to her; and the traveler may yet inquire for the site of London, as we now inquire for those of Nineveh and Babylon."[56] Failed Indian policies in North America and Australia, then, showcased Britain's supposed backwardness and proximity to demise. Such logic meant that the United States' own policies offered proof of American exceptionalism: the young republic was unique for its humanitarian treatment of Indigenous peoples, and it would thus endure.[57]

* * *

Despite the frequency with which rhetoric of philanthropy intersected with U.S. Indian policy, not all Americans agreed with officials' overtures of assistance and charity. By this time, many Whigs, the party of choice for many abolitionists, staunchly opposed Cass's and Jackson's removal plans. Yet, as with missionaries, the Whigs were not a monolith: various opinions existed within their ranks. Some Whigs actually supported removal and participated in Americans' settler colonialism. John Johnston—an eventual Whig who was removed from his post by Jackson in 1829—admitted that removal was perhaps Native peoples' best hope for endurance, and, as seen above, he often linked removal with ideas of benevolence in his letters. "Depredations committed on [Natives'] property by our Citizens," Johnston noted in 1827, "are rapidly increasing . . . and after a considerable part of my life spent in managing this description of persons I am free to declare, that in my judgment there is no adequate remedy but removal to a Country of their own, where a suitable Government could be established over them. Whatever speculative benevolence may urge to the contrary, their race must perish under the present management."[58] Johnston's argument was based upon the assumption that Americans could not—and should not—engage in self-denial when it came to Indigenous lands. The "depredations" that he documented could not be resolved by punishing settlers, but rather by removing Native peoples. Here, then, Johnston contrasted "speculative benevolence" with that of removal, a policy that, to his mind, offered the truest form of aid to Native peoples, that of survival. Yet Johnston's disdain for "speculative benevolence" contrasted with the very real speculative philanthropy in which he engaged. Johnston, too, engaged ideas of philanthropy by trying to "save" Native people from the "depredations committed" by white settlers, and he did so in order to remove Native people from his jurisdiction, thereby clearing the way for white settlement in the same. Johnston's plan for removal was not that of Cass or Jackson, but his language reveals in stark terms his participation in American settler colonialism.

While John Johnston wove ideas of poor relief and mercy into his appeals to Cass, other reformers, often members of Johnston's Whig party, vehemently denounced U.S. Indian policies by the later 1820s and 1830s. Such divergence on the removal issue must remind us that those who supported removal were by no means simply "products of their time." Ohio Quaker Elisha Bates, for example, lamented in 1836 that he had "thought it possible that some plan might be adopted by which sections of territory (intermixed) might be obtained by Europeans, without at all unsettling the natives from those spots on which they might be disposed to locate themselves."[59] Reformers such as Catharine Beecher, Lydia Maria Child, Jeremiah Evarts, George B. Cheever, John Greenleaf Whittier, and others, meanwhile, also denounced the U.S. government's Indian policies while also juxtaposing the Indian problem and slavery.[60] These individuals, in newspapers and in petitions, understood and articulated the violence of U.S. policies in Indian Country as inherently linked with the expansion of slavery and, as they did with the problem of slavery, denounced the United States for refusing to extend freedom, citizenship, and humanity to all. Religious denominations published their dissent in their periodicals, often associating pro-removal individuals with greed and the quest for Native land and resources.[61]

Indeed, by Jackson's presidency, religious-minded individuals and missionaries frequently articulated their misgivings regarding removal policies. Evarts, affiliated with the ABCFM, penned a series of widely circulated essays denouncing Jackson's Indian Removal bill. His *William Penn Essays* argued that treaties had established Native people as legal owners of their lands and that the United States was violating the principles of law.[62] By the time of Jackson's bill, women increasingly penned petitions and published their views in Christian periodicals with a vast readership.[63] Female missionaries in Georgia, meanwhile, spearheaded efforts to maintain mission schools as that state imprisoned their male counterparts who refused to swear an oath to the state—and, in turn, its laws regarding Native people and their lands—and obtain a license.[64] By and large, by the dawn of the 1830s, evangelicals and missionaries felt that Jackson had betrayed the promise of their civilizing efforts—they offered evidence of various Native peoples' agriculture, infrastructure, and commercial activity to showcase how far they thought Native Americans had come and how wrong forced removal was. These religious individuals, like Quaker Henry Harvey who lamented the Shawnees' repeated removals, clearly thought that the work of civilization was distinct from that of removal. And, indeed, many—most, even—Quakers lamented the U.S. government's plans for removal by the 1830s and 1840s. Yet the consequences of civilization were clear: the infrastructure that missionaries pointed to in their efforts to showcase Natives' success contributed to settlers' desire for the land, and the rhetoric of mercy, charity, and government philanthropy offered U.S. officials ample means to combat the opposition.[65] What was more, historian William McLoughlin makes clear that despite earlier efforts, by 1832 "only one missionary, the Baptist, Evan Jones, continued to help the Cherokees resist removal."[66]

Of course, Native writers and intellectuals also had ideas regarding the United States' Indian policies and missionaries' benevolence—though, like those white Americans who spoke and wrote about U.S. Indian policy, their ideas were not homogenous. The Ojibwe writer and Methodist missionary George Copway supported and ardently advocated for mission schooling among his people and other nations. In privileging his Ojibwe identity over his Methodist and British and American ones in his autobiography, however, Copway experimented "with forms of survivance and cultural fluidity" and created "a space within his autobiography in which an Ojibwe person can also be both British and American, as well as a creative, intellectual figure and a devout Christian."[67] Indeed, despite his support for missionary works, Copway noted that "the white men have been like the greedy lion, pouncing upon and devouring its prey. They have driven us from our nation, our homes, and possessions."[68] Before Copway, it was it was the Mohegan missionary Samson Occom who considered his religious life, wielded his pen, and exposed the embrace of racial ideologies among Christians. Occom readily observed how little money he received for his services compared to his white missionary counterparts and remarked, "So I am *ready* to Say, they have used me thus, because I Can't Instruct the Indians so well as other missionaries; but I can assure them I have endeavoured to teach them as well as I know how;—but I *must Say*, 'I believe it is because I am a poor Indian.'"[69] And, of course, several years after Cass's own *Remarks*—yet nonetheless in the midst of ongoing imperial competition—Apess delivered his *Eulogy on King Philip* and reminded Euro-Americans about their own history. He reminded missionaries, too, of their work in supporting both British and American imperial schemes. The United States might claim a benevolent mantle in the world, but despite their differences, others—Copway, Occom, Apess—understood the darkness that undergirded that mantle.

* * *

After the American Revolution, the new United States struggled to pinpoint in precise terms the kind of polity it would be. Rhetoric was central to that defining process. The discourse of morality offered a means to compare the young republic with the empires of old, and it offered a powerful narrative by which early Americans could understand their place in the world while simultaneously grappling with their status as an imperial republic.

Ideas of race and class combined to create U.S. Indian policy in the nineteenth century, and missionaries and Indigenous peoples alike played fundamental roles in crafting both the character of those policies and the narrative that Americans spun when trying to contemplate and reconcile the immense violence that characterized their republican experiment. Organizations like the Society of Friends offered a means to provide "useful" education to Indigenous peoples, while U.S. officials endeavored to offer "merciful" American charity to those "deserving" of it. Together, they ultimately enabled U.S. officials to make claims regarding the benevolence of the American empire on a global stage. Native peoples, meanwhile, alternatively fought, outwitted, and endured—sometimes all three—and they forced the young republic to make sense of an inherent contradiction—that of how to be an empire of liberty that denied the liberty, rights, and humanity to many of North America's peoples.

Americans ultimately confronted that contradiction with additional contradictions. And they were powerful. The idea of a benevolent empire, one that could best Britain on the international stage, held purchase in the imaginations of many Americans. Whigs who disdained Jacksonian removal, along with Democrats who saw in it the future of the nation, each saw power in the rhetoric of humanitarianism and philanthropy. Even those reformers who fought removal at the ballot box and in the press found a solution in the maintenance of paternalistic "benevolence" into the twentieth century.[70] Such ideas would accompany U.S. imperialists as they turned their attention to lands beyond the Mississippi and even beyond the Kanaka Maoli homelands in Hawai'i to the islands of the Pacific and the Caribbean by the late nineteenth and early twentieth centuries.[71] In the formative period of the republic's generation, speculative philanthropy, manifested in large part thanks to missionaries' labors, became a tool by which white Americans crafted fictions that ultimately became inseparable from their national narrative and sense of selves as citizens of the world.

Epilogue

French aristocrat Alexis de Tocqueville traversed the Atlantic to visit the United States in 1831. His visit prompted him to publish, in 1835, the first volume of a revealing portrait of the republic in its adolescence. De Tocqueville devoted hundreds of pages of his *Democracy in America* to descriptions of American political structures, economics, and reform efforts, as well as to the situations of Africans, African-descended peoples, and Native Americans. With regard to the latter, the Frenchman explained that "the Spaniards, despite acts of unparalleled monstrousness that left them indelibly covered with shame, were unable to exterminate the Indian race or even prevent the Indians from sharing their rights. The Americans of the United States achieved both results with marvelous ease, quietly, legally, philanthropically, without bloodshed without violating a single one of the great principles of morality in the eyes of the world. To destroy human beings with greater respect for the laws of humanity would be impossible."[1] De Tocqueville's assessment of U.S. Indian affairs—perhaps tongue-in-cheek, perhaps not—captured on the page the reality that the United States shrouded its violent Indian policies in a garb of humanity and philanthropy. What the Frenchman failed to note, however, was how crucial that violence, and the speculative philanthropy that undergirded it, was to the creation and financing of the other marvels and tragedies that he saw—the canals, turnpikes, and railroads, as well as the plantations—and that were the markers of early American capitalism and the growing American empire.

The world in which de Tocqueville traveled was one marked by recent and dramatic change. During the one hundred years that spanned the mid-eighteenth to mid-nineteenth centuries, the Ohio Country, in particular, transformed in profound ways. Euro-American settlers, enslaved peoples, and Native Americans formed the core of the story throughout, yet the imperial powers and political economies that they created and interacted with changed in fundamental ways over time. Violence characterized a mid-eighteenth-century world of fur trading and competition between British, French, and Native power, and, eventually, French defeat in the Seven Years' War. Years later, British, American, and Native powers struggled to claim authority and land as the American Revolution reverberated into the heart of the continent and resulted in an intensifying of settler colonialism and violence. By the 1820s and 1830s, U.S. and Native polities continued to struggle for power and negotiate the terms of American imperial power in the Ohio Country as well as invest in the fertile lands that all coveted.

Missions and missionaries played no small role in these changes, and theirs was the work that could, as de Tocqueville described, so "philanthropically" exact violence on Native peoples. Missionaries adapted to the realities of U.S. imperialism, even as they helped to birth the same. Following their paths, their connections, and their labors assists in grounding the story of imperial and economic change in the lands and lives of the Miamis, Shawnees, Potawatomis, settlers, and government officials who negotiated imperial power on a daily basis. Understanding the material consequences of "civilizing" Native peoples through agricultural education and the cultivation of lands—a policy choice to which missionaries gave life—offers a glimpse of the ideas of race and superiority that guided missionaries and Euro-Americans more broadly in their projects. It also reveals, however, the ways in which the civilizing project was part and parcel of the growth of a U.S. empire that gained power from its ability to grow an economy that reaped its profits from the land and from individuals'—enslaved, Indigenous, and white—labor. It reveals how missions served as nodes in a network of shipping and manufacturing interests—a mission complex—that aided in the growth of markets and that encouraged Euro-American population growth in the region—growth that further fueled investments in the transportation technologies that remade the landscape and the political economy of the United States. It shows that philanthropy could be speculative: a desire to "do good" could be—and often was—intimately linked with a desire to make profit.

Following missionaries beyond the 1830s and into the heart of the continent reveals quite clearly that not all proved to be "winners" in the story of transportation revolution and economic change. It troubles the idea of "progress" to its core. A story of "market revolution" and a "transition to capitalism" obscures the fact that such changes were—quite literally—*built* on Native peoples' lands alongside their abandoned homes and fields, and at the cost of what some, like Shawnees at Wapakoneta, thought would be their investments in their futures. A railroad ultimately traversed Wapakoneta's lands, and it resulted in profits for white investors and settlers. At the same time, that railroad and others like it encouraged Shawnees' repeated removals and the resultant devastation that Quaker Henry Harvey documented and ultimately lamented. Shawnees' disaster translated into white Euro-Americans' profits.

Yet that citizens of the Myaamia Tribe of Oklahoma and other nations still remain in what is now Indiana troubles any declension narrative of peoples engulfed and swept away by removals, and it troubles de Tocqueville's assessment of Native peoples as a race "exterminated." The early years of the American empire in Indian Country laid the foundations for what followed as that empire grew to the Pacific and beyond, but there is no straight line that extends from the early nineteenth-century Ohio Country and its story of Indian removal, speculative philanthropy, and profit to the twenty-first century, though there are many resonances. Individuals acted, negotiated, and struggled during the intervening years. The mission complex and speculative philanthropy accompanied and undergirded the growth of the American empire over time and across space, yet so, too, did Indigenous peoples' own politics, interests, and struggles. Their efforts—crucial to what Gerald Vizenor terms "survivance"—had ramifications that reverberated across time and space, and they point to a pattern of Indigenous peoples working within and against ideological and political paradigms created as a result of U.S.-Native negotiation.[2]

Americans continued to adapt their Indian policies to Native peoples' politics of persistence throughout the nineteenth and twentieth centuries. Policies shifted between—and sometimes combined—civilization, removal, allotment, boarding schools, termination, and, thanks to Indigenous peoples' activist work during the height of "Red Power" and the American Indian Movement, a slow recognition of Indigenous rights and sovereignty by the later twentieth century. The Society of Friends, too, remained central to such policies and ultimately became pivotal to President Ulysses S. Grant's "Peace Policy" after the U.S. Civil War, acting as superintendents of Indian affairs during that period. Such shifts were due in no small part to Indigenous peoples' refusal to disappear.

In many ways, the story of profit, empire, and the rhetoric of benevolence remains at the heart of the United States' relationships with the sovereign Indigenous nations of North America today. So, too, does Native peoples' negotiation. When citizens of the Standing Rock Sioux Tribe directed the attention of the American public and the world to Energy Transfer Partners' quest to build the Dakota Access Pipeline (DAPL) near their reservation beginning in 2016, they highlighted the lingering colonial relationship that exists between Native nations and the United States. The DAPL stood poised to threaten Standing Rock's water supply at Lake Oahe as well as disrupt historical and sacred lands. When environmental allies joined SRS citizens to protest the construction, appeals to the public good—the environment—intersected with Native peoples' efforts to both survive and assert their sovereignty. Just as relationships with missionaries could assist in both making claims upon the state and surviving removals in the nineteenth century, the SRS's partnerships with environmental allies proved effective in garnering international attention and an easement from President Obama in 2016 to halt construction. Citizens of the Standing Rock Sioux Tribe continued Native peoples' centuries-long efforts to resist the quest to harvest profits from Indigenous lands.[3]

As the events at Standing Rock revealed, Native individuals continue to carry the memories of historical violence, while also remaining, thriving, and enduring more violence. To borrow from Christina Sharpe's trenchant analysis of "the wake"—how the past traumas of slavery live and affect African-descended peoples in the present—Native peoples, too, must live with the ever-present nature of a violent past.[4] Yet the work of the Myaamia Center, a collaboration between citizens of the Miami Tribe, their allies, and Miami University in Ohio, nonetheless demonstrates the power of Native peoples' survivance. Citizens are working to ensure that language, games, and histories are maintained, preserved, and given new life. Such work, and that of other nations, looks toward "a traditional future"—a future that is forward-looking, modern, and yet built upon a rich tapestry of Indigenous ways of knowing and engaging the world.[5] The story of speculative philanthropy and empire offers a backdrop for understanding the foundations of Native peoples' ongoing struggle to negotiate U.S. power, and it also illuminates the enduring nature of their survivance.

NOTES

Introduction

1. Karim Tiro, "Denominated 'SAVAGE': Methodism, Writing, and Identity in the Works of William Apess, a Pequot," *American Quarterly* 48, no. 4 (December 1996): 659–679, 668.

2. Lisa Brooks powerfully reads Apess and his *Eulogy* as an effort to establish "New England as Native space into which Europeans entered" (199). She writes, "In the *Eulogy*, he attempted to build a conceptual space from within New England that could potentially include all of the lands' inhabitants and would serve justice to those who were disempowered within it, including his closest relations" (198–199). See Lisa Brooks, *The Common Pot: The Recovery of Native Space in the Northeast* (Minneapolis: University of Minnesota Press, 2007), 198–218.

3. As Susan Ryan notes, the discourse of benevolence supported a number of positions—including some that were repugnant then and now. See Susan Ryan, *The Grammar of Good Intentions: Race and the Antebellum Culture of Benevolence* (Ithaca, NY: Cornell University Press, 2003).

4. Tiro, "Denominated 'SAVAGE,'" 655.

5. William Apess, *Eulogy on King Philip, as Pronounced at the Odeon, in Federal Street, Boston* in Barry O'Connell, ed., *On Our Own Ground: The Complete Writings of William Apess, a Pequot* (Amherst: University of Massachusetts Press, 1992), 310.

6. Ibid., 287.

7. Ibid.

8. For additional treatments of the U.S. as an empire, see Michael Witgen, "A Nation of Settlers: The Early American Republic and the Colonization of the Northwest Territory," *William and Mary Quarterly* 76, no. 3 (July 2019): 391–398; and Michael Witgen, "Seeing Red: Race, Citizenship, and Indigeneity in the Old Northwest," *Journal of the Early Republic* 38, no. 4 (Winter 2018): 581–611.

9. See Daniel K. Richter, "'Believing That Many of the Red People Suffer Much for the Want of Food': Hunting, Agriculture, and a Quaker Construction of Indianness in the Early Republic," *Journal of the Early Republic* 19, no. 4 (Winter 1999): 601–628; Kathleen DuVal, "Debating Identity, Sovereignty, and Civilization: The Arkansas Valley After the Louisiana Purchase," *Journal of the Early Republic* (Spring 2006): 25–59; Francis Paul Prucha, *The Great Father: The United States Government and American Indians* (Lincoln: University of Nebraska Press, 1984); Bernard W. Sheehan, *Seeds of Extinction: Jeffersonian Philanthropy and the American Indian* (Chapel Hill: University of North Carolina, 1973); Reginald Horsman, *Expansion and American Indian Policy, 1783–1812* (East Lansing, MI: Michigan State University Press, 1967); and Reginald Horsman, *Race and Manifest Destiny: Origins of American Racial Anglo-Saxonism* (Cambridge, MA: Harvard University Press, 1981).

10. Emily Conroy-Krutz's work on "Christian Imperialism" in the early republic likewise situates missionaries as part of an American imperial project. See Emily Conroy-Krutz, *Christian Imperialism: Converting the World in the Early American Republic* (Ithaca, NY: Cornell University Press, 2015).

11. For a historiographical overview of the "imperial state," see Gautham Rao, "The New Historiography of the Early Federal Government: Institutions, Contexts, and the Imperial State," *William and Mary Quarterly* 77, no. 1 (2020): 97–128. Scholars often position missions as sites of cultural negotiation, leaving space to consider them more fully as hinges for economic and political change in the early republic. For studies of Friends' missions, see Jill Kinney, "'Letters, Pen, and Tilling the Field': Quaker Schools Among the Seneca Indians on the Allegany River, 1798–1852" (PhD diss., University of Rochester, 2009); Diane Rothenberg, "Friends Like These: An Ethnohistorical Analysis of the Interaction Between Allegany Senecas and Quakers, 1798–1823" (PhD diss., City College of New York, 1976); Matthew Dennis, *Seneca Possessed: Indians, Witchcraft, and Power in the Early American Republic* (Philadelphia: University of Pennsylvania Press, 2010); and Karim Tiro, "'We Wish to Do You Good': The Quaker Mission to the Oneida Nation, 1790–1840," *Journal of the Early Republic* 26, no. 3 (Fall 2006): 353–376.

12. For a history of racial capitalism in a global context, see Cedric J. Robinson, *Black Marxism: The Making of the Black Radical Tradition* (Chapel Hill: University of North Carolina Press, 1981, 2000). Sarah E. K. Fong offers the terminology of "racial-settler capitalism" to understand the ways in which philanthropy, land, and labor intersected in the late nineteenth century. Sarah E. K. Fong, "Racial-Settler Capitalism: Character Building and the Accumulation of Land and Labor in the Late Nineteenth Century," *American Indian Culture and Research Journal* 43, no. 2 (2019): 25–48.

13. There was always the risk, from Euro-Americans' perspectives, that Native peoples would take advantage of civilizing labor and infrastructure for their own purposes or that philanthropists' peers might question their motivations.

14. Such linkages between philanthropy and profit were not novel. Eighteenth-century Moravians in Pennsylvania, for example, linked religion, commerce, and profit in order to finance their far-flung missionary projects, and Quakers, too, forged connections between religion and economy. Nonetheless, the ongoing development of market capitalism in the late eighteenth and early nineteenth century—and with it speculative philanthropy—linked religion and profit even more tightly during the era of the early republic. By uniting the history of missions with that of capitalism and philanthropy, analyzing missionaries' civilizing efforts—during an era when agricultural mission work took place on Indigenous lands coveted by both settlers and speculators—becomes crucially important for understanding the linkages between imperialism and capitalism in the early United States. For connections between religion and profit, see Katherine Carté Engel, *Religion and Profit: Moravians in Early America* (Philadelphia: University of Pennsylvania Press, 2009); and Kristen Block, "Cultivating Inner and Outer Plantations: Property, Industry, and Slavery in Early Quaker Migration to the New World," *Early American Studies* 8, no. 3 (Fall 2010): 515–548.

15. Andrew Woolford says it well: "Benevolence and destruction are understood not as pure opposites but as potentially related terms, since perceived acts of benevolence, guided by an absolute moral certainty, can be experienced by the targets of such benevolence as painful and destructive." See Andrew Woolford, *This Benevolent Experiment: Indigenous Boarding Schools, Genocide, and Redress in Canada and the United States* (Lincoln: University of Nebraska Press, 2015), 3.

16. Christopher Leslie Brown's analysis of the ways in which reformers in early nineteenth-century Britain sought to accumulate "moral capital" and political clout by working for the abolition of slavery is useful for considering the intersections of philanthropy and capitalism in diverse contexts. Brown's work, too, shows that the accumulation of social capital undergirded reform. See Christopher Leslie Brown, *Moral Capital: Foundations of British Abolitionism* (Chapel Hill: University of North Carolina Press, 2006). Kathleen D. McCarthy, meanwhile, shows that economic development, the rise of civil society, and philanthropic projects went hand in hand in the eighteenth century and during the era of the early republic. See Kathleen D. McCarthy, *American Creed: Philanthropy and the Rise of Civil Society, 1700–1865* (Chicago: University of Chicago Press, 2003). On philanthropy in the Atlantic world, see Amanda B. Moniz's masterful *From Empire to Humanity: The American Revolution and the Origins of Humanitarianism* (Oxford: Oxford University Press, 2016). For philanthropy in Indian Country, see Sheehan, *Seeds of Extinction*.

17. Speculative philanthropy also offers a means to analyze the foundations of what scholars today term "philanthrocapitalism"—philanthropy organized and executed in a manner that models the for-profit world of capitalist business. Framing this history as foundational to such later developments helps make plain the crucial role that capitalism played in the development of the U.S. state and its culture of "civilizing" people of color in the name of humanitarianism.

18. On the state and its size, scope, and visibility, see Brian Balogh, *A Government Out of Sight: The Mystery of National Authority in Nineteenth-Century America* (Cambridge: Cambridge University Press, 2009); William J. Novak, "The Myth of the 'Weak' American State," *American Historical Review* 113, no. 3 (June 2008): 752–772; Stephen Skowronek, "Present at the Creation: The State in Early American Political History," *Journal of the Early Republic* 38, no. 1 (2018): 95–103; and Richard R. John, "Rethinking the Early American State," *Polity* 40, no. 3 (July 2008): 332–339. For historiographical overviews of the debates regarding the state, see Rao, "New Historiography"; and Richard R. John, "Governmental Institutions as Agents of Change: Rethinking American Political Development in the Early Republic, 1787–1835," *Studies in American Political Development* 11 (Fall 1997): 347–380.

19. For works that center Indian affairs and settler colonialism in their studies of the state, see Stephen J. Rockwell, *Indian Affairs and the Administrative State in the Nineteenth Century* (Cambridge: Cambridge University Press, 2010); Bethel Saler, *The Settler's Empire: Colonialism and State Formation in America's Old Northwest* (Philadelphia: University of Pennsylvania Press, 2014); and William H. Bergmann, *The American National State and the Early West* (Cambridge: Cambridge University Press, 2012).

20. Novak, "'Weak' American State," 754.

21. Max Edling highlights war as a crucial piece of the early American state's power. See Max E. Edling, *A Hercules in the Cradle: War, Money, and the American State, 1783–1867* (Chicago: University of Chicago Press, 2014).

22. Other scholars, too, examine Native negotiation of and resistance to U.S. expansion. See, for example, Jeffrey Ostler, *Surviving Genocide: Native Nations and the United States from the American Revolution to Bleeding Kansas* (New Haven, CT: Yale University Press, 2019); Jeffrey Ostler, *The Plains Sioux and U.S. Colonialism from Lewis and Clark to Wounded Knee* (Cambridge: Cambridge University Press, 2004); Gregory Evans Dowd, *A Spirited Resistance: The North American Indian Struggle for Unity, 1745–1815* (Baltimore: Johns Hopkins University Press, 1993); Witgen, "Seeing Red."

23. Works by Emilie Connolly and Michael Blaakman further flesh out the ways in which a variety of actors helped make the early U.S. state and its economy. See Emilie Connolly, "Panic, State Power, and Chickasaw Dispossession," *Journal of the Early Republic* 40, no. 4 (Winter 2020): 683–689; and Michael A. Blaakman, "'Haughty Republicans,' Native Land, and the Promise of Preemption," *William and Mary Quarterly* 78, no. 2 (April 2021): 243–250.

24. For power on the edge of empire, see Rachel St. John, "State Power in the West in the Early American Republic," *Journal of the Early Republic* 38, no. 1 (2018): 87–94. For a social history of the state and capitalism, see Andrew Shankman, "Toward a Social History of Federalism: The State and Capitalism To and From the American Revolution," *Journal of the Early Republic* 37, no. 4 (Winter 2017): 615–653. For succinctly describing the state as "blended," I am indebted to feedback and conversation with Andy Shankman during a discussion of a chapter of this book at the McNeil Center for Early American Studies in 2017.

25. Other scholars offer similar ideas regarding the U.S. imperial state. See Rao, "New Historiography"; and Serena Zabin, "Conclusion: Writing To and From the Revolution," *Journal of the Early Republic* 74, no. 4 (2017): 753–764.

26. On negotiated authority, see Gautham Rao, *National Duties: Customs Houses and the Making of the American State* (Chicago: University of Chicago Press, 2016); Shankman, "Toward a Social History of Federalism"; and Jack P. Greene, "Transatlantic Colonization and the Redefinition of Empire in the Early Modern Era: The British-American Experience," in Jack P. Greene, *Creating the British Atlantic: Essays on Transplantation, Adaptation, and Continuity* (Charlottesville: University of Virginia Press, 2013): 83–100 ; David Andrew Nichols, *Engines of Diplomacy: Indian Trading Factories and the Negotiation of American Empire* (Chapel Hill: University of North Carolina Press, 2016).

27. Civilization Fund Act, March 3, 1819, in Francis Paul Prucha, ed., *Documents of United States Indian Policy*, 3rd. edition (Lincoln: University of Nebraska Press, 2000), 33.

28. See Carol Nackenoff with Allison Hrabar, "Quaker Roles in Making and Implementing Federal Indian Policy: From Grant's Peace Policy through the Early Dawes Act Era (1869–1900)," in Ignacio Gallup-Diaz and Geoffrey Plank, eds., *Quakers and Native Americans* (Leiden: Brill, 2019), 271–292; and Joan Greene, "Civilize the Indian: Government Policies, Quakers, and Cherokee Education," *Journal of Cherokee Studies* 10, no. 2 (1985): 192–204.

29. Such analysis adds to recent scholarship on slavery and capitalism that also charts the connections between economy, race, and the development of the United States. For recent scholarship on slavery and capitalism, see Walter Johnson, *River of Dark Dreams: Slavery and Empire in the Cotton Kingdom* (Cambridge, MA: Harvard University Press, 2013); Edward E. Baptist, *The Half Has Never Been Told: Slavery and the Making of American Capitalism* (New York: Basic Books, 2014); Sven Beckert, *Empire of Cotton: A Global History* (New York: Knopf, 2014); Caitlin Rosenthal, *Accounting for Slavery: Masters and Management* (Cambridge, MA: Harvard University Press, 2018); and Seth Rockman, "What Makes the History of Capitalism Newsworthy?" *Journal of the Early Republic* 34, no. 3 (Fall 2014): 439–466. For calls to include Native peoples in broader economic histories, see Stephen Aron, "The Significance of the Frontier in the Transition to Capitalism," in Christopher Clark, ed., "The Transition to Capitalism in America: A Panel Discussion," *History Teacher* 27, no. 3 (May 1994): 263–288; and Alexandra Harmon, Colleen O'Neill, and Paul C. Rosier, "Interwoven Economic Histories: American Indians in a Capitalist America," *Journal of American History* (December 2011): 698–722. Work by Harry Scheiber, too, examines the linking of government and economy. Scheiber notes the existence of "activist officialdom"—putting to rest any claims that the federal government was not involved in economic policy (59). Scheiber notes, however, that the federal government's

interventions were in specific areas—leaving a space to examine how economic change and government policy went hand in hand in Indian Country—and not only due to land sales (87–88). See Harry N. Scheiber, "Federalism and the American Economic Order, 1789–1910," *Law & Society Review* 10 (1975): 57–118.

30. See Robinson, *Black Marxism*, especially Chapter 8; Jody A. Byrd, Alyosha Goldstein, Jodi Melamed, and Chandan Reddy, "Predatory Value: Economies of Dispossession and Disturbed Relationalities," *Social Text* 36, no. 2 (June 2018): 1–18; Winona LaDuke and Deborah Cowen, "Beyond Wiindigo Infrastructure," *South Atlantic Quarterly* 119, no. 2 (April 2020): 243–268; and Eric Williams, *Capitalism and Slavery* (Chapel Hill: University of North Carolina Press, 1944, 1994).

31. Coxe was an ardent supporter of an economy that married manufacturing and farming interests. Jefferson, on the other hand, envisioned a thoroughly agrarian republic. See Tench Coxe, *Observations on the Agriculture, Manufactures and Commerce of the United States* (New York: Childs & Swaine, 1789); Jacob E. Cooke, "Tench Coxe, Alexander Hamilton, and the Encouragement of American Manufactures," *William and Mary Quarterly*, 3rd Series, 32, no. 3 (July 1975): 369–392; and Jacob E. Cooke, *Tench Coxe and the Early Republic* (Chapel Hill: University of North Carolina Press, 1978). Jefferson offered his clearest articulation of his agrarian idealism in *Notes on a State of Virginia*. See Thomas Jefferson, *Notes on a State of Virginia* in Merrill D. Peterson, ed., *Thomas Jefferson: Writings: Autobiography/Notes on the State of Virginia/Public and Private Papers/Addresses/Letters* (Library of America) (New York: Penguin Putnam Inc., 1984), 123–325. See also Peter S. Onuf, *Jefferson's Empire: The Language of American Nationhood* (Charlottesville: University of Virginia Press, 2000).

32. Laurence Hauptman's work on what is now western New York is an important exception to this. See Laurence M. Hauptman, *Conspiracy of Interests: Iroquois Dispossession and the Rise of New York State* (Syracuse, NY: Syracuse University Press, 1999). For works on market revolution, see, for example, Harry N. Scheiber, *Ohio Canal Era: A Case Study of Government and the Economy* (Athens: Ohio University Press, 1969), 4; Charles Sellers, *The Market Revolution: Jacksonian America, 1815–1846* (Oxford: Oxford University Press, 1994); Daniel Walker Howe, *What Hath God Wrought: The Transformation of America, 1815–1848* (Oxford: Oxford University Press, 2007); and John Lauritz Larson, *The Market Revolution in America: Liberty, Ambition, and the Eclipse of the Common Good* (Cambridge: Cambridge University Press, 2009).

33. Though missing the history of Indian removals, Harry Scheiber's work nonetheless remains excellent for understanding the connections between government and economic change—pushing against what was then a historiographical tendency to understand the nineteenth century as a laissez-faire moment in government and economic policy. See Scheiber, *Ohio Canal Era*.

34. Rao, *National Duties*, 106, 119–120.

35. That railroad was also connected with the Union Bank of Maryland, the bank in which Thomas and other members of the committee invested Indian Concerns Committee funds. What was more, Thomas Ellicott—relative of the many Ellicotts who served on the Indian Concerns Committee—was president of that same Union Bank of Maryland from 1819 through to the end of the infamous Bank War. On the connection between the B&O Railroad and the Union Bank of Maryland, see James D. Dilts, *The Great Road: The Building of the Baltimore and Ohio, the Nation's First Railroad, 1828–1853* (Stanford, CA: Stanford University Press, 1993), 171–172. For the investment of Indian Concerns Committee funds, see Minutes of the Baltimore Yearly Meeting Standing Committee on Indian Concern (hereafter BYMCIC), minutes 1795-1815, 3 month 12 [March 12], 1809, 227 (Friends Historical Library, Swarthmore College,

Swarthmore, PA). On Thomas Ellicott and the Bank War, see Frank Otto Gatell, "Secretary Taney and the Baltimore Pets: A Study in Banking and Politics," *Business History Review* 39, no. 2 (Summer 1965): 205–227.

36. "Philip E. Thomas: Founder of the American Railway System. Phrenological Character and Biography," *American Phrenological Journal: A Repository of Science, Literature, General Intelligence* 31, no. 6 (June 1860): 81–83; Brown, *Moral Capital.*

37. For an analysis of this phenomenon in the later nineteenth century, see Noam Maggor, *Brahmin Capitalism: Frontiers of Wealth and Populism in America's First Gilded Age* (Cambridge, MA: Harvard University Press, 2017).

38. Robin D. G. Kelley, "Introduction," Race, Capitalism, Justice Forum 1, *Boston Review* (2017): 7.

39. A number of scholars working in the fields of Native American Studies and history are similarly highlighting the ways in which U.S. Indian policies both grew out of and contributed to the development of the U.S. economy. Jodi Byrd et al., for example, endeavor to analyze the ways in which "colonialism and racial capitalism have been historically co-constitutive," and the authors observe that "colonization and the economies of racial subjection serve as conditions of possibility in the United States for the ways in which financial institutions and land and market speculators have produced and profited from those most economically disenfranchised." See Byrd et al., "Predatory Value," 2. On the relationship between capitalism and dispossession, see Claudio Saunt, "Financing Dispossession: Stocks, Bonds, and the Deportation of Native Peoples in the Antebellum United States," *Journal of American History* 106 (September 2019): 315–337; and Connolly, "Panic." Michael Witgen's work, too, addresses these issues. See Witgen, "Seeing Red."

40. Ryan, *Grammar of Good Intentions*, 16.

41. For new histories of capitalism, see, for example, Daina Ramey Berry, *The Price for Their Pound of Flesh: The Value of the Enslaved, from Womb to Grave, in the Building of a Nation* (Boston: Beacon Press, 2017); Rosenthal, *Accounting for Slavery*; Baptist, *Half Has Never Been Told.*

42. Julie L. Reed, *Serving the Nation: Cherokee Sovereignty and Social Welfare, 1800–1907* (Norman: University of Oklahoma Press, 2016), 5.

43. Vizenor defines "survivance" as being "an active sense of presence" that entails more than mere survival, but rather a thriving. See Gerald Vizenor, "Aesthetics of Survivance: Literary Theory and Practice," in Gerald Vizenor, ed., *Survivance: Narratives of Native Presence* (Lincoln: University of Nebraska Press, 2008), 1.

44. William Clark to John C. Calhoun, St. Louis, September 5, 1823, National Archives, RG 107, Secretary of War, Letters Received, C-149 (17) in Shawnee file, IU Ethnohistory archive, 1823, folder 1 of 1.

45. Such work allows us to link policy history with Indigenous histories more fully and robustly. An inexhaustive sampling of this vast literature—some of which forces early American historians to think critically about methodology—includes Ned Blackhawk, *Violence over the Land: Indians and Empires in the Early American West* (Cambridge, MA: Harvard University Press, 2006); Brian DeLay, *The War of a Thousand Deserts: Indian Raids and the U.S.-Mexican War* (New Haven, CT: Yale University Press, 2008); Saler, *Settlers' Empire*; Ostler, *Plains Sioux and U.S. Colonialism*; Michael Witgen, *An Infinity of Nations: How the Native New World Shaped Early North America* (Philadelphia: University of Pennsylvania Press, 2011) Nichols, *Engines of Diplomacy*; Kathleen DuVal, *The Native Ground: Indians and Colonists in the Heart of the Continent* (Philadelphia: University of Pennsylvania Press, 2006); Christina Snyder, *Great Crossings: Indians,*

Settlers & Slaves in the Age of Jackson (Oxford: Oxford University Press, 2017); Lisa Brooks, *Our Beloved Kin: A New History of King Philip's War* (New Haven, CT: Yale University Press, 2019); Jean O'Brien, *Firsting and Lasting: Writing Indians Out of Existence in New England* (Minneapolis: University of Minnesota Press, 2010); and Daniel K. Richter, *Facing East from Indian Country: A Native History of Early America* (Cambridge, MA: Harvard University Press, 2001).

46. Adam Rothman's work is excellent on this point for the South. See Adam Rothman, *Slave Country: American Expansion and the Origins of the Deep South* (Cambridge, MA: Harvard University Press, 2005).

47. For work on the Ohio Valley and Trans-Appalachian West, see Michael N. McConnell, *A Country Between: The Upper Ohio Valley and Its Peoples, 1724–1774* (Lincoln: University of Nebraska Press, 1992); John P. Bowes, *Exiles and Pioneers: Eastern Indians in the Trans-Mississippi West* (Cambridge: Cambridge University Press, 2007); Stephen Aron, *How the West Was Lost: The Transformation of Kentucky from Daniel Boone to Henry Clay* (Baltimore: Johns Hopkins University Press, 1996); Eric Hinderaker, *Elusive Empires: Constructing Colonialism in the Ohio Valley, 1673–1800* (Cambridge: Cambridge University Press, 1997); Andrew R. L. Cayton, *Frontier Indiana* (Bloomington: Indiana University Press, 1996); and Andrew R. L. Cayton and Stuart D. Hobbs, eds., *The Center of a Great Empire: The Ohio Country in the Early American Republic* (Athens: Ohio University Press, 2005). For efforts to link regional histories with broader perspectives, see Andrew R. L. Cayton and Peter S. Onuf, *The Midwest and the Nation: Rethinking the History of an American Region* (Bloomington: Indiana University Press, 1990).

48. For a direct and thorough comparison of these territories, see Gregory Ablavsky, *Federal Ground: Governing Property and Violence in the First U.S. Territories* (Oxford: Oxford University Press, 2021). Thanks to Gregory Ablavsky for generously sharing his manuscript with me prior to its publication.

Chapter 1

1. Minutes of the Baltimore Yearly Meeting Standing Committee on Indian Concern (hereafter BYMCIC) Minutes, 1795–1815, 10th month 5 [October 5], 1804, 76–77 (Friends Historical Library, Swarthmore College, Swarthmore, PA).

2. Henry Knox to George Washington, July 7, 1789, in Walter Lowrie, Walter S. Franklin, and Matthew St. Clair Clarke, eds., *American State Papers, Indian Affairs, Vol. 1, Documents, Legislative and Executive of the Congress of the United States* (Washington, DC: Gales and Seaton, 1832), 53–54.

3. Such thinking was in dialogue with ideas of race. See Daniel K. Richter, "'Believing That Many of the Red People Suffer Much for the Want of Food': A Quaker View of Indians in the Early Republic," *Journal of the Early Republic* 19, no. 4 (Winter, 1999): 601–628.

4. On Indigenous prosperity in the Ohio Valley—and the centrality of Native women to the creation of that prosperity—see Susan Sleeper-Smith, *Indigenous Prosperity and American Conquest: Indian Women of the Ohio River Valley, 1690–1792* (Chapel Hill: University of North Carolina Press, by the Omohundro Institute of Early American History and Culture, 2018). On Indigenous prosperity, wealth, and market engagement in a variety of contexts, see Alexandra Harmon, *Rich Indians: Native People and the Problem of Wealth in American History* (Chapel Hill: University of North Carolina Press, 2010); and Daniel H. Usner Jr., *Indians, Settlers & Slaves in a Frontier Exchange Economy: The Lower Mississippi Valley Before 1783* (Chapel Hill: University of North Carolina Press, by the Omohundro Institute of Early American History and Culture, 1992).

5. On the Washington administration's Indian policies and Knox, see Colin G. Calloway, *The Indian World of George Washington: The First President, The First Americans, and the Birth of the Nation* (Oxford: Oxford University Press, 2018).

6. Ibid.

7. Ibid., 455–468.

8. Robert F. Berkhofer Jr., *Salvation and the Savage: An Analysis of Protestant Missions and American Indian Response, 1787–1862* (Lexington, KY: University of Kentucky Press, 1965), 72.

9. The Choctaw Academy and the Foreign Missionary School founded by the ABCFM in 1817 in Cornwall, CT, were prominent examples of larger-scale manual-labor boarding schools. See Christina Snyder, *Great Crossings: Indians, Settlers & Slaves in the Age of Jackson* (Oxford: Oxford University Press, 2017); and John Putnam Demos, *The Heathen School: A Story of Hope and Betrayal in the Age of the Early Republic* (New York: Alfred A. Knopf, 2014). See also Berkhofer Jr., *Salvation and the Savage*, 77.

10. And, indeed, such was the case beyond North America: in the Ottoman Empire, for example, missionaries were likewise crucial to imperial projects.

11. While it is vital that we connect earlier North American imperial history to that of the United States, we should take care to highlight both the connections and distinctions that marked the various histories and refrain from framing pre-1776 history as a mere prelude. For a discussion of these issues, see the April 2021 issue of the *William and Mary Quarterly*. In particular, see Eliga Gould and Rosemarie Zagarri, "Situating the United States in Vast Early America: Introduction"; Jessica Choppin Roney, "Containing Multitudes: Time, Space, the United States, and Vast Early America"; and Annette Gordon-Reed and Peter S. Onuf, "The Nation-State in a Changing World: Epilogue," *William and Mary Quarterly*, 3rd Series, 78, no. 2 (April 2021): 275–280.

12. On settler colonialism, see Patrick Wolfe, "Settler Colonialism and the Elimination of the Native," *Journal of Genocide Research* 8, no. 4 (December 2006): 387–409; Lorenzo Veracini, *Settler Colonialism: A Theoretical Overview* (New York: Palgrave Macmillan, 2010); and Lisa Ford, *Settler Sovereignty: Jurisdiction and Indigenous People in America and Australia, 1788–1836* (Cambridge, MA: Harvard University Press, 2010).

13. Amy Bushnell Turner, "Missions and Moral Judgement," *OAH Magazine of History* 14, no. 4, The Spanish Frontier in North America (Summer 2000): 23.

14. See, for example, Tracy Neal Leavelle, *The Catholic Calumet: Colonial Conversions in French and Indian North America* (Philadelphia: University of Pennsylvania Press, 2012); Bronwen McShea, *Apostles of Empire: The Jesuits of New France* (Lincoln: University of Nebraska Press, 2019); Katherine Carté Engel, *Religion and Profit: Moravians in Early America* (Philadelphia: University of Pennsylvania Press, 2009); Ramón A. Gutiérrez, *When Jesus Came, the Corn Mothers Went Away: Marriage, Sexuality, and Power in New Mexico, 1500–1846* (Stanford, CA: Stanford University Press, 1991); David J. Silverman, *Faith and Boundaries: Colonists, Christianity, and Community Among the Wampanoag Indians of Martha's Vineyard, 1600–1871* (Cambridge: Cambridge University Press, 2005); Laura Stevens, *The Poor Indians: British Missionaries, Native Americans, and Colonial Sensibility* (Philadelphia: University of Pennsylvania Press, 2004); Demos, *Heathen School*; Snyder, *Great Crossings*; and Katharine Gerbner, *Christian Slavery: Conversion and Race in the Protestant Atlantic World* (Philadelphia: University of Pennsylvania Press, 2018).

15. Carla Gardina Pestana's work on the British Empire and Protestantism illustrates the ways in which Protestantism facilitated British imperialism, and it also shows that Protestantism

was diverse. Colonial encounters could both change others' beliefs as well as change those of Protestants themselves. See Carla Gardina Pestana, *Protestant Empire: Religion and the Making of the British Atlantic World* (Philadelphia: University of Pennsylvania Press, 2009); and Carla Gardina Pestana, "The Missionary Impulse in the Atlantic World, 1500–1800: Or How Protestants Learned to Be Missionaries," *Social Sciences and Missions* 26 (2013): 9–39.

16. On smuggling, see, for example, Jesse Cromwell, *The Smugglers' World: Illicit Trade and Atlantic Communities in Eighteenth-Century Venezuela* (Chapel Hill: University of North Carolina Press, Omohundro Institute of Early American History and Culture, 2018).

17. Pestana, "Missionary Impulse," 12.

18. Kent G. Lightfoot, Lee M. Panich, Tsim D. Schneider, Sara L. Gonzalez, Matthew A. Russell, Darren Modzelewski, Theresa Molino, and Elliot H. Blair , "The Study of Indigenous Political Economies and Colonialism in Native California: Implications for Contemporary Tribal Groups and Federal Recognition," *American Antiquity* 78, no. 1 (January 2013): 95.

19. Lisbeth Haas, *Saints and Citizens: Indigenous Histories of Colonial Missions and Mexican California* (Berkeley: University of California Press, 2014), 5.

20. Marie Christine Duggan, "With and Without an Empire: Financing for California Missions Before and After 1810," *Pacific Historical Review* 85, no. 1 (February 2016): 23–71.

21. Haas, *Saints and Citizens*. Lisbeth Haas's work combines Indigenous oral histories and visual culture with European-produced documents to offer a glimpse of the ways in which Indigenous authority, memory, and identity survived within mission spaces.

22. McShea, *Apostles of Empire*, xvii.

23. McShea, *Apostles of Empire*. McShea's work builds upon earlier scholars' treatments of the Jesuits—treatments that historically showcased the religious men's missionary and ethnographic undertakings—by underscoring that Jesuits were simultaneously agents of Christianity and agents of empire. For these earlier treatments, see, in particular, Allan Greer, *The Mohawk Saint: Catherine Tekakwitha and the Jesuits* (Oxford: Oxford University Press, 2004).

24. Michael Witgen, in particular, illuminates this world of Indigenous power. See Michael Witgen, *An Infinity of Nations: How the Native New World Shaped Early North America* (Philadelphia: University of Pennsylvania Press, 2011).

25. Susan Sleeper-Smith, *Indian Women and French Men: Rethinking Cultural Encounter in the Western Great Lakes* (Amherst: University of Massachusetts Press, 2001); and Susan Sleeper-Smith, "Women, Kin, and Catholicism: New Perspectives on the Fur Trade," *Ethnohistory* 47, no. 2 (Spring 2000): 423–452. Lucy Murphy's work on the lead-mining industry in what is now Wisconsin and western Illinois likewise reveals that Native women created networks, often through intermarriage with European men. Through marriage and the assertion of their own expectations, they held power to welcome or turn away European men if they deemed them untrustworthy: "Native communities insisted on marriage because it created the assurance of mutuality and reciprocal obligations between the spouses' families. If a man refused to take a wife who had kin ties to the community with which he wanted to do business, he was not trusted." See Lucy Murphy, *A Gathering of Rivers: Indians, Métis, and Mining in the Western Great Lakes, 1737–1832* (Lincoln: University of Nebraska Press, 2000), 85.

26. Pestana, "Missionary Impulse," 20.

27. Ibid., 22. Nonetheless, as Pestana notes, Eliot's experiment was novel in that it was a corporation financed by monies raised by other congregations.

28. Ibid., 34–39.

29. Ibid., 35–36.

30. Berkhofer Jr., *Salvation and the Savage*, 2–6.

31. Pestana, "Missionary Impulse."

32. Laura Stevens, in particular, notes that while conversions were few, British missionary writing was plentiful and played a crucial role in cultivating a culture of sensibility and sense of self in the British Empire. See Stevens, *Poor Indians*.

33. Pestana, *Protestant Empire*, 6–8.

34. Pestana, "Missionary Impulse," 22.

35. Engel, *Religion and Profit*.

36. Margaret Connell Szasz provides an overview of mission schooling before 1800. See Margaret Connell Szasz, *Indian Education in the American Colonies, 1607–1783* (Lincoln: University of Nebraska Press, 1988).

37. See Gerbner, *Christian Slavery*; and Travis Glasson, *Missionary Anglicanism and Slavery in the Atlantic World* (Oxford: Oxford University Press, 2011).

38. Jon F. Sensbach, *A Separate Canaan: The Making of an Afro-Moravian World in North Carolina* (Chapel Hill: University of North Carolina Press, 1998), xvii–xviii.

39. Engel, *Religion and Profit*, 91.

40. See William Apess, "Eulogy on King Philip, as Pronounced at the Odeon, in Federal Street, Boston" in Barry O'Connell, ed., *On Our Own Ground: The Complete Writings of William Apess, a Pequot* (Amherst: University of Massachusetts Press, 1992), 310; and Karim Tiro, "Denominated 'SAVAGE': Methodism, Writing, and Identity in the Works of William Apess, a Pequot," *American Quarterly* 48, no. 4 (December 1996): 653–679.

41. See Gutiérrez, *When Jesus Came*; and Carroll L. Riley, *The Kachina and the Cross: Indians and Spaniards in the Early Southwest* (Salt Lake City: University of Utah Press, 1999).

42. David J. Silverman, "Indians, Missionaries, and Religious Translation: Creating Wampanoag Christianity in Seventeenth-Century Martha's Vineyard," *William and Mary Quarterly*, 3rd Series, 62, no. 2 (April 2005): 141–174.

43. Ibid., 159, 155.

44. Edward E. Andrews, *Native Apostles: Black and Indian Missionaries in the British Atlantic World* (Cambridge, MA: Harvard University Press, 2013).

45. Greer, *Mohawk Saint*.

46. Lee M. Panich and Tsim D. Schneider articulate the ways in which missions were Indigenous spaces in Indigenous landscapes in their edited volume on missions in what is now California. See "Native Agency at the Margins of Empire: Indigenous Landscapes, Spanish Missions, and Contested Histories," in Lee M. Panich and Tsim D. Schneider, eds., *Indigenous Landscapes and Spanish Missions: New Perspectives from Archaeology and Ethnohistory* (Tucson: University of Arizona Press, 2014): 5–22.

47. On Indigenous peoples' negotiations and survivance in boarding schools, see Brenda J. Child, *Boarding School Seasons: American Indian Families, 1900–1940* (Lincoln: University of Nebraska Press, 1998); K. Tsianina Lomawaima, *They Called It Prairie Light: The Story of Chilocco Indian School* (Lincoln: University of Nebraska Press, 1994).

48. Such work is especially prominent with regard to California missions, where the California Indian History Curriculum Coalition is working to change California curriculums to accurately reflect the history of missions. See Khal Schneider, Dale Allender, Margarita Berta-Avila, Rose Borunda, Gregg Castro, Amy Murray, and Jenna Porter, "More Than Missions: Native Californians and Allies Changing the Story of California History," *Journal of American Indian Education* 58, no. 3 (Fall 2019): 58–77. For educational initiatives that clearly assert Native

presence, see Louellyn White, *Free to Be Mohawk: Indigenous Education at the Akwesasne Freedom School* (Norman: University of Oklahoma Press, 2015); and Julie L. Davis, *Survival Schools: The American Indian Movement and Community Education in the Twin Cities* (Minneapolis: University of Minnesota Press, 2013).

49. Emily Conroy-Krutz, *Christian Imperialism: Converting the World in the Early American Republic* (Ithaca, NY: Cornell University Press, 2015).

50. James H. Merrell, *Into the American Woods: Negotiations on the Pennsylvania Frontier* (New York: W. W. Norton & Company, 1999).

51. On Teedyuscung, see Anthony F. C. Wallace, *King of the Delawares: Teedyuscung, 1700–1763* (Syracuse, NY: Syracuse University Press, 1949).

52. *Minutes of Conferences held with the Indians at Easton, in the months of July and November, 1756; together with two messages sent by the government to the Indians residing on the Susquehannah; and report of the committee appointed by the assembly to attend the governor at the last of the said conferences* (Philadelphia: B. Franklin, 1757), 4.

53. Hermann Wellenreuther, "The Political Dilemma of the Quakers in Pennsylvania, 1681–1748," *Pennsylvania Magazine of History and Biography* 94, no. 2 (1970): 135–172.

54. Samuel Parrish, *Some chapters in the history of the Friendly Association for Regaining and Preserving the Peace with the Indians by Pacific Measures* (Philadelphia: Friends' Historical Association, 1877), 29.

55. Julius H. Rubin, *Perishing Heathens: Stories of Protestant Missionaries and Christian Indians in Antebellum America* (Lincoln: University of Nebraska Press, 2017), 76.

56. On the writing and circulation of texts in the English and British context, see Stevens, *Poor Indians*. For a wide-ranging tour of the Black Legend and its contexts, see Margert R. Greer, Walter D. Mignolo, and Maureen Quilligan, eds., *Rereading the Black Legend: The Discourses of Religion and Racial Difference in Renaissance Empires* (Chicago: University of Chicago Press, 2007).

57. Karen Halttunen, "Humanitarianism and the Pornography of Pain in Anglo-American Culture," *American Historical Review* 100, no. 2 (April 1995): 303–334.

58. Travel writing has a long history of shaping the European imaginary. Jennifer L. Morgan, in particular, shows how such writing contributed to ideas of and associations between Indigenous women, Black women, and the monstrous. See Jennifer L. Morgan, "'Some Could Suckle over Their Shoulder': Male Travelers, Female Bodies, and the Gendering of Racial Ideology, 1500–1770," *William and Mary Quarterly* 54, no. 1 (January 1997): 167–192. Konstantin Dierks, meanwhile, demonstrates the power of letters to shape a white middle class in the British Empire, further separating in the white imaginary white Britons from Indigenous peoples and enslaved Africans and African-descended peoples. See Konstantin Dierks, *In My Power: Letter Writing and Communications in Early America* (Philadelphia: University of Pennsylvania Press, 2009).

59. See Stevens, *Poor Indians*.

60. Witgen, *Infinity of Nations*.

61. Daniel H. Usner Jr. sketches the growth of the "frontier exchange economy" in the Lower Mississippi, for example, in the eighteenth century. Other scholars, from Michael Witgen to Susan Sleeper-Smith to Lucy Murphy, have offered works that are similarly illuminating regarding the ways in which markets and trade linked Indigenous and European peoples of North America together during the centuries preceding the emergence of the United States. They highlight, too, how Native peoples adapted their economies to changing economic

landscapes. See Usner Jr., *Indians, Settlers & Slaves*; Witgen, *Infinity of Nations*; and Murphy, *Gathering of Rivers*.

62. Wolfe, "Settler Colonialism," 387–409.

63. On the Northwest Ordinance, see Peter S. Onuf, *Statehood and Union: A History of the Northwest Ordinance* (Bloomington: Indiana University Press, 1987); and R. Douglas Hurt, "Historians and the Northwest Ordinance," *Western Historical Quarterly* 20, no. 3 (1989): 261–280.

64. Northwest Ordinance, July 13, 1787 (National Archives Microfilm Publication M332, roll 9); Miscellaneous Papers of the Continental Congress, 1774–1789; Records of the Continental and Confederation Congresses and the Constitutional Convention, 1774–1789, Record Group 360; National Archives.

65. Ibid., section eleven.

66. Ibid., section twelve.

67. Tiya Miles's discussion of the Northwest Ordinance and slavery is particularly illuminative, and her work transforms our understanding of the document. See Tiya Miles, *The Dawn of Detroit: A Chronicle of Bondage and Freedom in the City of the Straits* (New York: New Press, 2017). On slavery in the Ohio Country, see M. Scott Heerman, *The Alchemy of Slavery: Human Bondage and Emancipation in the Illinois Country, 1730–1865* (Philadelphia: University of Pennsylvania Press, 2018); Matthew Salafia, *Slavery's Borderland: Freedom and Bondage Along the Ohio River* (Philadelphia: University of Pennsylvania Press, 2013); and Paul Finkelman, "Slavery and the Northwest Ordinance: A Study in Ambiguity," *Journal of the Early Republic* 6, no. 4 (1986): 343–370.

68. Gordon Wood presents the crisis of the 1780s as part of a breakdown of republican political theory and, indeed, the 1787 legislation reveals that government policymakers were attempting to redefine the authority of the federal government. See Gordon S. Wood, *The Creation of the American Republic, 1776–1787* (Chapel Hill: University of North Carolina Press, 1969).

69. Gregory Ablavsky, "The Savage Constitution," *Duke Law Journal* 63, no. 5 (February 2014): 1006–1007, quotation on 1007.

70. Northwest Ordinance, article 3.

71. Ostler on NW Ordinance; Jeffrey Ostler, "'Just and lawful war' as Genocidal War in the (United States) Northwest Ordinance and Northwest Territory, 1787–1832," *Journal of Genocide Research* 18, no. 1 (2016): 1–20.

72. Gregory Ablavsky, *Federal Ground: Governing Property and Violence in the First U.S. Territories* (Oxford: Oxford University Press, 2021), 87 (unpublished proofs).

73. Ibid.

74. Lisa Brooks, *The Common Pot: The Recovery of Native Space in the Northeast* (Minneapolis: University of Minnesota Press, 2007), 106–162.

75. While the United States issued the Trade and Intercourse Acts in an attempt to ward off British traders and regulate settler colonization of Indian lands, the acts also exposed both the republic's commitment to building its fledgling economy and the centrality of Indian Country to that process. Indian affairs became a crucial piece not only of the engineering required to build an empire and a federal state, but also to the financing of imperial growth. On early federal economic policies, see Gautham Rao, *National Duties: Customs Houses and the Making of the American State* (Chicago: University of Chicago Press, 2016), 119–120; and Douglas A. Irwin, "Revenue or Reciprocity?: Founding Feuds over Early U.S. Trade Policy," in Douglas A. Irwin and Richard Sylla, eds., *Founding Choices: American Economic Policy in the 1790s* (Chicago: University of Chicago Press, 2009), 89–120.

76. For histories of the Trade and Intercourse Act, see Francis Paul Prucha, *American Indian Policy in the Formative Years: The Indian Trade and Intercourse Acts 1790–1834* (Cambridge, MA: Harvard University Press, 1962); for "civilized arts," see 55–56.

77. On the military and authority, see Andrew R. L. Cayton, "'Separate Interests' and the Nation-State: The Washington Administration and the Origins of Regionalism in the Trans-Appalachian West," *Journal of American History* 79, no. 1 (June 1992): 39–67.

78. On Friends' changing political involvement in North America, see Jack D. Marietta, *The Reformation of American Quakerism, 1748–1783* (Philadelphia: University of Pennsylvania Press, 1984).

79. Brown, *Moral Capital.*

80. Karim M. Tiro, "'We Wish to Do You Good': The Quaker Mission to the Oneida Nation, 1790–1840," *Journal of the Early Republic* 26, no. 3 (Fall 2006): 356–358.

81. Ibid., 363–364.

82. Richter, "'Believing,'" 616; see also Tiro, "'We Wish to Do You Good.'"

83. Tiro, "'We Wish to Do You Good,'"366.

84. Ibid., 371, 373.

85. Ibid., 371–372.

86. Ibid., 373–376.

87. William McLoughlin, *Champions of the Cherokees: Evan and John B. Jones* (Princeton, NJ: Princeton University Press, 1990), 18.

88. Charles S. Maier, *Among Empires: American Ascendancy and Its Predecessors* (Cambridge, MA: Harvard University Press, 2006). As Michael Krenn demonstrates, race would continue to undergird U.S. empire into the present. See Michael L. Krenn, *The Color of Empire: Race and American Foreign Relations* (Lincoln, NE: University of Nebraska Press, 2006).

89. Berkhofer Jr., *Salvation and the Savage*, 7, 49–50.

90. Timothy Pickering to St. Clair, May 31, 1796 (Quaker Collection, Magill Library, Haverford College, Haverford, PA). The letter is also, however, included in BYMCIC, Minutes, 1795–1815.

Chapter 2

1. John Parrish, "Concerning Treaty at Newtown Point Indian Treaty, 1791," 6th month 30 [June 30] 1791, John Parrish Journals, 1790–1793, William L. Clements Library, University of Michigan, Ann Arbor, MI. This journal hereafter referred to as John Parrish Journals Vol. 2. John Parrish compiled a memoir (Vol. 1) and five other journals between c. 1790 and 1793. Each contains his observations during several treaty councils as well as his thoughts on slavery. The consistency of dating styles and pagination vary within each volume. Parrish often recorded the day of the week (e.g. "4th day") and month (e.g. "the 30th" or "30") for most entries; I have included dates in standard style in brackets and page numbers when possible.

2. John Parrish Journals, Vol. 2, 5th day 30 [June 30], 1791.

3. Alyssa Mt. Pleasant notes that U.S. commissioners needed instruction in Haudenosaunee protocols and that some individuals, such as Red Jacket, did, indeed, attempt to educate white Americans like Pickering. See Alyssa Mt. Pleasant, "Independence for Whom?" in Andrew Shankman, ed., *The World of the Revolutionary American Republic: Land, Labor, and the Conflict for a Continent* (New York: Routledge, 2014), 121–122, 126.

4. Reginald Horsman, "American Indian Policy in the Old Northwest, 1783–1812," *William and Mary Quarterly* 18, no. 1 (January 1961): 35–53.

5. Parrish was one among several other missionary brokers during this period: the Moravian John Heckewelder and other members of the Society of Friends were also occasionally among the government's dinner guests during the violence of the 1790s.

6. Historian Leonard Sadosky's work on early American diplomacy likewise situates both Indian affairs and U.S. relations with European empires in a single conversation. See Leonard Sadosky, *Revolutionary Negotiations: Indians, Empires, and Diplomats in the Founding of America* (Jeffersonian America) (Charlottesville: University of Virginia Press, 2010), in particular, Chapter 5.

7. Eliga Gould, *Among the Powers of the Earth: The American Revolution and the Making of a New World Empire* (Cambridge, MA: Harvard University Press, 2012).

8. For an excellent, transnational analysis of consuls and empire, see Simeon Andonov Simeonov, "'With What Right Are They Sending a Consul': Unauthorized Consulship, U.S. Expansion, and the Transformation of the Spanish American Empire, 1795–1808," *Journal of the Early Republic* 40, no. 1 (Spring 2020): 19–44.

9. The ongoing Spanish presence in Florida after the American Revolution enabled the Creeks to continue to play imperial powers off of one another. See Thomas D. Watson, "Strivings for Sovereignty: Alexander McGillivray, Creek Warfare, and Diplomacy, 1783–1790," *Florida Historical Quarterly* 58, no. 4 (April 1980): 400–414.

10. Horsman, "American Indian Policy."

11. Shannon Bontrager likewise demonstrates this in her study of the Wyandots in the early republic. She draws upon borderlands historiography to show that Wyandots "constructed a complex interdependent set of borders that allowed them significant control over their own destiny." See Shannon Bontrager, "'From a Nation of Drunkards, We Have Become a Sober People': The Wyandot Experience in the Ohio Valley During the Early Republic," *Journal of the Early Republic* 32, no. 4 (Winter 2012): 606.

12. Though his work stops short of the 1790s, Michael McConnell's work on the region before the Revolution is useful for understanding the changing, international landscape that Delawares, Shawnees, and their neighbors made. See Michael N. McConnell, *A Country Between: The Upper Ohio Valley and Its Peoples, 1724–1774* (Lincoln: University of Nebraska, 1992).

13. Patrick Bottiger, *The Borderland of Fear: Vincennes, Prophetstown, and the Invasion of the Miami Homeland* (Lincoln: University of Nebraska Press, 2016), 32.

14. Ibid., 34.

15. Ibid., 34.

16. Ibid., 30–31.

17. Ibid., 36–37.

18. For women's roles in the fur trade, see Susan Sleeper-Smith, *Indian Women and French Men: Rethinking Cultural Encounter in the Great Lakes* (Amherst: University of Massachusetts, 2001).

19. For a detailed view of the Glaize and the demography of the region, see Helen Hornbeck Tanner, "The Glaize in 1792: A Composite Indian Community," *Ethnohistory* 25, no. 1 (Winter 1978): 15–39.

20. Susan Sleeper-Smith, *Indigenous Prosperity and American Conquest: Indian Women of the Ohio River Valley, 1690–1792* (Chapel Hill: University of North Carolina Press, 2018), 310. Though much of Theda Perdue's work focuses on the Cherokees, it is nonetheless instructive here. See Theda Perdue, *Cherokee Women: Gender and Culture Change, 1700–1835* (Lincoln: University of Nebraska Press, 1998). For a broader look of individual Indigenous women's

lives, see Theda Perdue, ed., *Sifters: Native American Women's Lives* (Oxford: Oxford University Press, 2001).

21. Sleeper-Smith, *Indigenous Prosperity*, 309–310.

22. Noteworthy here, too, is that Aupaumut and Joseph Brant met as well. As Lisa Brooks notes, the two men approached the situation in the Ohio Country differently. For Aupaumut and Joseph Brant, see Lisa Brooks, *The Common Pot: The Recovery of Native Space in the Northeast* (Minneapolis: University of Minnesota Press, 2008), 106–162.

23. Alyssa Mt. Pleasant explains that this approach was due to two things: one, the Haudenosaunee were still reeling and recovering from the devastation wrought by the United States during Sullivan's Campaign; and, two, the Great Law of Peace guided much of Haudenosaunee efforts and diplomacy. See Mt. Pleasant, "Independence for Whom?" 124–125.

24. John Parrish Journals, Vol. 2, 4th day, the 13th [July 13], 1791.

25. Ibid.

26. Hendrick Aupaumut, "Narratives of his mission to the Western tribes of Indians undated," 1, 4, Am. 573, Historical Society of Pennsylvania, Philadelphia, Pennsylvania. For more on Aupaumut, see Rachel Wheeler, "Hendrick Aupaumut: Christian-Mahican Prophet," *Journal of the Early Republic* 25, no. 2 (Summer 2005): 187–220; Alan Taylor, "Captain Hendrick Aupaumut: The Dilemmas of an Intercultural Broker," *Ethnohistory* 43, no. 3 (Summer 1996): 431–457.

27. Aupaumut, "Narratives," 30.

28. Ibid.

29. Sleeper-Smith, *Indigenous Prosperity*, 304–309.

30. Aupaumut, "Narratives," 59.

31. John Parrish Journals, Vol. 2, 4th day, the 29th [June 29], 1791.

32. Ibid., 6th of the 7th month [July 6], 1791.

33. Like dress, these military parades were central to performing diplomacy. See Timothy J. Shannon, "Dressing for Success on the Mohawk Frontier: Hendrick, William Johnson, and the Indian Fashion," *William and Mary Quarterly*, 3rd Series, 53, no. 1, Material Culture in Early America (January 1996), 13–42.

34. John Parrish Journals, Vol. 4, 3rd day, the 9th, [July 9], 1793, 43.

35. John Parrish Journals, Vol. 2, 6th day, the 1st, 7th month [July 1], 1791.

36. In 1808, for example, Baltimore Friends Elisha Tyson and James Gillingham traveled to the Ohio Country in order to see the progress of their society's philanthropy firsthand. Before they embarked on their tour, Secretary Dearborn inquired, "If Mr Tyson & Mr Gillingham should find it convenient, while on their visit to the Western Indians, to spend a day or two at Greenville, with a party of Indians at that place, under the direction of an Indian called the Prophet." Dearborn wanted "to have such enquiries made . . . as to the real views and Intentions of those people & especially of their leader." He also informed the Quakers that it would "be very desirable to have similar enquiries made among the Wiandots [*sic*] at Sandusky as to the actual Conduct & apparent views of that People, in relation to the Interests of the U.S." Henry Dearborn to Elisha Tyson and James Gillingham, March 24, 1808 (M15, reel 2, RG 75, NARA); for British traders, see, for example, William Henry Harrison to Henry Dearborn, February 19, 1802, in Logan Esarey, ed., *Governors Messages and Letters*, vol. 1 (Indianapolis: Indiana Historical Bureau, 1922), 38–39.

37. One of these Friends, William Hartshorne, attended the treaty councils near Detroit in 1793, and his journal, though less detailed, corroborates those of John Parrish. See

W. M. Hartshorne's Journal of Journey to Detroit, 1793, vol. 1, MSS 003/152 (Friends Historical Library, Swarthmore College, Swarthmore, PA).

38. Larry Brent Hershey, "Peace through Conversation: William Penn, Israel Pemberton, and the Shaping of Quaker-Indian Relations, 1681–1757" (master's thesis, University of Iowa, 2008).

39. *Baltimore Evening Post* (Baltimore, Maryland), November, 23, 1792, Vol. 1, Issue 115, 3.

40. On Native peoples' migrations in the region, see, in particular, Laura Keenan Spero, "'Stout, bold, cunning and the greatest travellers in America': The Colonial Shawnee Diaspora" (PhD diss., University of Pennsylvania, 2010); and Stephen Warren, *The Shawnees and Their Neighbors, 1795–1870* (Champaign: University of Illinois Press, 2008). For Delawares' travels, see Dawn Marsh, "Creating Delaware Homelands in the Ohio Country," *Ohio History* 116 (2009): 26–40.

41. John Parrish Journals, Vol. 4, 5th day, the 4th [July 4], 1793.

42. Thomas Brainerd, *The Life of John Brainerd, the Brother of David Brainerd, and His Successor as Missionary to the Indians of New Jersey* (Philadelphia: Presbyterian Publication Committee, 1865), 234–235.

43. John Parrish Journals, Vol. 3, May 1793; John Parrish Journals, Vol. 1,"Memoir," undated [c. 1790]; John Parrish Journals, Vol. 4, the 29th [June 29], 1793, 19–20.

44. John Parrish Journals, Vol. 4, 29 and 7 of the week [June 29], 1793, 15.

45. Francis Jennings, *The History and Culture of Iroquois Diplomacy: An Interdisciplinary Guide to the Treaties of the Six Nations and Their League* (Syracuse, NY: Syracuse University Press, 1985); Mt. Pleasant, "Independence for Whom?" 128; Daniel K. Richter and James H. Merrell, eds., *Beyond the Covenant Chain: The Iroquois and Their Neighbors in Indian North America, 1600–1800* (State College: Penn State University Press, 2003); Daniel K. Richter, *The Ordeal of the Longhouse: The Peoples of the Iroquois League in the Era of European Colonization* (Chapel Hill: University of North Carolina Press, by the Omohundro Institute of Early American History and Culture, 1992).

The metaphor was widely understood and used: Colonels William Preston and William Fleming wrote to the Shawnees in 1778, "The Governor and Council will appoint Commissioners to talk with you, and endeavour to Cover the Blood that has been Spilt upon the Path of Peace, and brighten the Chain of Friendship." Col. William Preston and Col. William Fleming, April 3, 1778, "Address to the Shawnee," in Reuben Gold Thwaites and Louise Phelps Kellogg, eds., *Frontier Defense on the Upper Ohio, 1777–1778* (Madison: Wisconsin Historical Society, 1912), 260.

46. John Parrish Journals, Vol. 2, 1st day, the 10th [July 10], 1791.

47. BYMCIC, Minutes, 1795–1815, 3 mo. 23 [March 23] 1799, 34–35.

48. Ibid., 3 mo. 24 [March 24] 1799, 34–35; For Teedyuscung, see Francis Jennings, *Empire of Fortune: Crowns, Colonies, and Tribes in the Seven Years War in America* (New York: W. W. Norton & Company, 1988), 274.

49. Anthony F. C. Wallace, *King of the Delawares: Teedyuscung, 1700–1763* (Syracuse, NY: Syracuse University Press, 1949).

50. The Friendly Association for Regaining and Preserving Peace with the Indians, active during the Seven Years' War in Pennsylvania, for example, published and circulated numerous pamphlets detailing their efforts among Delawares during the 1750s and 1760s. See, for example, Charles Thomson, *An Enquiry in the causes of the alienation of the Delaware and Shawanese Indians from the British interest . . . who thereupon abandoned the fort and country* (London: J. Wilkie, 1759). Such documentation survived into the nineteenth century as in, for example, Samuel

Parrish, *Some Chapters in the History of the Friendly Association for Regaining and Preserving Peace with the Indians by Pacific Measures* (Philadelphia: Friends' Historical Association, 1877).

51. See John Heckewelder, *History, Manners, and Customs of the Indian Nations Who Once Inhabited Pennsylvania and the Neighboring States* (New York: Arno Press Inc., 1971); and David Zeisberger, *Diary of David Zeisberger, a Moravian Missionary Among the Indians of Ohio*, edited and translated by Eugene F. Bliss (Cincinnati: R. Clarke & Co., 1885).

52. For the Putnam-Heckewelder partnership, see Sleeper-Smith, *Indigenous Prosperity*, 296–301.

53. Ibid.

54. Unlike Heckewelder, other Moravians, such as Abraham Luckenbach and John Peter Kluge, failed to cultivate workable relations among Native peoples. These two men ultimately abandoned their mission among the Delawares in 1806 Indiana Territory after Delawares drove them away in the aftermath of a deadly witch hunt. See *The Moravian Indian mission on White River; diaries and letters, May 5, 1799, to November 12, 1806*, edited by Lawrence Henry Gipson, translated by Harry Emilius Stocker, Herman T. Frueauff, Samuel C. Zeller (Indianapolis: Indiana Historical Bureau, 1938).

55. Stephanie Gamble, "'Strong Expressions of Regard': Native Diplomats and Quakers in Early National Philadelphia," in Ignacio Gallup-Diaz and Geoffrey Plank, eds., *Quakers and Native Americans* (Leiden: Brill, 2018): 93–114.

56. Parrish, vol. 3, May 1793.

57. Ibid.

58. John Parrish Journals, Vol. 1, [c. 1790].

59. John Parrish Journals, Vol. 3 [May 1793].

60. Entries dated August 8, August 10 [Unknown Quaker woman], 1761 August 4–12, Journal [Easton, PA] (Quaker Collection, William L. Clements Library, University of Michigan, Ann Arbor, MI.

61. Joseph Patterson notebooks, April 29, 1802, vol. 3, 17 (William L. Clements Library, University of Michigan, Ann Arbor, MI).

62. John Parrish Journals, Vol. 2, 4th day, 13 [July 13], 1791.

63. Scholarship on gift-giving in early America reveals that gift-giving was intricately connected with assertions of Native power. See, for example, Joseph M. Hall Jr., *Zamumo's Gifts: Indian-European Exchange in the Colonial Southeast* (Philadelphia: University of Pennsylvania Press, 2009); Richard White, *The Middle Ground: Indians, Empires, and Republics in the Great Lakes Region, 1650–1815* (Cambridge: Cambridge University Press, 1991); and David Murray, *Indian Giving: Economies of Power in Indian-white Exchanges* (Amherst: University of Massachusetts Press, 2000).

64. John Parrish Journals, Vol. 4, 6th month 25 [June 25], 1793, 1, 50.

65. Ibid. For the significance of food exchange, see Michael A. LaCombe, *Political Gastronomy: Food and Authority in the English Atlantic World* (Philadelphia: University of Pennsylvania Press, 2012).

66. John Parrish Journals, Vol. 1, [c. 1790].

67. John Parrish Journals, Vol. 2, 7th month, the 6th [July 6], 1791.

68. Ibid., 7th day, 16 [July 16], 1791.

69. Ibid., 7th month, the 6th [July 6].

70. John Parrish Journals, Vol. 3 [May 1793].

71. John Parrish Journals, Vol. 4, 19th of the 8th month [August 19], 76.

72. Ibid.

73. John Parrish Journals, Vol. 3, [May 1793].

74. John Parrish Journals, Vol. 2, April 30, 1793—June 1, 1793; Ibid., n.d., n.p., 29–31.

75. Ibid., 6th day of 7th month [July 6], 1791.

76. John Parrish Journals, Vol. 4, 2nd and 3rd of the 7th month [July 2–3], 1793, 24.

77. John Parrish Journals, Vol. 4, 3rd day, the 9th [August 9], 1793, 42–43.

Chapter 3

1. Joseph Lancaster, *Improvements in Education, as it Respects the Industrious Classes of the Community: Containing Among other Important Particulars, An Account of the Institution for the Education of One Thousand Poor Children, Borough Road, Southwark; and of the New System of Education on which it is Conducted. From the Third London Edition, with Additions. To which is Prefixed a Sketch of the New-York Free School* (New York: Collins and Perkins, 1807), xix.

2. Ibid., xviii.

3. Ibid., xix. Friends in North America had similar concerns for their own children and, in consequence, expended great energy in considering the schooling of Quaker children more generally. Owen Biddle penned a narrative in 1790, for example, that discussed the possibility of modeling John Fothergill's London Quaker school in Philadelphia. See Owen Biddle, *A Plan for a School on an Establishment similar to that at Ackworth, in Yorkshire, Great-Britain, varied to suit the Circumstances of the Youth within the Limits of the Yearly-Meeting For Pennsylvania and New-Jersey: Introduced with the Sense of Friends in New-England, on the Subject of Education; and an Account of some Schools in Great-Britain: To which is Added, Observations and Remarks, Intended for the Consideration of Friends* (Philadelphia: Joseph Crukshank, 1790).

4. For the use of Lancaster's methods in Indian Country, see Robert F. Berkhofer Jr., *Salvation and the Savage: An Analysis of Protestant Missions and American Indian Response, 1787–1862* (New York: Atheneum, 1972), 25–28.

5. Secretary of War Henry Dearborn to Henry Drinker, May 22, 1801, National Archives I, M15, Letters Sent by the Secretary of War, Records of the Office of the Secretary of War (reel 1, NARA, Washington, DC) (hereafter referred to as NARA).

6. Jessica Choppin Roney shows how during the eighteenth century, civic action could be a means to engage in the political, particularly for white men. See Jessica Choppin Roney, *Governed by a Spirit of Opposition: The Origins of American Political Practice in Colonial Philadelphia* (Baltimore: Johns Hopkins University Press, 2014).

7. John S. Tyson, *Life of Elisha Tyson, the Philanthropist* (Baltimore: B. Lundy, 1825), 3.

8. Christopher L. Brown, *Moral Capital: Foundations of British Abolitionism* (Chapel Hill: University of North Carolina Press, Omohundro Institute of Early American History and Culture, 2006). Susan Ryan also notes that for white individuals, benevolence was seen as a duty of citizenship. See Susan Ryan, *The Grammar of Good Intentions: Race and the Antebellum Culture of Benevolence* (Ithaca, NY: Cornell University Press, 2003), 7.

9. For a broad overview of the terms surrounding philanthropy and benevolence, see Ryan, *Grammar of Good Intentions*, 9–10.

10. As Mark Boonshoft argues, however, more expansive ideas regarding education emerged after a period of elite education, centered in academies. See Mark Boonshoft, *Aristocratic Education and the Making of the American Republic* (Chapel Hill, NC: University of North Carolina Press, 2020). For early republic ideas regarding education, see Benjamin Rush, "Thoughts Upon the Mode of Education Proper in a Republic" (1786); Thomas Jefferson, "Second

Inaugural Address," March 4, 1805, in Merrill D. Peterson, ed., *Thomas Jefferson: Writings* (New York: Viking Press, 1984), 520–521; see also "Letter to Peter Carr," September 7, 1814, 1348, in the same; Thomas Jefferson, "A Bill for the More General Diffusion of Knowledge," in Julian P. Boyd, ed., *The Papers of Thomas Jefferson, vol. 2, 1777–18 June 1779* (Princeton, NJ: Princeton University Press, 1950), 526–535; Carl F. Kaestle, *Pillars of the Republic: Common Schools and American Society, 1780–1860* (New York: Hill and Wang, 1983); and Keith Whitescarver, "Creating Citizens for the Republic: Education in Georgia, 1776–1810," *Journal of the Early Republic* 13, no. 4 (Winter 1993): 455–479. Whitescarver's work points out the links between developing ideas of U.S. citizenship, nationalism, and education in the early republic.

11. With regard to the military, by 1826 the secretary of war, James Barbour, proclaimed citizens' labor to be more important than military service. He wrote that "at least a million and a half of our most useful citizens would be relieved from the unprofitable pageantry of military parade . . . constituting so injurious a draft on their industry." "Annual Report of the Secretary of War, Showing the Operations of the Military Establishment of the United States in 1826"; and "Report of the Board of Officers on the Organization of the Militia," December 4, 1826, *American State Papers* Class V (Military Affairs) vol. 3 (Washington: Gales and Seaton, 1832–61), 388–389, in John Dwiggins, "The Military Establishment and Democratic Politics in the United States, 1783–1848" (PhD diss., University of Pennsylvania, 2012).

Far from performing intensive manual labor themselves, several prominent members of the Baltimore meeting's Committee on Indian Concerns instead spent their evenings debating just what constituted "useful knowledge." For the "Society for the Attainment of Useful Knowledge," a social group to which several members of the Baltimore Friends' Committee on Indian Concerns belonged, "useful knowledge" could mean a number of things, and their schooling in literature, history, and the like meant that their own "usefulness" was quite different than that of others. Their meeting minutes offer a glimpse into the questions that were, at the time, both deemed worthy of debate and crucial to prominent Baltimorean men's "attainment of useful knowledge." On January 6, 1798, for example, the men asked, "Is a Man of Good morals & Sound Constitution—Justifiable in passing the prime of life in a State of Celibacy?" After lively discussion, they decided in the negative; procreation was, instead, advisable. Similar deliberation ensued when, on October 28, 1797, the men debated whether "In Case of a general emancipation of the Slaves in the United States by Law—Ought Government to indemnify the present Holders." Debate ended with an answer in the affirmative. Over the course of the group's three-year existence, the men debated the issues of a land tax, the armament of merchant vessels, debt prison, and "the mental faculties of the Ladies" (they found, according to Enlightenment principles, that "the Ladies" were the mental equals of men). See Society for the Attainment of Useful Knowledge, *Minute Book, 1797–1800*; and *The Constitution By-laws and Minutes of the Society for the Attainment of Useful Knowledge Baltimore, 1797–1800* (Baltimore: Maryland Historical Society), 32–33; 19–20; 57.

12. See especially Sarah Knott, *Sensibility and the American Revolution* (Chapel Hill: University of North Carolina Press, Omohundro Institute of Early American History and Culture, 2009), Chapter 2.

13. Much of this discussion is informed by Lynn Hunt's work. See Lynn Hunt, *Inventing Human Rights: A History* (New York: Norton, 2007); in particular, see 35–69. See also Knott, *Sensibility and the American Revolution.*

14. Samuel Fothergill quoted in Frederick B. Tolles, *Meeting House and Counting House: The Quaker Merchants of Colonial Philadelphia, 1682–1763* (Chapel Hill: University of North

Carolina Press, Omohundro Institute of Early American History and Culture, 1948), 4. Kristen Block explores slaveholding among early Quakers in Barbados and the Middle Colonies and its role in Friends' efforts to balance their "inner" (spiritual) and "outer" (economic) "plantations." See Kristen Block, "Cultivating Inner and Outer Plantations: Property, Industry, and Slavery in Early Quaker Migration to the New World," *Early American Studies* 8, no. 3, Special Forum (Fall 2010): 515–548.

15. See Jack Marietta, *The Reformation of American Quakerism, 1748–1783* (Philadelphia: University of Pennsylvania Press, 2007.

16. Tolles, *Meeting House and Counting House.*

17. Roney, *Governed by a Spirit of Opposition.*

18. Seth Rockman, *Scraping By: Wage Labor, Slavery, and Survival in Early Baltimore* (Baltimore: Johns Hopkins University Press, 2008), 1–15; for statistics, see Terry D. Bilhartz, *Urban Religion and the Second Great Awakening: Church and Society in Early National Baltimore* (London: Associated University Press, 1986), 12.

19. Rockman, *Scraping By*, 13.

20. Ibid., 7.

21. David Brion Davis insists that "Quakers' decision to disengage themselves from slavery was not an inevitable outgrowth of George Fox's advice in 1657 to treat slaves with Christian mercy and if possible limit their terms of bondage to thirty years." Instead, he points to Friends' relatively slow route toward abolition. See David Brion Davis, *The Problem of Slavery in the Age of Revolution, 1770–1825* (Ithaca, NY: Cornell University Press, 1975), 214, n 1. Philadelphia Yearly Meeting disowned slave-holding Friends beginning in 1774. See Gary Nash, "Slaves and Slaveholders in Colonial Philadelphia," *William and Mary Quarterly*, 3rd Series, 30 (April 1973): 223–256.

22. Seth Rockman, "Work, Wages, and Welfare at Baltimore's School of Industry," *Maryland Historical Magazine* 102, no. 1 (Spring 2007): 572–607.

23. Historian Seth Rockman argues that the school "suggests a second, seemingly contradictory pattern in the emergence of a wage-economy—the persistence of coercive labor relations. The School of Industry sought to add the city's 'free' wage-earners to the ranks of enslaved, indentured, and imprisoned laborers from whom work had long been compelled." See Seth Rockman, "Work, Wages, and Welfare," 575.

24. Demos, *The Heathen School*; on the Choctaw Academy's academy, see Christina Snyder, *Great Crossings: Indians, Settlers & Slaves in the Age of Jackson* (Oxford: Oxford University Press, 2017).

25. Friends in Wilmington, Delaware, were in many ways the most ardent in their philanthropic work, and they managed to raise impressive sums of money that ensured that children who experienced poverty—African-descended and Euro-American alike—could attend Quaker-run schools. Philadelphia Quakers, with whom the Baltimore Committee on Indian Concerns corresponded regularly, likewise participated in numerous efforts to provide poor relief and charity schooling. See Sydney V. James, *A People Among Peoples: Quaker Benevolence in Eighteenth-Century America* (Cambridge, MA: Harvard University Press, 1963), 274.

26. See Lancaster, *Improvements in Education.* A particularly thoughtful piece on the Lancasterian schools in the United States is Dell Upton's on the schools and "spatial imagination." See Dell Upton, "Lancasterian Schools, Republican Citizenship, and the Spatial Imagination in Early Nineteenth-Century America," *Journal of the Society of Architectural Historians* 55, no. 3 (September 1996): 238–253.

27. William C. Kashatus III, "The Inner Light and Popular Enlightenment: Philadelphia Quakers and Charity Schooling, 1790–1820," *Pennsylvania Magazine of History and Biography* 118, no. 1/2 (January 1994): 87–116, quotation, 100.

28. Ibid.

29. Bilhartz, *Urban Religion*, 38–51.

30. Rockman, *Scraping By*, 17, 19; see BYMCIC minutes for membership lists. Thomas, for example, served as clerk of the Committee on Indian Concerns for a time.

31. Thomas Ellicott—relative of the many Ellicotts who served on the Committee on Indian Concerns—was president of the Union Bank of Maryland from 1819 through to the end of the infamous Bank War, and both the Committee on Indian Concerns and Philip E. Thomas invested in that bank. On the connection between the B&O Railroad and the Union Bank of Maryland, see James D. Dilts, *The Great Road: The Building of the Baltimore and Ohio, the Nation's First Railroad, 1828–1853* (Stanford, CA: Stanford University Press, 1993), 171–172. For the investment of the Committee on Indian Concerns funds, see BYMCIC minutes, Vol. I, 3 month 12, 1809, 227.

32. Brown, *Moral Capital*. Brown's analysis reminds scholars to consider the myriad personalities, beliefs, and motivations that fueled not only abolitionism but reform efforts more generally. See also James Walvin, *The Quakers: Money and Morals* (London: John Murray, 1997).

33. See Marietta, *Reformation of American Quakerism*.

34. Timothy Pickering to St. Clair, May 31, 1796 (Quaker Collection, Magill Library, Haverford College, Haverford, PA). The letter is also included in an entry dated 10th month, 1796, BYMCIC minutes, 13–14.

35. BYMCIC, Minutes, 1795–1815, 10th month, 1795, 1. For practical education among women, see Margaret Nash, "Rethinking Republican Motherhood: Benjamin Rush and the Young Ladies' Academy of Philadelphia," *Journal of the Early Republic* 17, no. 2 (Summer 1997): 171–191; see also Mary Kelley, *Learning to Stand and Speak: Women, Education, and Public Life in America's* Republic (Chapel Hill: University of North Carolina Press, Omohundro Institute of Early American History and Culture, 2008).

36. Timothy Pickering to Arthur St. Clair, May 31, 1796 (Quaker Collection, Magill Library, Haverford College, Haverford, PA). Karim Tiro likewise argues that Pickering endorsed Quaker missionaries because they focused on agricultural rather than theological instruction. Friends' early references to providing "religious instruction" (which, by 1796, disappear from the minutes) may suggest, however, that they were at first open to the possibility of providing more than agricultural education. See Karim Tiro, "'We Wish to Do You Good.': The Quaker Mission to the Oneida Nation, 1790–1840" *Journal of the Early Republic*, vol. 26, no. 3 (Fall, 2006): 353–376.

37. On this broader discourse, see, for example, George Boudreau, "'Highly Valuable & Extensively Useful': Community and Readership Among the Eighteenth Century Philadelphia Middling Sort," *Pennsylvania History* 63, no. 3 (July 1996): 302–329.

38. William Kirk to Henry Dearborn, July 20, 1807, Letters Received by the Secretary of War, Main Series, Records of the Office of the Secretary of War (Record Group 107), NARA, Washington, DC.

39. Society of Friends, Baltimore Yearly Meeting, *A Brief Account of the Proceedings of the Committee, Appointed by the Yearly Meeting of Friends, Held in Baltimore, for Promoting the Improvement and Civilization of the Indian Natives*, 6–8.

40. "Notes of a Journey taken by Elisha Tyson and James Gillingham on a visit to some Indians in the neighbourhood of Fort Wayne" (Friends Historical Library, Swarthmore College, Swarthmore, PA), 1808, 27th of 4th month [April 27].

41. 3 mo. 19 [Mar. 19], 1808, BYMCIC minutes, 177.

42. Society of Friends, Baltimore Yearly Meeting, *A Brief Account of the Proceedings*, 14.

43. 11 mo. 15 [Nov. 15], 1811, BYMCIC minutes.

44. 3 mo. 12 1809 [Mar. 12], BYMCIC minutes, 198–199.

45. See Berkhofer Jr., *Salvation and the Savage*, 28; John Putnam Demos, *The Heathen School: A Story of Hope and Betrayal in the Age of the Early Republic* (New York: Alfred A. Knopf, 2014).

46. See, for example, Christine Stansell, *City of Women: Sex and Class in New York, 1789–1860* (Urbana: University of Illinois Press, 1987).

47. See Jeanne Boydston, *Home and Work: Housework, Wages, and the Ideology of Labor in the Early Republic* (Oxford: Oxford University Press, 1994); and Karin Wulf, *Not All Wives: Women of Colonial Philadelphia* (Philadelphia: University of Pennsylvania Press, 2005). Wulf's work examines single women in eighteenth-century Philadelphia and ultimately traces masculinity's association with economic and political culture by the end of the eighteenth century.

48. David D. Smits, "The Squaw Drudge: A Prime Index of Savagism," *Ethnohistory* 29, no. 4 (Autumn 1982): 281–306. Such images were part of a broader Euro-American tradition of exoticizing the bodies of women of color. See, for example, Jennifer L. Morgan, "'Some Could Suckle over Their Shoulder'": Male Travelers, Female Bodies, and the Gendering of Racial Ideology, 1500–1770," *William and Mary Quarterly* 54, no. 1 (January 1997): 167–192.

49. As has been well documented, this was in direct tension with many Native peoples' own conceptions regarding gendered divisions of labor. In Haudenosaunee villages, Daniel K. Richter notes that "an Iroquois town was largely a female world" as women "tended the fields" and men, as hunters and warriors, "dispersed to locales near and far." Daniel K. Richter, *The Ordeal of the Longhouse: The Peoples of the Iroquois League in the Era of European Colonization* (Chapel Hill: University of North Carolina Press, Omohundro Institute of Early American History and Culture, 1992), 22–23; Theda Perdue, *Cherokee Women: Gender and Culture Change, 1700–1835* (Lincoln: University of Nebraska Press, 1998).

50. Gerard T. Hopkins, Journal, 1804–1805, Historical Society of Pennsylvania, Philadelphia, April 10, 1804; this passage is Hopkins's recording of a speech given to Miamis and Potawatomis.

51. See BYMCIC membership list, 1815, vol. 2.

52. Revealing their lack of understanding—and inclusion—of Indigenous women in their efforts, non-conformist Quaker women of the 1840s (Quaker abolitionist and proponent of women's rights Lucretia Mott among them) viewed Native women's labor in the fields as evidence of their servility; they believed that female Natives' liberation would come about through spinning and other such work in the home. Nonetheless the Quaker Joint Indian Committee declared in 1842, "History confirms the deeply interesting fact, that no people ever yet were elevated to the rank of civilization while their females were held in a servile condition." Lucretia Mott served with the women of this Joint Indian Committee. See Carol Faulkner, *Lucretia Mott's Heresy: Abolition and Women's Rights in Nineteenth-Century America* (Philadelphia: University of Pennsylvania Press, 2011), 135. On women and reform more broadly, see Lori D. Ginzberg, *Women and the Work of Benevolence: Morality, Politics, and Class in the Nineteenth-Century United States* (New Haven, CT: Yale University Press, 1990).

This reorganization of gender roles also corresponded to efforts to organize the United States' non-native population according to patriarchic norms. Among the non-Indians in the United States, men were most often the individuals with whom the government formed an explicit relationship. Census records, for example, usually placed the eldest male as the "head of household," and beneath his name were listed the others living in his home and under his care. The federal government's partnership with Quakers in the Ohio Country—particularly once Quaker women began accompanying their husbands to the region to teach spinning and weaving in 1815—facilitated the exportation of this system of governing. Moreover, like the white, "middling" women whose domestic labor supported men's wage labor outside of the home, Baltimore Friends encouraged Native women to support their husbands' work by laboring within the home.

The language of treaties between the United States and Native Americans, moreover, involved rhetoric of protection, promises of peace, and broad notions of friendship—all of which implicitly challenged Native masculine diplomatic roles. An 1805 treaty with the Wyandots, for example, states that "the said Indian nations do again acknowledge themselves and all their tribes, to be in friendship with, and under the protection of the United States." Treaty with the Wyandot, Etc., 1805. July 4, 1805, in Charles J. Kappler, ed., *Indian Affairs, Laws and Treaties*, vol. II (Washington: Government Printing Office, 1904), 77. The United States thus presupposed both that Native Americans required "the protection of the United States" and that they desired friendship with the U.S. government. With the United States demanding peace from Native people and presuming friendship, Native peoples' own diplomatic powers of making war and crafting military alliances were, according to treaty rhetoric, subjugated beneath U.S. authority.

53. 5th month 22 [May 22], 1796, BYMCIC minutes, 3–7.

54. Anonymous Friend, "A Journey to the Northwestern terretory the 2d of the 10th mo 1797," MSS 003/005 (Friends Historical Library, Swarthmore College, Swarthmore, PA).

55. Lancaster, *Improvements in Education*, xix.

56. Tyson, *Life of Elisha Tyson*.

57. Ibid. Indeed, even John Tyson's subtitle for the Elisha Tyson biography, "the Philanthropist," indicates the importance of such work in cultivating a legacy.

58. Tyson, *Life of Elisha Tyson*, preface.

59. Ibid., 3.

60. Ibid., 3.

61. Ibid., 58.

62. Jessica Choppin Roney, "'Effective Men' and Early Voluntary Associations in Philadelphia, 1725–1775," in Thomas A. Foster, ed., *New Men: Manliness in Early America* (New York: New York University Press, 2011); Bruce Dorsey, *Reforming Men and Women: Gender in the Antebellum City* (Ithaca, NY: Cornell University Press, 2002).

63. Tyson, *Life of Elisha Tyson*, 59.

64. Ibid., 72.

65. Ibid., 72.

Chapter 4

1. This revised chapter was originally published as "The Mission Complex: Economic Development, 'Civilization,' and Empire in the Early Republic," *Journal of the Early Republic* 36, no. 3 (Fall 2016): 467–491. Reprinted with permission. For foundational examinations of missions, civilization efforts, and the consequences of these in the early republic, see Francis Paul Prucha, *The Great Father: The United States Government and the American Indians* (Lincoln: University of Nebraska Press,1986); Jill Kinney, "'Letters, Pen, and Tilling the Field': Quaker Schools Among the Seneca Indians on the Allegany River, 1798–1852" (PhD diss., University

of Rochester, 2009); Diane Rothenberg, "Friends Like These: An Ethnohistorical Analysis of the Interaction Between Allegany Senecas and Quakers, 1798–1823," (PhD diss., City College of New York, 1976); Matthew Dennis, *Seneca Possessed: Indians, Witchcraft, and Power in the Early American Republic* (Philadelphia: University of Pennsylvania Press, 2010); Claudio Saunt, *A New Order of Things: Property, Power, and the Transformation of the Creek Indians, 1733–1816* (Cambridge: Cambridge University Press, 1999).

2. On the logic of settler colonialism, see Lorenzo Veracini, *Settler Colonialism: A Theoretical Overview* (New York: Palgrave Macmillan, 2010); and Patrick Wolfe, "Settler Colonialism and the Elimination of the Native," *Journal of Genocide Research* 8, no. 4 (December 2006): 387–409.

3. On this revolution in transportation and economy, see Charles Sellers, *The Market Revolution: Jacksonian America, 1815–1846* (New York: Oxford University Press, 1991); Daniel Walker Howe, *What Hath God Wrought: The Transformation of America, 1815–1848* (New York: Oxford University Press, 2007); and John Lauritz Larson, *The Market Revolution in America: Liberty, Ambition, and the Eclipse of the Common Good* (Cambridge: Cambridge University Press, 2009).

4. Anonymous Friend, A Journey to the Northwestern terretory the 2d of the 10th mo [Oct 2] 1797, MSS 003/005 (Friends Historical Library, Swarthmore College, Swarthmore, PA).

5. Anonymous, Diary, 1807 9 mo 10-10 mo 12, Journals (MSS) MSS 003/8 (Friends Historical Library, Swarthmore College, Swarthmore, PA).

6. On regional political economies, see Christopher Clark, "Ohio Country in the Political Economy of Nation Building," in Andrew R. L. Cayton and Stuart D. Hobbs, *The Center of a Great Empire: The Ohio Country in the Early Republic* (Athens, OH: Ohio University Press, 2005); Andrew R. L. Cayton and Peter S. Onuf, *The Midwest and the Nation: Rethinking the History of an American Region* (Bloomington: Indiana University Press, 1990); Andrew R. L. Cayton, *Frontier Republic: Ideology and Politics in the Ohio Country, 1780–1825* (Kent, OH: Kent State University Press, 1989); Susan Sleeper-Smith, *Indigenous Prosperity and American Conquest: Indian Women of the Ohio River Valley, 1690–1792* (Chapel Hill: University of North Carolina Press, 2018).

7. Henry Dearborn to Isaac Tyson, April 16, 1808, Miscellaneous Letters Sent by the Secretary of War, 1800–1809, Records of the Office of the Secretary of War (M370, reel 3, NARA, Washington, DC).

8. Anonymous Friend, A Journey to the Northwestern territory, the 2d of the 10th mo [Oct 2] 1797, MSS 003/005 (Friends Historical Library, Swarthmore College, Swarthmore, PA).

9. Ibid. In 1804, for example, Hopkins and his Quaker companion Philip Dennis hired "an old Indian and his Squaw" to guide them across a river. Gerard T. Hopkins, Journal, 1804–05, March 29, 1804 (Historical Society of Pennsylvania, Philadelphia, PA).

10. See Eric Hinderaker, *Elusive Empires: Constructing Colonialism in the Ohio Valley, 1673–1800* (Cambridge: Cambridge University Press, 1999), 247–249; David C. Klingman and Richard K. Vedder, eds., *Essays on the Economy of the Old Northwest* (Athens, OH: Ohio University Press, 1987); Scott Key, "Economics or Education: The Establishment of American Land-Grant Universities," *Journal of Higher Education* 67, no. 2 (March–April 1996): 199–205; James A. Henretta, "The 'Market' in the Early Republic," *Journal of the Early Republic* 18, no. 2 (Summer 1998): 289–304, see especially 292–294; Max M. Edling, "'So Immense a Power in the Affairs of War': Alexander Hamilton and the Restoration of Public Credit," *William and Mary Quarterly*, 3rd Series, 64, no. 2 (April 2007): 287–326.

11. Thomas Jefferson to William Henry Harrison, February 27, 1803, in Logan Esarey, ed., *Messages and Letters of William Henry Harrison, Vol. 1, 1800–1811* (Indianapolis: Indiana

Historical Commission, 1922), 70. See also Patrick Griffin, "The Ideological Origins of Indian Removal," in Cayton and Hobbs, *Center of a Great Empire.*

12. For population growth, see Christopher Clark, "The Ohio Country in the Political Economy of Nation Building," in Cayton and Hobbs, *Center of a Great Empire*, 151.

13. William Wells to John Armstrong, January 12, 1801, John Armstrong Papers, Box 4, Folder 5 (Indiana Historical Society, Indianapolis, IN); William Wells to John Armstrong, May 4, 1801, John Armstrong Papers, Box 4, Folder 6.

14. Shifting federal policies reveal the problems of finance in the period and offer opportunities to examine how the state and individuals created economic change by confronting those problems. See, for example, Paul A. Gilje, "The Rise of Capitalism in the Early Republic," *Journal of the Early Republic* 16, no. 2, Special Issue (Summer 1996), 159–181; Max M. Edling and Mark Kaplanoff, "Alexander Hamilton's Fiscal Reform: Transforming the Structure of Taxation in the Early Republic," *William and Mary Quarterly*, 3rd Series, 61, no. 4 (October 2004): 713–744; Gautham Rao, *National Duties: Custom Houses and the Making of the American State* (Chicago: University of Chicago Press, 2016).

15. William Henry Harrison to Secretary of War, July 15, 1801, in Esarey, ed., *Messages and Letters*, 29–30.

16. Henry Knox to George Washington, July 7, 1789, in *American State Papers*, Vol. IV, *Indian Affairs* (Washington: Gales and Seaton, 1832), 53–54.

17. Kathleen McCarthy likewise reveals the vast amount of money available to civic associations and argues, in a manner applicable to Friends, that associations offered disenfranchised groups a means to engage with the political world. Other scholars similarly see reformers as central to nation building. See Kathleen D. McCarthy, *American Creed: Philanthropy and the Rise of Civil Society, 1700–1865* (Chicago: University of Chicago Press, 2003); Steven Mintz, *Moralists and Modernizers: America's Pre-Civil War Reformers* (Baltimore: Johns Hopkins University Press, 1995); Lori D. Ginzberg, "The Nation's Mission: Social Movements and Nation-Building in the United States," *Social History/Histoire Sociale* 33, no. 66 (2000): 325–341.

18. Michel Foucault, *Discipline and Punish: The Birth of the Prison*, translated by Alan Sheridan (New York: Random House, 1977).

19. For the founding of Dennis's Station, see Hopkins journal, 1804; see also BYMCIC, Minutes, 1795–1815, Swarthmore College, Friends Historical Library, Swarthmore, PA.

20. Ibid.

21. BYMCIC, Minutes, 1795–1815, 87; For this correspondence, see Henry Dearborn to Henry Drinker, October 24, 1806, Miscellaneous Letters Sent by the Secretary of War, 1800–1809, Records of the Office of the Secretary of War (National Archives Microfilm Publication M370, roll 3, 229), Record Group 107, National Archives Building, Washington, DC (hereafter referred to as M370); Henry Dearborn to William Kirk, November 24, 1806, M370, roll 2; William Kirk to Henry Dearborn, July 20, 1807, Letters Received (Main Series), 1801–1889, Records of the Office of the Secretary of War (National Archives Microfilm M221, roll 8), Record Group 107, National Archives, Washington, DC; BYMCIC, Minutes, 1815–1847, 14–15.

22. William Eustis to John Johnston, January 16, 1810, John Johnston Papers, 1801–1860 (MIC125, reel 1, Ohio Historical Society, Columbus, OH).

23. John Johnston to P. E. Thomas, April 15, 1809, in Gayle Thornbrough, ed., *Letter Book of the Indian Agency at Fort Wayne, 1809–1815* (Indianapolis: Indiana Historical Society, 1961), 40–42.

24. BYCMIC, minutes 1795–1815, 10 mo 12 [October 12], 1813, 258–259.

25. Friends report that the Shawnees had planted about two hundred fifty acres of corn at Wapakoneta, putting the average yield per acre between twenty-eight and thirty-two bushels. These yields approximate the average reported through the first half of the nineteenth century. An 1820s family farm, for example, yielded thirty bushels of corn per acre. See David M. Strothers and Patrick M. Tucker, "The Dunlap Farmstead: A Market-Dependent Farm in the Early History of the Maumee Valley of Ohio," *Archaeology of Eastern North America* 30 (2002): 155–188; see page 178 for a chart on 1820s farm production.

26. For Fort Wayne accounts, see Bert J. Griswold, ed., *Fort Wayne, Gateway to the West, 1802–1813* (Indianapolis: Historical Bureau of the Indiana Library and Historical Department, 1927), 405–663; see page 458 for 1806 figure. Factory stores existed until 1822. On the factory system, see Ora Brooks Peake, *A History of the United States Indian Factory System, 1795–1822* (Denver: Sage Books, 1954); David Andrew Nichols, *Engines of Diplomacy: Indian Trading Factories and the Negotiation of American Empire* (Chapel Hill: University of North Carolina Press, 2016); and William H. Bergmann, *The American National State and the Early West* (Cambridge: Cambridge University Press, 2012); and Stephen J. Rockwell, *Indian Affairs and the Administrative State in the Nineteenth Century* (New York: Cambridge University Press, 2010).

27. See Secretary of War Henry Dearborn to Tench Coxe, February 10, 1804 (M15, reel 1, RG 75, NARA, Washington, DC); Tench Coxe, "An Address to an Assembly of the Friends of American Manufactures convened for the purpose of establishing a Society for the Encouragement of Manufactures and the Useful Arts, read in the University of Pennsylvania, on Thursday the 9th of August 1787," (Philadelphia: R. Aitken & Son, 1787), 29–30; and Tench Coxe, *Observations on the Agriculture, Manufactures and Commerce of the United States* (New York: Francis Childs and John Swaine, 1789), 12. Tench Coxe, the first to procure goods for the U.S. Indian trade, set the model for later superintendents. His ideological support of the intertwining of U.S. agricultural and manufacturing sectors thus translated into policy. See Jacob E. Cooke, *Tench Coxe and the Early Republic* (Chapel Hill: University of North Carolina Press, 1978); Jacob E. Cooke, "Tench Coxe, Alexander Hamilton, and the Encouragement of American Manufactures," *William and Mary Quarterly*, 3rd Series, 32, no. 3 (July 1975): 369–392.

28. Coxe family papers, 1638–1897, call no. 2049, Series I, vol. 28, 23–25 (Historical Society of Pennsylvania, Philadelphia, PA).

29. John Mason to John Armstrong, March 8, 1814, 198–199, Letters Sent by the Superintendent of Indian Trade, 1807–1823, Records of the Office of Indian Trade (National Archives Microfilm Publication M16, roll 3, 198–199), National Archives, Washington, DC (hereafter referred to as M16).

30. Henry Dearborn to Israel Whelen, June 5, 1802, M15, roll 1, 222–223.

31. Ibid.

32. John Mason to John Johnston, January 3, 1808, M16, roll 1, 196.

33. For accounts, see Griswold, ed., *Fort Wayne*, 405–663.

34. For Quaker-run stores in Alaska, see Nicholas E. Flanders, "Missionaries and Professional Infidels: Religion and Government in Western Alaska," *Arctic Anthropology* 28, no. 2 (1991): 44–62.

35. On arms manufacturing, see Andrew J. B. Fagal, "American Arms Manufacturing and the Onset of the War of 1812," *New England Quarterly* 87 (September 2014): 526–537.

36. Though some argue to the contrary, Bernard Sheehan and Reginald Horsman rightly see continuity between Federalist and Jeffersonian Indian policies. Both emphasize the intellectual impulses behind federal Indian policy. See Bernard W. Sheehan, *Seeds of Extinction:*

Jeffersonian Philanthropy and the American Indian (Chapel Hill: University of North Carolina Press, 1974); and Reginald Horsman, *Expansion and American Indian Policy, 1783–1812* (East Lansing, MI: Michigan State University Press, 1967). Anthony Wallace, on the other hand, argues that Jeffersonian policies departed from those of the Federalists. Anthony F. C. Wallace, *Jefferson and the Indians: The Tragic Fate of the First Americans* (Cambridge: Harvard University Press, 1999).

37. For benevolence and U.S. empire over time, see, for example, Anders Stephanson, *Manifest Destiny: American Expansionism and the Empire of Right* (New York: Hill and Wang, 1995).

38. For correspondence with Wells, see BYMIC minutes, vol. 1, 10 mo 15 [October 15] 1805, 109–113; P. E. William Wells's presence in the region, however, was mired in controversy. See R. David Edmunds, "'Evil Men Who Add to Our Difficulties': Shawnees, Quakers, and William Wells, 1807–1808," *American Indian Culture and Research Journal* 14, no. 4 (1990): 1–14.

39. Thomas to John Johnston Baltimore, February 20, 1809, John Johnston Papers, reel 1.

40. See Henry Dearborn to Governor William Hull, John Johnston, Samuel Tripper, March 24, 1808 (M15, reel 2, RG 75, NARA, Washington, DC). For additional letters restricting missionaries' movements, see, for example, Henry Dearborn to William Ewing, March 18, 1805 (M15, reel 2, RG 75, NARA, Washington, DC).

The control of movement extended to the region's Native people as well. The government required "passports" for traveling Native Americans who wished to venture to Washington, DC. In 1802, Secretary Dearborn informed his Indian agents that they were "directed not to furnish any Indians with the means of travelling to the Seat of Government unless they have passports." The reason for the passports, Dearborn claimed, was to minimize the "many inconveniences arising from Indians travelling through the country to the Seat of Government without passports." By 1806, the president of the United States claimed he would only see traveling Native leaders during four months of the year—May, June, October, and November—since he deemed it "expedient to decline receiving visits from his red children, while Congress are in session. See Henry Dearborn to J. W. Brownson, April 19, 1802 (M15, reel 1, RG 75, NARA, Washington, DC); Henry Dearborn to Charles Jouett, September 6, 1802 (M15, reel 1, RG 75, NARA, Washington, DC; Henry Dearborn to William Wells, November 3, 1806 (M15, reel 2, RG 75, NARA, Washington, DC).

41. For John Shaw, see P. E. Thomas to John Johnston, February 20, 1809, John Johnston Papers, reel 1. The Miamis refused Quaker William Kirk's assistance in 1807, and so Kirk moved on to assist the Shawnees at Wapakoneta. Friends' reputation among Native peoples in the region was generally strong, and thus many of Kirk's contemporaries as well as present-day historians believe that Wells played a role in souring Kirk's reputation among the Miamis. This bureaucratic battle, stemming from William Wells's jealousy of Kirk's newfound power in the region, resulted in Kirk's dismissal from his post by secretary of war Henry Dearborn in 1808. See Edmunds, "'Evil Men Who Add to Our Difficulties.'"

42. P. E. Thomas to John Johnston Baltimore, 2 mo 20th 1809, John Johnston Papers (Ohio Historical Society, Columbus, OH).

43. Henry Dearborn to Captain Hendrick [Aupaumut], December 27, 1808 (M15, reel 2, RG75, NARA, Washington, DC). For more on Aupaumut, see Wheeler, "Hendrick Aupaumut: Christian-Mahican Prophet"; and Alan Taylor, "Captain Hendrick Aupaumut: The Dilemmas of an Intercultural Broker" *Ethnohistory* 43, no. 3 (Summer, 1996): 431–457.

44. For more on Shawnee, Miami, and other regional economies, see Stephen Warren, *The Shawnees and Their Neighbors, 1795–1870* (Champaign, IL: University of Illinois Press, 2008);

Stewart Rafert, *The Miami Indians of Indiana: A Persistent People* (Indianapolis: Indiana Historical Society, 1996), see especially Chapters 1 and 2; Hinderaker, *Elusive Empires*. For kinship, marriage, and trade, see Susan Sleeper-Smith, *Indian Women and French Men: Rethinking Cultural Encounter in the Western Great Lakes* (Amherst, MA: University of Massachusetts Press, 2001). The Miami leader Richardville, for example, was the son of a Frenchman and a prominent Miami woman, and he used his connections with both the French and Miamis (and government agents) to cultivate wealth and political power during the early nineteenth century. See Bradley J. Birzer, "Entangling Empires, Fracturing Frontiers: Jean Baptiste Richardville and the Quest for Miami Autonomy, 1760–1841" (PhD diss., Indiana University, 1998).

45. BYCMIC minutes, "The address of the Committee of the Yearly meeting of Baltimore dated 19th of the third month 1808," included in the minutes, vol. 1, 3 mo 19 [March 19] 1808, 180–189.

46. For the "civil war of 1812," see Alan Taylor, *The Civil War of 1812: American Citizens, British Subjects, Irish Rebels, & Indian Allies* (New York: Knopf Doubleday, 2010).

47. John Johnston to William Henry Harrison, June 24, 1810, in Esarey, ed., *Messages and Letters*, 431.

48. For more on the terms "accommodationist" and "nativist," see Gregory Evans Dowd, *A Spirited Resistance: The North American Indian Struggle for Unity, 1745–1815* (Baltimore: Johns Hopkins University Press, 1991). Works by Kathleen DuVal, Stephen Warren, and Patrick Bottiger illuminate the many options, problems, and opportunities presented to Native peoples as a consequence of U.S. Indian policies and how they in turn confronted and shaped federal policies. See Kathleen DuVal, *The Native Ground: Indians and Colonists in the Heart of the Continent* (Philadelphia: University of Pennsylvania Press, 2006); Warren, *Shawnees and Their Neighbors*; and Patrick Bottiger, "Prophetstown for Their Own Purposes: The French, Miamis, and Cultural Identities in the Wabash-Maumee Valley," *Journal of the Early Republic* 33, no. 1 (Spring 2013): 29–60. R. David Edmunds's call for a reinterpretation of those leaders who cultivated relationships with the United States in order to benefit their own peoples, now decades old, is still pertinent. See R. David Edmunds, "Redefining Red Patriotism: Five Medals of the Potawatomies," *Red River Valley Historical Review* 5, no. 2 (March 1980): 13–24.

49. Journal of the Proceedings at the Indian Treaty at Fort Wayne and Vincennes September 1 to October 27, 1809, in Esarey, ed., *Messages and Letters*, 362–378, see especially 370–371.

50. On Shawnees' political efforts during the years surrounding the War of 1812, see R. David Edmunds, *The Shawnee Prophet* (Lincoln: University of Nebraska Press, 1983); Patrick Bottiger, "Prophetstown for Their Own Purposes"; Warren, *Shawnees and Their Neighbors*.

51. United States DS to the Wyandots of Solomons Town [Ohio]; Quarter Master's Department, North-Western Army, ca. 1812, War of 1812 Collection, Box 2 (William L. Clements Library, University of Michigan, Ann Arbor, MI); B.F. Stickney ALS, ADS to Jacob Fowler; McPherson's Block House, February 10 and May 3, 1813, War of 1812 Collection, Box 2 (William L. Clements Library, University of Michigan, Ann Arbor, MI); Joseph Richardville to Jean B. Richardville, April 26, 1824 in *John Tipton Papers*, Vol. 1, 1809–1827 (Indianapolis, Indiana Historical Bureau, 1942), 357, 485.

52. For Miamis' experiences during the war, see Rafert, *Miami Indians of Indiana*, 73–76.

53. Johnston to Genl. John Mason (Supt. of Indian Trade), January 4, 1813, T58 (NARA, Washington, DC).

54. William Henry Harrison to the General Assembly, July 29, 1805, in Esarey, ed., *Messages and Letters*, 152–158.

55. For the petition, see Congressional Document Series #181, document 74 (Ethnohistory Collection, Indiana University). For Miamis forced removals and the use of a canal to do so, see George Strack, George Ironstrack, Daryl Baldwin, Kristina Fox, Julie Olds, Robbyn Abbitt, and Melissa Rinehart, *Myaamiaki Aancihsaaciki: A Cultural Exploration of the Myaamia Removal Route* (Miami: Miami Tribe of Oklahoma, 2011).

Chapter 5

Note to epigraph: This revised chapter was originally published as "'A Damnd Rebelious Race': The U.S. Civilization Plan and Native Authority," in Ignacio Gallup-Diaz and Geoffrey Plank, eds., *Quakers and American Indians* (Brill Academic Press: Leiden, 2019). Reprinted with permission. Hugh B. McKeen to John Tipton, June 28, 1826, *John Tipton Papers, Vol. 1* (Indianapolis: Indiana Historical Bureau, 1942), 547.</>

1. May 20, 1817, Western Emigration Society Papers, VFM 519 (Ohio Historical Society, Columbus, OH).

2. Samuel Todd, Post-Script in Nathan Guilford to William Avril, Western Emigration Society Papers, VFM (Ohio Historical Society, Columbus, OH).

3. May 20, 1817, Western Emigration Society Papers.

4. Ibid.

5. 10 month 11 [October 11], 1815, BYMCIC, Minutes, 1815–1847.

6. Ibid.

7. James Ellicott and Philip E. Thomas, August 1, 1816, Report on feasibility of introducing farming and other civilising activities among the Indians at Waupaghkonnetta and Lewis Town by the Society of Friends at Baltimore, NARA RG 107, Secretary of War, Letters Received, Shawnee File, Box #8027, folder 1 of 1 (1816), Ethnohistory Collection, IU.

8. Ibid. Friends reported a similar situation at Sears' Town. Wyandots near Upper Sandusky, meanwhile, received annuities from the government and were reportedly anxious "to receive instruction in their farming business."

9. Ibid.

10. Ibid.

11. Ibid.

12. George C. Johnston, Book of promissory notes, 1829–1831 (Ohio Historical Society, Columbus, OH).

13. John Johnston's Fort Wayne factory account books similarly reveal that Native individuals were responsible for more than one-third of the debts owed the factory store in 1806. See Bert J. Griswold, ed., *Fort Wayne, Gateway to the West, 1802–1813* (Indianapolis: Historical Bureau of the Indiana Library and Historical Department, 1927), 405–663; see page 458 for 1806 figure.

14. See Thomas Jefferson to William Henry Harrison, February 27, 1803, in Logan Esarey, ed., *Governors' messages and letters: messages and letters of William Henry Harrison* Vol. 1, 1800-1811 (Indianapolis: Indiana Historical Commission, 1922), 70–73.

15. Johnston, Book of promissory notes.

16. Jeanne Boydston, *Home and Work: Housework, Wages, and the Ideology of Labor in the Early Republic* (New York: Oxford University Press, 1990), see especially Chapter 5.

17. Henry Harvey, *History of the Shawnee Indians from the Year 1681 to 1854, Inclusive* (Cincinnati: Ephraim Morgan & Sons, 1855), 187.

18. John Johnston to William H. Crawford Piqua, October 22, 1816, Shawnee File, 1813–1816, Box #8027, folder 1 of 1 (1816), Ethnohistory Collection.

19. Ibid.

20. Miami and Eel River Indians, Receipt, Annuity Payment, August 24—December 23, 1829, in N. Robertson and D. Ricker, eds., *John Tipton Papers*, Vol. 2, (Indianapolis: Indiana Historical Bureau, 1942), 186–189, Miami File, 1829–1847, Box #5023, folder 1 of 1 (1829), Ethnohistory Collection.

21. John Tipton, Abstract of Payments for Labor at Miami Villages, 1829, in N. Robertson and D. Ricker, eds., *John Tipton Papers*, Vol. 2, 238, Miami File, Box #5023, folder 1 of 1 (1829), Ethnohistory Collection. The "Thorntown" Miamis were Eel River Miamis who once lived on the Thorntown Reserve lands that were ceded to the United States in 1828.

22. While census data is inconclusive, the men who labored on Miami lands were likely from nearby lands and had recently moved there. United States Census, 1820C NARA M33, National Archives and Records Administration, Washington D. C.

23. Stephen Warren, *The Shawnees and Their Neighbors, 1795–1870*, (Champaign: University of Illinois Press, 2005), 43–68.

24. Bradley J. Birzer, "Entangling Empires, Fracturing Frontiers: Jean Baptiste Richardville and the Quest for Miami Autonomy, 1760–1841," Ph.D. Dissertation, Indiana University, 1998.

25. Joseph Richardville to Jean B. Richardville, April 26, 1824, *John Tipton Papers*, Vol. 1, 1809–1827 (Indianapolis: Indiana Historical Bureau, 1942), 357, 485.

26. Stewart Rafert, *The Miami Indians of Indiana: A Persistent People, 1654–1994* (Indianapolis: Indiana Historical Society, 1996), 96.

27. John Tipton to Comparet and Coquillard, September 1, 1824, *John Tipton Papers*, Vol. 1, 391.

28. Lewis Cass to Tipton, October 14, 1824, *John Tipton Papers*, Vol. 1, 398. In 1826, Richardville's political ally, Meehcikilita, supported Richardville's economic pursuits, and he worked closely with Richardville to confront U.S. power in the region. Meehcikilita advocated on behalf of Jean Baptiste's request for the license, and he further informed secretary of war James Barbour, "We wish you would let Richardville have goods and the exclusive right to trade with our Nation, in order to prevent as much as possible the impositions practised on the Indians in that country by the traders." Le Gros's support of Richardville's trading business was in part political. Richardville's relations with Euro-American traders and federal officials translated into political power for the nation, and granting him the exclusive right to trade with the nation meant that the Miamis could more easily control their own economy and their peoples' access to alcohol. Importantly, however, this was not part of an effort to isolate the Miamis' economy from global trade. It was, rather, a quest to regulate trade, and it combined older notions of leadership grounded in ideas of reciprocity with emerging ideas of private property, profit, and political economy more generally. Richardville stood to profit handsomely by controlling trade with the Miami nation, but he also stood poised to ensure that his people would receive both fair treatment and pricing. Though Le Gros's appeal to grant Richardville exclusive trading rights with the Miamis in Indiana ultimately failed, it nonetheless reflected Miami leaders' awareness of their bargaining power—Richardville did, after all, acquire a trading license.

29. John B. Boure to John Tipton, December 24, 1829, in N. Robertson and D. Ricker, eds., *John Tipton Papers*, Vol. 2, 230, Miami File, Box #5023, folder 1 (1829), Ethnohistory Collection, IU.

30. Ibid.

31. Miami Indians to Lewis Cass, 1830, National Archives, RG 75, Letters Received, Miami File, Box #5023, folder 1 of 2 (1830–1833), Ethnohistory Collection.

32. Ibid.

33. John Tipton to John H. Eaton, February 15, 1830, in N. Robertson and D. Ricker, eds., *John Tipton Papers*, Vol. 2, 250–251, Miami File, Box #5023, folder 1 of 2 (1830–1833), Ethnohistory Collection.

34. Ibid.

35. William G. Ewing to John Tipton, February 3, 1830, in N. Robertson and D. Ricker, eds., *John Tipton Papers*, Vol. 2, 244–247, Miami File, Box #5023, folder 1 of 2 (1830–1833), Ethnohistory Collection; For Indiana memorials, see "Memorial of the Legislature of Indiana" (from Cong. Doc. Series #181, document 74) and "Memorial of the General Assembly of Indiana" (from Cong. Doc. Series #193, Doc. 79), Miami File, Box #5023, folder 1 of 2 (1830–1833), Ethnohistory Collection.

36. Ibid.

37. Whigs were generally in favor of internal improvement programs, while Democrats generally opposed them. The debate was especially intense in places like Ohio that seemed prime for improvement projects thanks to growing population numbers and an expanding economy. On overcoming "the tyranny of distance" through improvement projects, see Daniel Walker Howe, *What Hath God Wrought: The Transformation of America, 1815–1848*, (Oxford: Oxford University Press, 2007), 211–242.

38. G. B. Porter to Fort Wayne Cass, August 23, 1833, National Archives, RG 75, O.I.A., Letters Received, Miami File, Box #5023, folder 2 of 2 (1830–1833), Ethnohistory Collection.

39. John Tipton to John H. Eaton, February 15, 1830, in N. Robertson and D. Ricker, eds., *John Tipton Papers*, Vol. 2, 250–251, Miami File, Box #5023, folder 1 of 2 (1830–1833), Ethnohistory Collection.

40. For report on Martha Rhodes's death and Black Hoof's sympathies, see 10 mo 16 [October 16], 1817, BYMCIC, Minutes, 1815–1847.

41. See BYMCIC, Minutes, 1815–1847.

42. 10 mo 29 [October 29], 1823, BYMCIC, Minutes, 1815–1847, 88.

43. Stephanie McCurry's work on women in the Civil War South offers excellent analysis on the role of petitions in forming bonds with the state. See Stephanie McCurry, *Confederate Reckoning: Power and Politics in the Civil War South* (Cambridge, MA: Harvard University Press, 2010).

44. Le Gros [Meehcikilita] to James Barbour, January 27, 1826, in N. Robertson and D. Ricker, eds., *John Tipton Papers*, Vol. 1, 517–518.

45. Ibid.

46. Thomas L. McKenney to Le Gros, February 2, 1826, in N. Robertson and D. Ricker, eds., *John Tipton Papers*, Vol. 1, 519–520; Hugh B. McKeen to John Tipton, June 28, 1826, in N. Robertson and D. Ricker, eds., *John Tipton Papers*, Vol. 1, 546–547.

47. Chief Le Gros [Meehcikilita] to Gov. Lewis Cass, October 12, 1826, in Rafert, *Miami Indians of Indiana*, 77.

48. Yael Ben-zvi, *Native Land Talk: Indigenous and Arrivant Rights Theories* (Hanover, NH: Dartmouth College Press, 2018).

49. September 16, 1820, Shawnee and Delaware Indians, Talk to the President of the United States, Principal Town on Apple Creek, State of Missouri, RG 107, M-92 (14), NARA, Delaware File, Box #1524 (1820–1827), folder 1 of 2 (July 1820–1821), Ethnohistory Collection.

50. Treaty of Peace and Friendship Between the Osage, and Delaware, Shawnee, Wea, Piankashaw, Peoria and Kickapoo, September 21, 1822, RG 75, Letters Received, Secretary

of War, NARA, Shawnee File, Box #8029 (1821–1829), folder 1 of 1 (1822–1823), Ethnohistory Collection.

51. September 16, 1820, Shawnee and Delaware Indians, Talk to the President of the United States, Principal Town on Apple Creek, State of Missouri, RG 107, M-92 (14), NARA, Delaware File, Box #1524 (1820–1827), folder 1 of 2 (July 1820–1821), Ethnohistory Collection.

52. Ibid.

53. Claudio Saunt, *A New Order of Things: Property, Power, and the Transformation of the Creek Indians, 1733–1816* (New York: Cambridge University Press, 1999).

54. Treaty with the Delawares (Treaty of St. Mary's), 1818 in Charles J. Kappler, ed., *Indian Affairs, Laws and Treaties*, vol. 2 (Washington: Government Printing Office, 1904, 170-171.

55. A Petition from Hendrick Aupaumet, Sachem to the President and Congress of the U.S. for a location of lands. Signed by Hendrick Aupaumet, Sachem [signed from N. Stockbridge], November 16, 1819, Stockbridge Papers, Folder 5 (Cornell University, Ithaca, NY).

56. Ibid.

57. Ibid.

58. Ibid.

59. Ibid.

60. Ibid.

61. The most thorough history of the Stockbridge Indians is David J. Silverman, *Red Brethren: The Brothertown and Stockbridge Indians and the Problem of Race in Early America* (Ithaca, NY: Cornell University Press, 2010).

62. Letter of the Stockbridge Indians, by Rev. J. Miner to the ABCFM, October 30, 1827, Stockbridge Papers, Folder 9A (Cornell University, Ithaca, NY).

63. John Johnston to Thomas L. McKenney, Wapaghkonetta, July 18, 1825, National Archives, RG 75, Records of the Bureau of Indian Affairs, Letters Received, Piqua Agency 1825 (Roll #3, Ohio Historical Society), Shawnee File, Box #8029, folder 1 of 1 (1825–1826), Ethnohistory Collection.

64. John Johnston to Thomas L. McKenney Piqua, February 20, 1827 (with enclosures), Collection Archives, RG 75, Records of the Bureau of Indian Affairs, Letters Received, Piqua Agency 1827 (Roll #3, Ohio Historical Society), Shawnee File, Box #8029, folder 1 of 1 (1827–1828), Ethnohistory Collection, IU.

65. Ibid.

66. Ibid.

67. Ibid.

68. John Johnston to Thomas L. McKenney, January 17, 1828, National Archives, RG 75, Records of the Bureau of Indian Affairs, Letters Received, Piqua Agency 1828 (Roll #3, Ohio Historical Society), Shawnee File, Box #8029, folder 1 of 1 (1827–1828), Ethnohistory Collection, IU.

69. John Johnston to Thomas L. McKenney Piqua, February 20, 1827 (with enclosures), National Archives, RG 75, Records of the Bureau of Indian Affairs, Letters Received, Piqua Agency 1827 (Roll #3, Ohio Historical Society), Shawnee File, Box #8029, folder 1 of 1 (1827–1828), Ethnohistory Collection.

Chapter 6

1. John Johnston to Thomas L. McKenney, Upper Piqua, January 29, 1828, National Archives, RG 75, Records of the Bureau of Indian Affairs, Letters Received, Piqua Agency 1828 (Roll #3, Ohio Historical Society, Columbus, OH), Ethnohistory Collection.

2. Johnston informed McKenney on January 17, 1828, that he was in Columbus "attending as Canal Commissioner and will return to Piqua as soon as the Board adjourn." John Johnston to Thomas L. McKenney, January 17, 1828, National Archives, RG 75, Records of the Bureau of Indian Affairs, Letters Received, Piqua Agency 1828 (Roll #3, Ohio Historical Society, Columbus, OH) in Ethnohistory Collection. Harry Scheiber notes that Johnston was particularly aggressive among the canal commissioners—pushing hard to have the canal system extend from Dayton through his holdings at Piqua. See Harry N. Scheiber, *Ohio Canal Era: A Case Study of Government and the Economy, 1820–1861* (Athens: Ohio University Press, 1969), 97–98.

3. George Strack, George Ironstrack, Daryl Baldwin, Kristina Fox, Julie Olds, Robbyn Abbitt, and Melissa Rinehart, *Myaamiaki Aancihsaaciki: A Cultural Exploration of the Myaamia Removal Route* (Miami: Miami Tribe of Oklahoma, 2011), 3.

4. On such technological developments, see, for example, Scheiber, *Ohio Canal Era*; Howe, *What Hath God Wrought*; Sellers, *The Market Revolution*; Andrew R. L. Cayton and Peter S. Onuf, *The Midwest and the Nation: Rethinking the History of an American Region* (Bloomington: Indiana University Press, 1990); Christopher Clark, "Ohio Country in the Political Economy of Nation Building," in Andrew R. L. Cayton and Stuart D. Hobbs, *The Center of a Great Empire: The Ohio Country in the Early Republic* (Athens, OH: Ohio University Press, 2005).

5. Daniel Walker Howe, *What Hath God Wrought: The Transformation of America, 1815–1848* (Oxford: Oxford University Press, 2007).

6. Howe, 47.

7. Civilization Fund Act, March 3, 1819, in Francis Paul Prucha, ed., *Documents of United States Indian Policy*, 3rd. edition (Lincoln: University of Nebraska Press, 2000), 33.

8. The ABCFM included under its auspices Congregationalist, Presbyterian, and other Protestant denominations. Emily Conroy-Krutz's work offers a much-needed corrective to the history of missionaries and U.S. imperialism abroad by pushing the timeline back to the early nineteenth century. Her work also links the continental and global in important ways. See Emily Conroy-Krutz, *Christian Imperialism: Converting the World in the Early American Republic* (Ithaca: Cornell University Press, 2016). The growing number of societies undertaking missionary work should also be understood within the context of the Second Great Awakening, a phenomenon that was particularly present in Ohio and western New York. See Whitney R. Cross, *The Burned-Over District: The Social and Intellectual History of Enthusiastic Religion in Western New York, 1800–1850* (Ithaca, NY: Cornell University Press, 1950); Nathan O. Hatch, *The Democratization of American Christianity* (New Haven, CT: Yale University Press, 1989); and Christine Leigh Heyrman, *Southern Cross: The Beginnings of the Bible Belt* (Chapel Hill: University of North Carolina Press, 1998).

9. Students at a school in Cornwall, CT, for example, spent two and a half days laboring on the "school's agricultural property." See John Demos, *The Heathen School: A Story of Hope and Betrayal in the Age of the Early Republic* (New York: Alfred A. Knopf, 2014), 72.

10. February 29, 1820, Regulations for the Civilization of the Indians, Department of War. NARA M15, National Archives and Records Administration, Washington, D.C., 379.

11. There does seem to have been some confusion, on the part of some missionaries, as to how the funds could be spent. In 1824, Thomas L. McKenney rejected Baptists' request to repair mills at their mission site, stating that they were not considered a school building. That the Baptists assumed that the War Department would cover the repair costs almost certainly means that they had used the funds to build the mills at the outset. See William McLoughlin, *Champions of the Cherokees: Evan and John B. Jones* (Princeton, NJ: Princeton University Press, 1990), 49.

12. Henry Clay's "American System," proposed in 1824, was a key example of policymakers' attempts to find ways to fund infrastructure. Pamela Baker, for instance, sees the period between 1814 and Jackson's presidency as one of three major periods in the federal government's expansion of its role in economic policy (along with Reconstruction and the New Deal). See Pamela Baker, "The Washington Road Bill and the Struggle to Adopt a Federal System of Internal Improvement," *Journal of the Early Republic* 22, no. 3 (Autumn 2002): 437–464.

13. Laurence Hauptman's work is excellent on this point for Haudenosaunee Country. See Laurence Hauptman, *A Conspiracy of Interests: Iroquois Dispossession and the Rise of New York* State (Syracuse, NY: Syracuse University Press, 1999).

14. It is worth noting that much of the literature on the transportation revolution elides the reality that Indigenous dispossession undergirded such changes. See Jeremy Atack, Fred Bateman, Michael Haines, and Robert A. Margo, "Did Railroads Induce or Follow Economic Growth? Urbanization and Population Growth in the American Midwest, 1850–1860," *Social Science History* 34, no. 2 (Summer 2010): 184–185.

15. Ibid.

16. James Ellicott and Philip E. Thomas, "Report on feasibility of introducing farming and other civilizing activities among the Indians at Waupaghkonnetta and Lewis Town by the Society of Friends at Baltimore," August 1, 1816, NARA in Shawnee Box #8027, Ethnohistory Collection.

17. Isaac McCoy to J. C. Calhoun, Fort Wayne, October 1, 1821, Secretary of War, Letters Received, M-145 (15), RG 107, NARA in Shawnee File, Box #8029, folder 1 of 1 (1821), Ethnohistory Collection.

18. Ibid.

19. Ibid.

20. Lucien Bolles letters, ABMU, June 8, 1826, in McLoughlin, *Champions of the Cherokees*, 51.

21. Isaac McCoy, *Remarks on the Practicability of Indian Reform, Embracing Their Colonization* (Boston: Lincoln & Edmands, Washington-Street, 1827).

22. Nicholas Guyatt discusses McCoy in the context of creating racial segregation in the early republic. See Nicholas Guyatt, *Bind Us Apart: How Enlightened Americans Invented Racial Segregation* (New York: Basic Books, 2016), especially Chapter 11. For a biography of McCoy, see George A. Schultz, *An Indian Canaan: Isaac McCoy and the Vision of an Indian State* (Norman: University of Oklahoma Press, 1972).

23. See Francis Paul Prucha, *The Great Father: The United States Government and the American Indians* (Lincoln: University of Nebraska Press, 1984), 304–305.

24. McCoy, *Remarks on the Practicability of Indian Reform*, 11.

25. Ibid., 14, 17.

26. Ibid., 21.

27. Ibid., 22.

28. Ibid., 32.

29. Ibid.

30. Ibid., 34.

31. Ibid., 21.

32. Ibid., 23.

33. Timothy S. Smith, "Missionary abominations unmasked: or, A view of Carey mission containing an unmasking of the missionary abominations practiced among the Indians of

St. Joseph Country at the celebrated missionary establishment known as Carey mission under the superintendence of the Rev. Isaac McCoy" (South Bend, IN: Printed at Beacon Office, 1833), 7–8.

34. Ibid.

35. Isaac McCoy, *History of Baptist Indian Missions: Embracing Remarks on the Former and Present Condition of the Aboriginal Tribes; Their Settlement within the Indian Territory, and their Future Prospects* (Washington: William M. Morrison; New York: H. and S. Raynor, 1840), 79.

36. Ibid.

37. Lucius Bolles to Jesse Mercer, ABMU, March 16, 1827, in McLoughlin, *Champions of the Cherokees*, 50.

38. Ora Brooks Peake, *A History of the United States Indian Factory System, 1795–1822* (Denver: Sage Books, 1954); David Andrew Nichols, *Engines of Diplomacy: Indian Trading Factories and the Negotiation of American Empire* (Chapel Hill: University of North Carolina Press, 2016); William H. Bergmann, *The American National State and the Early West* (Cambridge: Cambridge University Press, 2012); Stephen J. Rockwell, *Indian Affairs and the Administrative State in the Nineteenth Century* (New York: Cambridge University Press, 2010).

39. Lucius Bolles to Jesse Mercer, ABMU, March 16, 1827, in McLoughlin, *Champions of the Cherokees*, 50.

40. John Johnston to William H. Crawford, October 22, 1816, NARA RG 107, J-264 in Shawnee File, Ethnohistory Collection.

41. Hauptman, *Conspiracy of Interests*.

42. *Proceedings of Sundry Citizens of Baltimore, Convened for the Purpose of Devising the Most Efficient Means of Improving the Intercourse Between That City and the Western States* (Baltimore: Printed by William Wooddy, 1827), 23.

43. Ibid.

44. Ibid., 30.

45. Ibid.

46. Matthew Pawson to Jonathan Ellicott and Others, Deed, May 12, 1804, MSS 1825, Deeds and Land Papers (Maryland Historical Society, Baltimore, MD).

47. James Corrie to Jonathan Ellicott and Others, May 26, 1804, Deed, MSS 1825 Deeds and Land Papers (Maryland Historical Society, Baltimore, MD).

48. The Ellicotts bought "Helm's Pick," for example, in 1794, and they purchased additional lands near Gwinn's Falls in 1800. Andrew Ellicott, a surveyor for the U.S. government, purchased lands near Baltimore as early as 1780. See MSS 1825, Lands and Deed Papers (Maryland Historical Society, Baltimore, MD).

49. The Ellicotts purchased these plots in 1807 for a total of $15,133. See 1807 Deed, MSS 1825, Deeds and Land Papers (Maryland Historical Society, Baltimore, MD).

50. Ibid.

51. *Proceedings of Sundry Citizens of Baltimore, Convened for the Purpose of Devising the Most Efficient Means of Improving the Intercourse Between That City and the Western States*. The B&O station at Ellicott City—the oldest in the United States—still stands in the Ellicott Mill's District. On the connection between the B&O Railroad and the Union Bank of Maryland, see James D. Dilts, *The Great Road: The Building of the Baltimore and Ohio, the Nation's First Railroad, 1828–1853* (Stanford, CA: Stanford University Press, 1993), 171–172. For the investment of Indian Concerns Committee funds at the Union Bank of Maryland, see BYMCIC, Minutes, 1795–1815, 3 mo. [March 12], 1809, 227.

In 1812, the Ellicotts formerly partitioned the lands centered around and to the west of Gwynn's Falls (also shown on map) among themselves. See Indenture from 1812, MSS 1825 Deeds and Land Papers, Baltimore, MD, Maryland Historical Society.

52. John Scott to the Secretary of War, St. Genevieve, September 21, 1820, in Carter, *Territorial Papers*, Vol. 15, 645–646 in box #1524, Delaware, 1820–1827, Delaware, July 1820–1821, folder 1 of 2, Ethnohistory Collection.

53. McCoy, *History of Baptist Missions*, 79.

54. Ibid.

55. Christina Snyder, *Great Crossings: Indians, Settlers, and Slaves in the Age of Jackson* (New York: Oxford University Press, 2017), 71–72.

56. McCoy, *History of Baptist Missions*, 65.

57. October 11, 1826, "Proceedings, Potawatomi and Miami Treaty Negotiations," *John Tipton Papers*, Vol. 1 (Indianapolis: Indiana Historical Bureau, 1942), 584.

58. Congressional Document Series #181, document 74, Miami File, 1829–1864, Box #5023, Ethnohistory Collection.

59. Ibid.

60. Ibid.

61. Strack et al., *Myaamiaki Aancihsaaciki*; John P. Bowes, *Land Too Good for Indians: Northern Indian Removal* (Norman: University of Oklahoma Press, 2016), 65–77. Bowes employs a compelling framework of "adaptive resistance" to understand Miamis' efforts to remain in Indiana.

62. The Myaamia presence in what is now Ohio and Indiana is indeed thriving, as evidenced by their language revitalization and educational programs—a partnership between the Miami Tribe of Oklahoma and Miami University.

63. Treaty with the Wyandot, Etc. (Treaty of the Maumee Rapids) 1817, September 29, 1817, in Charles J. Kappler, ed., *Indian Affairs, Laws and Treaties*, vol. 2 (Washington: Government Printing Office, 1904), 160.

64. For a history of Shawnee removals, see Stephen Warren, *The Shawnees and Their Neighbors, 179501870* (Champaign, IL: University of Illinois Press, 2005).

65. Henry Harvey, *The History of the Shawnee Indians, from the Year 1681 to 1854, Inclusive* (Cincinnati: Ephraim Morgan & Sons, 1855), 168.

66. On gender and reform, see Bruce Dorsey, *Reforming Men and Women: Gender in the Antebellum City* (Ithaca, NY: Cornell University Press, 2002).

67. On the importance of white women to the U.S. settler-colonial project, see Laurel Clark Shire, *The Threshold of Manifest Destiny: Gender and National Expansion in Florida* (Philadelphia: University of Pennsylvania Press, 2016).

68. Henry Harvey, *History of the Shawnee Indians, From the Year 1681 to 1854, Inclusive* (Cincinnati: Ephraim Morgan & Sons, 1855), 169.

69. Ibid.

70. 10 mo. [October] 12, 1820, BYMCIC, Minutes, 1815–1847, 64–69.

71. 8 mo. [August] 13, 1821, BYMCIC, Minutes, 1815–1847, 72.

72. Ibid., 83.

73. Harvey, *History of the Shawnee Indians*, 179.

74. Ibid., 182.

75. Ibid.

76. Ibid., 194.

77. Ibid., 204. For the treaty, see Treaty with the Shawnee, 1831, August 8, 1831, in Kappler, ed., *Indian Affairs*.

78. Harvey, *History of the Shawnee Indians*, 205–206.

79. Ibid., 204–205.

80. Ibid., 212.

81. Ibid., 213.

82. Ibid., 215.

83. Ibid., 216.

84. Ibid., 234.

85. Ibid.

86. *Annual Report of the Commissioner of Indian Affairs, Transmitted with the Message of the President and the Opening of the Second Session of the Twenty-Eighth Congress* (Washington: C. Alexander, Printer, 1844), 134.

87. Ibid.

88. James Anderson, "The Methodist Shawnee Mission in Johnson County, Kansas, 1830–1862," in John Edward Hicks, ed., *The Trail Guide*, published occasionally by the Kansas City Posse, The Westerners, Kansas City, Missouri. Registrar of Brands, Vol. 1, January 1956, No. 2.

89. Harvey, *History of the Shawnee Indians*, 270.

90. Ibid., 274.

91. United States Office of Indian Affairs, Report of the Commissioner of Indian Affairs for the Year 1862 (Washington: Government Printing Office, 1863), 111.

92. In 2021, the remains of 215 Indigenous children were found on the grounds of the Kamloops Indian Residential School in British Columbia. At least 189 children are known to have been buried at Carlisle.

93. Harvey, *History of the Shawnee Indians*, 277.

94. Ibid., 145.

95. Ibid.

96. Bowes, *Land Too Good for Indians*; see especially the introduction.

Chapter 7

1. John Johnston to Lewis Cass, Piqua, October 1, 1820, National Archives, RG 75, Michigan Superintendence of Indian Affairs, Letters received by the Superintendent vol. 2, 331–334, microcopy 1, roll 7 in Box #1524, Delaware, 1820–1827, Delaware, July 1820–1821, folder 1 of 2, Ethnohistory Collection.

2. On rhetorical use of "poor Indians," albeit in a British context, see Laura Stevens, *Poor Indians: British Missionaries, Native Americans, and Colonial Sensibility* (Philadelphia: University of Pennsylvania Press, 2004).

3. Susan M. Ryan, *Grammar of Good Intentions: Race and the Antebellum Culture of Benevolence* (Ithaca: Cornell University Press, 2003).

4. Stevens, *Poor Indians*, 17.

5. On settler colonialism and disavowal of violence, see Lorenzo Veracini, *Settler Colonialism: A Theoretical Overview* (New York: Palgrave Macmillian, 2010), 76–86.

6. Susan Ryan's work makes clear the contested nature of benevolence in the 1820s and 1830s. See Ryan, *Grammar of Good Intentions*.

7. On evolution of poverty and poor relief see Dorsey, *Reforming Men and Women*; Seth Rockman, *Scraping By: Wage Labor, Slavery, and Survival in Early Baltimore* (Baltimore: Johns Hopkins University Press, 2009), especially Chapter 6.

8. For an interpretation of how "enlightened Americans invented segregation," see Nicholas Guyatt, *Bind Us Apart: How Enlightened Americans Invented Racial Segregation* (New York: Basic Books, 2016).

9. [unknown] to Superintendent of Indian Trade, November 6, 1818, National Archives, RG 75, T58. Letters Received by the Superintendent of Indian Trade, 1806–1824, National Archives and Records Administration, Washington D.C.

10. John Parrish, *Remarks on the Slavery of the Black People; Addressed to the Citizens of the United States, particularly to those who are in Legislative or Executive Stations in the General or State Governments; and also to such Individuals as Hold Them in Bondage* (Philadelphia: Kimber, Conrad, & Co., 1806), 43.

11. For Gabriel's Rebellion, see Douglas R. Egerton, *Gabriel's Rebellion: The Virginia Slave Conspiracies of 1800 and 1802* (Chapel Hill: University of North Carolina Press, 1993).

12. Christopher Leslie Brown, *Moral Capital: Foundations of British Abolitionism* (Chapel Hill: University of North Carolina Press, by the Omohundro Institute for Early American History and Culture, 2012), 260–262, 294–295; quotation 295.

13. On Liberia, see Beverly C. Tomek, *Colonization and Its Discontents: Emancipation, Emigration, and Antislavery in Antebellum Pennsylvania* (Early American Places, New York: New York University Press, 2012).

14. Stevens, *Poor Indians*.

15. Stevens, *Poor Indians*; while in a different context, Julie Reed's work on the Cherokees reveals in depth how Cherokees' ideas and practices regarding social welfare both supported their communities and changed over time. See Julie L. Reed, *Serving the Nation: Cherokee Sovereignty and Social Welfare, 1800–1907* (Norman, OK: Oklahoma University Press, 2016).

16. Matthew Dennis rightly argues that, while often political in nature, overtures of impoverishment should be understood as more stylistic than substantive. See Matthew Dennis, *Seneca Possessed: Indians, Witchcraft, and Power in the Early American Republic* (Philadelphia: University of Pennsylvania Press, 2010), 154–156.

17. Little Turtle to Baltimore Society of Friends, 1802, American Antiquarian Society, Worcester, MA. Bruce White's work is useful for understanding the cultural contexts of such rhetoric. See Bruce M. White, "'Give Us a Little Milk': The Social and Cultural meanings of Gift Giving in the Lake Superior Fur Trade," *Minnesota History* 48, no. 2 (Summer 1982): 62.

18. Little Turtle to Baltimore Society of Friends, 1802, American Antiquarian Society, Worcester, MA.

19. Fore more on how white women figured into welfare appeals, see Laurel Clark Shire, *Threshold of Manifest Destiny: Gender and National Expansion in Florida* (Philadelphia: University of Pennsylvania Press, 2016).

20. Thomas L. McKenney to Dr. Samuel Worcester, Extract of a letter from Thos. L. M'Kenney . . . to Dr. Samuel Worcester . . . of the American Board of Commissioners for Foreign Missionaries, October 30, 1817 (Newberry Library, Chicago, IL).

21. Ibid.

22. Thomas Loraine McKenney, *History of the Indian Tribes of North America, with biographical sketches and anecdotes of the principal chiefs, embellished with one hundred and twenty portraits,*

from the Indian Gallery in the Department of War, at Washington, three volumes (Philadelphia: J. T. Bowen, 1836–1844). For a biography of McKenney, see Herman J. Viola, *Thomas L. McKenney: Architect of America's Early Indian Policy: 1816–1830* (Chicago: Swallow Press, 1974).

23. Michael B. Katz, *The Undeserving Poor: From the War on Poverty to the War on Welfare* (New York: Pantheon Books, 1989), 11–15.

24. John Shaw to Cass, Upper Sandusky, March 27, 1821, Shawnee File, Box #8029, Shawnee 1821–1829, Shawnees, 1821, folder 1 of 1, Ethnohistory Collection, Indiana University, Bloomington, IN.

25. Ibid.

26. Ibid.

27. William Clark to Peter B. Porter, August 1, 1828, National Archives, RG 75, St. Louis Superintendency, Letters Received, Roll 748, Ethnohistory Collection.

28. John Johnston to Lewis Cass, Piqua, December 30, 1820, National Archives, RG 75, roll 1, roll 7, in Box #1524, Delaware, 1820–1827, Delaware, July 1820–1821, folder 1 of 2, Ethnohistory Collection.

29. December 3, 1825, "Statement shewing the number of Indian Schools, where established, by whom, the number of Teachers, the number of Pupils, and the amount annually allowed and paid to each, by the Government with remarks as to their condition," (Newberry Library, Chicago, IL).

30. Christina Snyder's work on the Choctaw Academy, a school whose pupils were often the children of regional tribes' most elite leaders, demonstrates the prominent role that ideas of race occupied at the school. Enslaved Africans provided much of the labor at this boarding school, yet here too, federal funds subsidized the school and its operation and intersected with regional political economy. Snyder, *Choctaw Academy*. See also Robert F. Berkhofer Jr., *Salvation and the Savage: An Analysis of Protestant Missions and American Indian Response, 1787–1862* (Lexington, KY: University of Kentucky Press, 1965), 26–27.

31. BYMCIC, Minutes, 1815–1847, 10 mo 16 [October 16] 1817, 33.

32. William E. Unrau, "An International Perspective on American Indian Policy: The South Australian Protector and Aborigines Protection Society," *Pacific Historical Review* 45, no. 4 (November 1976): 522–523.

33. Ibid., 526.

34. See, for example, Ford, *Settler Sovereignty*; Bethel Saler, *Settlers' Empire: Colonialism and State Formation in America's Old Northwest* (Philadelphia: University of Pennsylvania Press, 2014); Margaret Jacobs, *White Mother to a Dark Race: Settler Colonialism, Maternalism, and the Removal of Indigenous Children in the American West and Australia, 1880–1940* (Lincoln: University of Nebraska Press, 2009).

35. William E. Unrau, "An International Perspective on American Indian Policy: The South Australian Protector and Aborigines Protection Society" *Pacific Historical Review* 45, no. 4 (1976): 519–538, quotation 530.

36. For Cass, see Francis Paul Prucha, *Indian Policy in the United States: Historical Essays* (Lincoln: University of Nebraska Press, 1981); Frank B. Woodford, *Lewis Cass: The Last Jeffersonian* (New Brunswick, NJ: Rutgers University Press, 1950); and Willard Carl Klunder, *Lewis Cass and the Politics of Moderation* (Kent, OH: Kent State University Press, 1996).

37. Lewis Cass, *Remarks on the policy and practice of the United States and Great Britain in their treatment of the Indians* (Boston: F.T. Gray, 1827), 1.

38. Ibid., 45.

39. Ibid., 28.

40. On Cherokees and Creeks and slavery, see Miles, *Ties That Bind*; Claudio Saunt, *New Order of Things: Property, Power, and the Transformation of the Creek Indians, 1733–1816* (Cambridge: Cambridge University Press, 1999); and Theda Perdue, *Slavery and the Evolution of Cherokee Society, 1540–1866* (Knoxville: University of Tennessee Press, 1987).

41. Cass, *Remarks*, 37.

42. Ibid., 31.

43. Ibid., 29–30.

44. Ibid., 8.

45. Ibid.

46. Ibid., 26.

47. Ibid., 43.

48. Ibid.

49. Ibid., 47.

50. Ibid., 48; One should note that by 1836, the lieutenant governor of Upper Canada, Francis Bond Head, removed the Ottawas to Manitoulin Island. See Unrau, "International Perspective," 524–525.

51. Cass, *Remarks*, 48.

52. Ibid., 47.

53. Ibid., 7.

54. Ibid., 26.

55. Ibid.

56. Ibid., 80.

57. Anders Stephanson also notes this desire to be exceptional, and he notes that it dovetailed with the emerging idea of Manifest Destiny. White Americans' drew upon a Puritan past in order to claim the distinction of exceptional and thus uniquely positioned to realize a dream of Christian empire in the world. See Anders Stephanson, *Manifest Destiny: American Expansion and the Empire of Right* (New York: Hill and Wang, 1995).

58. John Johnston to Thomas L. McKenney, February 20, 1827, National Archives, RG 75 Records of the Bureau of Indian Affairs, Letters Received Piqua Agency 1827, Roll #3, Ohio Historical Society), in Ethnohistory Collection.

59. For quotation, see Unrau, "An International Perspective on American Indian Policy," 524.

60. Linda K. Kerber, "The Abolitionist Perception of the Indian," *Journal of American History* 62, no. 2 (September 1975): 271–295.

61. Mary Hershberger, "Mobilizing Women, Anticipating Abolition: The Struggle Against Indian Removal in the 1830s," *Journal of American History* 86, no. 1 (June 1999): 18.

62. Ibid., 23.

63. Ibid., 19.

64. Ibid., 31.

65. On missionary resistance to removal policies in Cherokee Country, see William McLoughlin, *Cherokees and Missionaries, 1789–1839* (New Haven, CT: Yale University Press, 1984).

66. William G. McLoughlin, *Champions of the Cherokees: Evan and John B. Jones* (Princeton, NJ: Princeton University Press, 1990), 51.

67. Cathy Rex, "Survivance and Fluidity: George Copway's The Life, History, and Travels of Kah-ge-ga-gah-bowh," *Studies in American Indian Literatures* 18, no. 2 (Summer 2006): 5, 3.

68. George Copway, *The Life, History, and Travels of Kah-ge-ga-gah-bowh (George Copway): A Young Indian Chief of the Ojebwa Nation* (Albany, NY: Weed & Parsons, 1847), 218–219.

69. Samson Occom, A Short Narrative of My Life, typescript, Dartmouth College Archives, in Bernd Peyer, *The Elders Wrote: An Anthology of Early Prose by North American Indians, 1768–1931* (Berlin: Dietrich Reimer Verlag, 1982).

70. Kerber, "Abolitionist Perception," 295.

71. In 1819, the same year that the U.S. federal government passed the Civilization Fund Act, the ABCFM sent its first missionaries to Hawai'i. By the mid-nineteenth century, missionaries were intricately involved with the islands' sugar plantation economies. Noenoe Silva explains that missionaries acted as crucial government and economic agents, gathering census data regarding the Kanaka Maoli in order to give investors an idea of the extent to which they could rely upon Indigenous agricultural labor should they develop a sugar plantation on Kanaka lands (49). Silva also points out that many of the missionaries who traveled to the islands themselves became plantation owners, offering one of the clearest examples of the speculative nature of philanthropy in this nineteenth-century moment. It was missionaries—and eventually their children and grandchildren—who were able to buy lands appropriate for plantations thanks to their government connections and elite status in the colonial society. These elite men and their families profited from the spoils of the colonial system that they helped to build, and they ensured that they irrevocably altered the lives and labor systems of the Kanaka Maoli, as well as their ability to cultivate the lands as they had done for centuries. Silva notes that a "discourse of work"—discourse that was bound up in the same ideas of civilization and labor as in eastern North America—"justified the subjugation and conversion of Kanaka Maoli into laborers" (53). Missionaries in Hawai'i profited off of their preaching of a Protestant labor regime, and, in doing so, ensured that theirs was a project of speculative philanthropy. The missionaries accumulated social, political, moral, and economic capital by virtue of their mission to Kanaka lands, and they laid the groundwork for U.S. annexation of Hawai'i by the end of the century. See Noenoe Silva, *Aloha Betrayed: Native Hawaiian Resistance to American Colonialism* (Durham, NC: Duke University Press, 2004).

Epilogue

1. Alexis de Tocqueville, *Democracy in America*, translated by Arthur Goldhammer (New York: Penguin Putnam Inc., 2004), 391.

2. Vizenor defines "survivance" as being "an active sense of presence" that entails more than mere survival. See Gerald Vizenor, "Aesthetics of Survivance: Literary Theory and Practice," in Gerald Vizenor, ed., *Survivance: Narratives of Native Presence* (Lincoln: University of Nebraska Press, 2008), 1.

3. Elizabeth Ellis, "Why We Must Not Forget Standing Rock," *Rewire*, May 8, 2017. Winona LaDuke and Deborah Cowen chart the centrality of infrastructure in the settler-colonial project, and they also highlight that "infrastructure is not inherently colonial—it is also essential for transformation; a pipe can carry fresh water as well as toxic sludge." See Winona LaDuke and Deborah Cowen, "Beyond Wiindigo Infrastructure," *South Atlantic Quarterly* 119, no. 2 (April 2020): 245. On DAPL, see also Nick Estes, *Our History is the Future: Standing Rock*

versus the Dakota Access Pipeline, and the Long Tradition of Indigenous Resistance (London: Verso, 2019).

4. Christina Sharpe, *In the Wake: On Blackness and Being* (Durham, NC: Duke University Press, 2016), 1–24.

5. Joshua Reid offers a compelling description of a "traditional future" in his masterful work on the Makahs. See Joshua L. Reid, *The Sea Is My Country: The Maritime World of the Makahs* (New Haven, CT: Yale University Press, 2015).

INDEX

ACKNOWLEDGMENTS

This book is the product of many years of friendship, collegiality, support, and generosity. As with so many scholarly endeavors, numerous individuals and institutions have made this work possible. I hope that this tallying of debts may serve as my thanks and as an acknowledgment of the wealth of advice, knowledge, and friendship that others have brought to this project and to me.

Several institutions supported this work. The Society of Historians of American Foreign Relations and the Clements Library at the University of Michigan offered me research fellowships. At the Clements, Jane Greene, in particular, was invaluable, while Wayne Huxhold at Indiana University's Glenn Black Laboratory and Library made my work in the archives there a delight. The University of Pennsylvania also offered several years of fellowship support, making both my advanced education and the dissertation that preceded this book possible. The *Journal of the Early Republic* and Brill Press previously published edited versions of Chapters 4 and 5, and I am grateful to be able to include those chapters here. The staff at the Historical Society of Pennsylvania, Swarthmore College, Haverford College, the Ohio History Center, Indiana Historical Society, Cornell University, the National Archives, and others were all vital to this project.

The McNeil Center for Early American Studies provided funds, community, and friends. My thanks for conversation, feedback, and camaraderie go to Dee Andrews, Jessica Blake, Daniel Couch, Christine Croxall, Demetri Debe, Elizabeth Eager, Elizabeth Ellis, Rachel Engl, Alexandra Finley, Brendan Gillis, Nicholas Gliserman, Sarah L. H. Gronningsater, Sonia Hazard, James Hill, Andrew Inchiosa, Christopher Jones, Lauren Kimball, Jessica Linker, Alexander Manevitz, Don James McLaughlin, Emily Merrill, Tony Perry, Tommy Richards, Gabriel Rocha, David Silverman, Laura Soderberg, and Rachel Walker.

The Bright Institute at Knox College offered me collegiality and funds, and it connected me to a community of individuals whom I was and am honored to learn from. These scholars know the challenges and rewards that come with teaching and writing at a small college, and they know, too, the importance of kindness in scholarly communities. For offering feedback on a portion of this manuscript and for their generosity on numerous fronts, my thanks go to Cathy Adams, Christian Crouch, Cate Denial, Josh Eyler, Chris Guilliard, Jonathan Hancock, Michael Hughes, Courtney Joseph, Carl Keyes, Angela Keysor, Will Mackintosh, Natalie Mendoza, Jennifer Morgan, Tamika Nunley, Monica Rico, Bryan Rindfleisch, Doug Sackman, Bridgett Williams-Searle, Michael Witgen, and Serena Zabin.

I am also grateful for feedback and conversations with Gregory Ablavsky, Emilie Connolly, Alexandra Montgomery, Gautham Rao, Bethel Saler, Timothy Shannon, Karim Tiro, and the late Andrew Cayton—at SHEAR, the McNeil Center, and various coffee shops alike. Thomas Lappas, meanwhile, read several chapters and offered encouragement and a much-needed critical eye along the way. Timothy Thibodeau offered support and conversation and has been a steadfast mentor since my days as an undergraduate. Participants in a 2015 Ohio History Seminar and a 2017 seminar at the McNeil Center for Early American Studies offered valuable feedback as I worked to both complete my dissertation and transform that project into this book.

George Ironstrack, Diane Hunter, and Dani Tippmann were generous with their time and expertise. I was fortunate enough to enjoy conversation with George and Diane during a research trip to the Fort Wayne area in 2017, and I am thankful that they shared their vast knowledge about Pinšiwa and the history of the Myaamia Tribe with me. Meanwhile, I am forever indebted to Dani Tippmann for giving me a tour of the land, for welcoming me into her home for a meal, and for sharing with me her story and experiences. My time with Dani shifted how I think about my work and this history, and I am so very grateful to her. While I was the beneficiary of George, Diane, and Dani's hospitality and knowledge, any and all errors in this book are, of course, my own.

Bob Lockhart at Penn Press patiently guided me through this publication process, always offered expert feedback and advice on my writing and ideas, and was understanding as we all navigated the upheaval of the COVID-19 pandemic. Jessica Choppin Roney and Katherine Carté each helped me to better articulate my ideas and balance my goals for the book. They are models for how we should all strive to engage one another as scholars.

During my time as a graduate student at Penn, Robert St. George pushed my thinking in creative and surprising directions. Kathleen Brown's feedback and mentorship was invaluable. Dan Richter was the dissertation adviser I needed and then some. His unflagging support, generosity, and willingness to give his time and advice—both in graduate school and now as I navigate life as a professor—provide an example that I always strive to emulate with my own students. Thanks, Dan, for telling me early on to work on my historiography.

At Ursinus, Susanna Throop supported me in my writing goals and always offered expert mentorship, even as she has assumed the weight of a department besieged by the loss of beloved colleagues. One such loss was Ross Doughty. Ross made me feel at home at Ursinus, and in the relatively brief time that we worked together, he made me a better historian. My conversations with him stayed with me as I completed this book. Edward Onaci took the time to read this book proposal, shared his own publishing experiences with me, and gave sage advice on numerous occasions. Glenda Chao and Johanna Mellis read excerpts of this work, while Margie Connor has patiently, and with good humor, guided me through the paperwork that made my research and travel possible. Ursinus College more generally provided financial support that enabled me to further develop this project. My student research assistant Sarah Johns's sophisticated research skills were invaluable, and I am indebted to her for our conversations about gender and history.

I am a firm believer in the power of a writing group, and I have been fortunate to be a part of a few. At Penn, Abigail Cooper, Elizabeth Della Zazzera, Danielle Holtz, and Emma Teitleman offered invaluable feedback. At Ursinus, Kara McShane and Rosa Abrahams have been the best colleagues, writing partners, and friends. They read this entire manuscript (some chapters more than once), and this book is so much better because of them. I am grateful to them both for keeping me going, on target, on time, and for laughing and eating great food with me.

Of course, while professional support has been crucial, my family and friends have filled my life with love, humor, and calm. I absolutely include my cats in this. Winston and Oscar, two of the most adorable friends that have blessed my life, always made sure that they kept my arms warm as I typed. Jackie, Jenn, Jesse, Alexander, Mackenzie, and Andrew: thanks for keeping me grounded and laughing. John and Marietta: thank you for opening your home to me and for welcoming me to the family so warmly. Kelli: thank you for the long walks and everything else in between. I cannot enumerate the ways in which you make my life better. Mom and Dad: thanks for your endless love and support. Mom, thanks for walking with me; Dad, thanks for talking about capitalism with me. Justin: thanks for being my rock, for making me laugh, for playing the games I always win, for picking up and echoing the jingles that I sing to the cats, and for your love. I'm so lucky and honored to have you by my side.